THE EMIGRANT:
ANCESTRY, AND SOME
DESCENDANTS

BY

BOSTON
1914

SIMON CROSBY THE EMIGRANT: HIS ENGLISH ANCESTRY, AND SOME OF HIS AMERICAN DESCENDANTS

BY

ELEANOR DAVIS CROSBY

Author of
"WILLIAM HOOPER, 1635"
"DOLOR DAVIS, 1634—RICHARD EVERETT, 1636," Etc.

BOSTON
PRESS OF GEO. H. ELLIS CO.
1914

CS71
.C75
1971

CONTENTS.

		PAGE
PREFACE		v
INTRODUCTION		ix
CHAPTER I.	THE ENGLISH ANCESTRY OF SIMON CROSBY THE EMIGRANT	1
CHAPTER II.	THOMAS CROSBY, FATHER OF SIMON THE EMIGRANT	19
CHAPTER III.	SIMON CROSBY THE EMIGRANT	43
CHAPTER IV.	SIMON CROSBY OF BILLERICA	66
CHAPTER V.	EARLY CROSBYS IN BILLERICA	92
CHAPTER VI.	TWO OF THE CROSBY FAMILY IN BILLERICA DURING THE REVOLUTIONARY PERIOD	110
CHAPTER VII.	THE FIRST MERCHANT IN THE FAMILY	131
CHAPTER VIII.	THE PRESENT-DAY CROSBYS OF THIS LINE OF THE FAMILY	138
APPENDICES		143

PREFACE.

This work on Simon Crosby the Emigrant, of Cambridge, Mass., is rendered chiefly important to those who bear the name of Crosby in America because here for the first time it has been possible to show whence came to this country the ancestor of the great majority of American Crosbys. Simon Crosby of Cambridge has always been known as the Emigrant to those who have made a special study of this subject, and while, strictly speaking, his father, Thomas Crosby, might be entitled to be known as the Emigrant because he belonged to a prior generation, but because he came to America at a later date than his son it has been thought advisable to continue the usage of the past, which has always known Simon of Cambridge as the Emigrant, and thus cause less confusion to present and future readers of this book.

During the past thirty-six years those records that pertain to the descendants of Simon Crosby that are here set forth were slowly collected from time to time. No attempt has naturally been made to give a complete history of the Crosby family in America, for as time goes on the name becomes more and more familiar; but that immediate branch of the family with which I am connected by marriage, alone has been the subject of interest to me. In so far, however, as nearly all the Crosbys in America are descended from some one of the generations here dealt with, it is hoped this work will have an interest much wider than the scope which was originally intended for it.

For such records as relate to the family in America I am indebted to the usual sources of genealogical data, too familiar to workers in this field to need special mention here. The records contained in public libraries and the New England Historic Genealogical Society are known to all. Town records have been carefully examined, and in many places special references are given. I am indebted to the services of Mr. J. Gardner Bartlett, a trained genealogist, for the research in English records which established for the first time the connecting link between the Crosbys of America and England, and for most of the material relating to the line in England, and the place in York County whence they owed their origin. Mr. Bartlett made a careful and painstaking search of York County records. To Mrs. Susie C. Tufts I am indebted for some references to records of the family in America. My son, Sumner Crosby, has furnished a general introduction and has revised the book.

My earnest wish is that this book may prove of interest to those who delve in the dark recesses of the past as they relate to one family, and be a stimulus for further work to future Crosby genealogists.

For those who are interested in the bibliography of the Crosby family in America, I will say that the earliest attempt to compile an extensive genealogy of the Crosbys in America was made about fifty years ago by Professor Howard Crosby, D.D., Chancellor of the University of New York, and Professor Alpheus Crosby of Dartmouth College and Salem, Mass. In a visit to England, Professor Howard Crosby also obtained some notes on English Crosbys, but he secured no data on the ancestry or place of origin of Simon Crosby, the Puritan colonist of Cambridge, Mass. These gentlemen did not complete their work, and their proposed genealogy was never published.

In 1877, Judge Nathan Crosby of Lowell, Mass., a brother of the above-named Professor Alpheus Crosby, published a 143-page volume, giving the descendants of Josiah Crosby, born at Billerica, Mass., 24 Nov. 1730, and briefly tracing the latter's ancestry back to Simon Crosby the Emigrant, of Cambridge, Mass. About four pages of miscellaneous Crosby items in England, which had been obtained by Professor Howard Crosby, also appear in this book; but no data are given as to the parentage or place of origin of the Emigrant Simon Crosby.

In 1898, Ernest Howard Crosby, Esq., of New York (son of Professor Howard Crosby before mentioned), from papers left by his father and his own researches, compiled a genealogy of the descendants of William Bedlow Crosby of New York, born 7 Feb. 1786, which appeared in the New York Genealogical and Biographical Record, vol. 29, pp. 183–190, and vol. 30, pp. 5–10, 73–79, and 146–152; this genealogy was later reprinted as a 24-page book. In this work the ancestry is traced back to Simon Crosby of Cambridge, Mass., and a few notes on English Crosbys are given; but Mr. Crosby stated that "every attempt to fix the place of Simon's English home has been unsuccessful."

In 1906, the Crosbys of Brattleboro, Vt., printed a pamphlet relating to their family, compiled by Mrs. Fannie (Crosby) Rice, but no data are given relating to the ancestry of Simon Crosby the Emigrant.

In 1912, Simon Percy Crosby, Esq., of St. Paul, Minn., published a 212-page volume he had compiled, principally of the descendants of Oliver Crosby, born in Billerica, Mass., 17 March 1769. The line is traced back briefly to

Simon Crosby of Cambridge, Mass.; but Mr. Crosby secured no knowledge of the ancestry of the Emigrant, and states, "I visited Great Britain in 1910, and again in 1912, and tried to ascertain from what resources I could get reliable information concerning our ancestry; but I found nothing more than had already been obtained."

Besides the four foregoing works, short accounts of various branches of the New England Crosby family may be found as follows:—

Crosbys of Massachusetts, in Paige's History of Cambridge, Mass., p. 519; Hazen's History of Billerica, Mass., Part II, pp. 27–32; Freeman's History of Cape Cod, vol. 2, pp. 213 and 365; Stearn's History of Ashburnham, Mass., pp. 656–660; Ward's History of Shrewsbury, Mass., pp. 255–258; and Early Rowley Settlers, in Essex Institute Historical Collections, vol. 20, pp. 230–231; Crosbys of New Hampshire, in Cutter's History of Jaffrey, N.H., pp. 257–260; Dow's History of Hampton, N.H., pp. 651–652; Saunderson's History of Charlestown, N.H., pp. 245–247 and 315–318; Ramsdell's History of Milford, N.H., pp. 650–660; and Secomb's History of Amherst, N.H., pp. 547–551; Crosbys of Maine, in the Bangor Historical Magazine, vol. 1, pp. 81–83, and vol. 2, pp. 105–112, and in the Maine Historical and Genealogical Recorder, vol. 4, pp. 153–160; Crosbys of Putnam County, N.Y., in the New York Genealogical and Biographical Records, vol. 18, pp. 87–88, and vol. 32, pp. 111–116, 161–163, 225–228.*

* None of these records gives any data on the ancestry of Simon Crosby the Emigrant of Cambridge, Mass.—E. D. C.

INTRODUCTION.

During the space of thirty-six years my mother has devoted her spare time to the compilation of the records of our branch of the Crosby family, and during that time so much material had been gathered from the usual public and private sources of information that it was deemed advisable to publish a book giving the facts collected a permanent shape for future generations of one branch of the family. But on the eve of publication one last attempt was made to unravel the mystery surrounding the ancestry of the Crosby family in England. For up to that time no one had been able to say whence came Simon Crosby the Emigrant to America, and all investigators of the subject had abandoned it as hopeless. However, one slight clue held out some hope, and upon this Mr. J. Gardner Bartlett, an expert genealogist of the New England Historical and Genealogical Committee, was commissioned to try to penetrate the mystery which surrounded the past, and that neither the clue nor Mr. Bartlett's efforts were unavailing is shown by the fact that now for the first time it is possible to trace the family back to 1440.

The clue referred to was the reference in the Cambridge Proprietors' Records of 1645 to the grant of six acres in small farm lots to one "Owld Crosby," and later, in 1646, of a grant of six acres of wood lots to Thomas Crosby. As Thomas Crosby died in Rowley, Mass., in 1661, at the age of eighty-five, he might well have been thought to be old in 1645, at the age of sixty-nine. As Simon the Emigrant had died in 1639, it is fair to suppose the two records above referred to Thomas Crosby. Therefore, finding him in Cambridge after the death of Simon Crosby, and finding him later in Rowley under the pastorate of Rev. Ezekiel Rogers, who founded that place, the inference became natural that Thomas Crosby was somehow connected with Simon Crosby, and both of them with Rev. Ezekiel Rogers. Simon Crosby had been accompanied to America in 1635 by his young wife Anne, and their young child Thomas, aged eight weeks. That he had named his son "Thomas" was very significant, for in those days it was quite customary to continue the given name of a family in alternate generations. The fact that Thomas Crosby, after the death of Simon Crosby, received grants of land in Cambridge, but for all that removed to Rowley, causes the inference that he was especially interested in the exploits of Rev. Rogers. Now it has been known that both Rev. Thomas Shepard and Rev. Ezekiel Rogers came from York County, England, and what was more natural than to suppose that also the Crosbys might have come from there? And, furthermore, as the Crosbys were people of ample means for those times it might well be supposed they shared the religious discontent of the times, which was the real motive of their emigration to America. Slight as this clue was, it was sufficiently justified, and in July, 1912, Mr. Bartlett started his investigations, with the result that he discovered in the Parish Register of Holme-on-Spalding-Moor, York County, England, that Simon Crosby had married Anne Brigham on April 21, 1634, and that on the 26th of February, 1634–35, their son Thomas was baptized. Thereupon Mr. Bartlett, having for the first time definitely cleared up the mystery surrounding the place from which the Emigrant Simon had come, received a

INTRODUCTION

commission to continue his researches, the results of which will be found in the first part of this book. In all, Mr. Bartlett examined nine hundred wills, and all the records pertaining to the Crosby family to which he could get access in York County.

In March, 1913, he wrote the following letter to my mother:—

LONDON, 28 March 1913.

My dear Mrs. Crosby,—I herewith submit report of the Crosby search, consisting of 237 type-written pages on the Crosby and allied families, 8 charts of the Crosbys and allied families of Lambert, Ellithorpe, Brigham, Sotheron, Millington, Watson and Belt, views of the church of Holme-on-Spalding-Moor and a map of Yorkshire.

As you will see, I have proved that Thomas Crosby, the emigrant to New England, came from Holme-on-Spalding-Moor; that he had 4 sons: 1. Anthony, who died in Holme in 1632, unmarried; 2. Thomas, who died at Holme in 1658, leaving two surviving daughters, and in his will names the 3 sons of his brother Simon; 3. William, who died probably in England before 1640, and left a child, later of Rowley, Mass.; 4. Simon, who came to New England in 1635. The "Widow Constance Crosby of Rowley, Mass., was by birth a Brigham and was sister of Anne who married on 21 April, 1634, at Holme, in Co. York, Simon Crosby."

J. GARDNER BARTLETT.

Crosby, a township in the parish of Bottesford in Northern Lincolnshire, is mentioned in Domesday Book in 1086, as follows: "Lands of Ivo Talbois in Lincolnshire. In Crosbi, Siward formerly had five oxgangs * of land to be taxed. There is [arable] land there for two ploughs. Five acres of land belong to the soke. Odo, a vassal of Ivo's, has there one plough and a half, six villanes,† one bordar ‡ with one

---

* An oxgang varied in size; but in Yorkshire and Lincolnshire was about twenty-five acres.

† A villane was a peasant serf of the lord of a manor.

‡ A bordar was a free peasant who held a cottage and garden, paying a rental to the lord in certain crops.

plough, three mills of 8 shillings, and eighteen acres of meadow. Value in King Edward's time 30 shillings, now 40 shillings." (Bawdwen's Domesday of Yorkshire and Lincolnshire, p. 486.) About 1181, Alice, daughter of Isabel de Crokesby, renders an account of one mark for rights in forty acres of land in Crokesby. She has paid into the Exchequer and is acquitted. (Great Roll of the Pipe, Lincolnshire, 28 Henry II. (1181-82.) Translated from the Latin.) This latter record is the earliest mention found of the use of a Crosby place as a family surname.

Crosby, a township in the parish of Leake in Yorkshire, is about thirty miles northwest of the city of York. This place also is named in the great Domesday Survey of 1086, in a schedule of the lands in Yorkshire of Earl Alan. "In Crocsbi to be taxed three carucates, and there may be one plough. Bernulf formerly held a manor there. The same now holds it of the Earl, and it is waste. The whole is two miles in length and half in breadth. There are moors there. Value in King Edward's time five shillings." (Bawdwen's Domesday of Yorkshire and Lincolnshire, p. 106.)

It appears that all the places called "Crosby" are found named on records as early as the twelfth century, and probably all of them were founded and named by the Danes during the tenth century, which was the period of their greatest activity in settling in England. Although but two of the places (those in Lincolnshire and Yorkshire) are found mentioned as early as Domesday Book (1086), it must be remembered that Domesday does not cover Westmoreland and Cumberland at all, nor parts of Lancashire, in which counties the other places named "Crosby" are located.

These very early mentions of the name of Crosby have only a certain historical value and are of no great importance in the history of a branch of a certain family except to the historically curious.

In like manner, for those interested in the subject of heraldry the following information is given:—

Among coats-of-arms of various Crosby families in England appear the following (all except the first are given in Burke's "General Armoury"):—

Sable, a chevron ermine, between three rams trippant argent, armed and hoofed or. These arms are on the tomb of Sir John Crosby, Knt., alderman of London, who died in 1475.

Sable, a chevron ermine, between three rams passant argent. Granted in 1771 to Brass Crosby, Lord Mayor of London.

Azure, on a chevron between three lambs passant or, as many roses proper. Confirmed in 1821 to Vinus H. Crosby, grand-nephew of Brass Crosby.

Argent, a lion rampant sable, between two dexter hands couped at the wrist gules. Crosby of Newcastle-on-Tyne, co. Northumberland, and of Yorkshire. (No other particulars given.)

Per chevron argent and sable, three guttées counterchanged. Crosby (no place or other particulars given).

Per chevron argent and sable, three unicorns' heads couped counterchanged. Crosby (no place or other particulars given).

Per chevron sable and argent, three goats passant counterchanged. Crosby (no place or other particulars given).

There are also several coats-of-arms assigned to Crosbie families of Ireland.

In like manner, reference is made to Matthew's "American Armoury and Blue Book," page 201, part 2, [1913].

INTRODUCTION

An extensive search has failed to show that the Crosbys of Alne and Holme-on-Spalding-Moor, Co. York, ancestors of Thomas[5] Crosby, the progenitor of the Crosbys of America, used or claimed any coat-of-arms; while they were of the best class of landowning yeomanry, they apparently were not of the armorial gentry, although the two daughters and coheiresses of Thomas[6] Crosby (eldest surviving son of Thomas[5] Crosby, the New England Puritan colonist) married into the armorial families of Belt and Bower of Yorkshire. It is therefore to be concluded that the American Crosbys are not entitled to a coat-of-arms.

The derivation of the name of "Crosby" seems to be generally given as coming from "cross," the symbol of Christianity, and the Danish termination "by," which suffix is equivalent to the "bury," "burg," or "borough" of other derivatives meaning a town or centre of population, and hence "Crosby" meant "the town of the Cross," or the town located near a cross or where a cross had been set up. Which might very well have been, for when Christianity made its appearance in England in 597 with the advent of Augustine* it is not too much a stretch of the imagination to suppose that the establishment of a large cross near any hamlet which up to then had not been of sufficient importance to bear a name might thereafter be designated as the "town of the cross," or "Cross-by"; or even that such establishment of a cross in days when Christianity had not generally been adapted in Britain was enough of a challenge to the rest of the country that those who dwelt in its shadow were of the Christian faith and no longer worshipped Woden † and "the gods of their fathers."‡

---

* Green's History of the English People, vol. 1, p. 48.
† Knight's History of England, vol. 1, p. 64 et seq.
‡ Green's History of the English People, vol. 1, p. 48.

There is little doubt in the minds of etymologists that such was the origin of the name of "Crosby," nor is there much doubt that the name attached itself to some town or towns before it came to be used as the surname of any family. For in early days in England among the middle and yeoman class and before the awakening of much family interest a man might be known as simply by his given name, such as Thomas, and, to designate him the better, he would be called Thomas of the town he lived in, as "Thomas of Crosby," and later, removing elsewhere, would still be known as "Thomas of Crosby," and then as Thomas Crosby; and hence began the use of the name as a family name. And this appears to be borne out by the fact that in all the very earliest references to the name it appears as "de Crosseby," which is the French way of saying "of Crosby," and was so used as the family name for over two hundred years, viz., 1204–1415, when for the first time, so far as recorded, the "de" is dropped. It is interesting, also, to note that in the spelling of the name in those days the derivation from "cross" is plainer than it is to-day, by spelling the name "Crosseby."

It must have been, of course, after the advent of William the Conqueror in 1066 that the use of the Norman "de" was started, and it was the very use of this French form that has led some to believe that the name of "Crosby" is of French origin, especially so as the name of the first Crosby of whom we have a record was Odo de Crosseby, the "Odo" being the same name as that of the brother of William himself. But this Odo de Crosseby is not mentioned until the reign of John in 1204, when the Norman influence was well established over Saxon Britain; and it must further be borne in mind that the existence of surnames at all in any general use did not come in until the eleventh century, which was coincident with the arrival of the Normans. Lower, in his excellent work on English surnames,* says: "It is certain that the practice of making the second name of the individual stationary and transmitting it to descendants came generally into use during the eleventh and three following centuries. By the middle of the twelfth it began, in the estimation of some, to be essential that persons of rank should bear some designation in addition to their baptismal name." Which would appear to explain why the "de" was used in 1204 when the Norman influence was still strongly felt. But that the name "Crosby" should be of Norman origin is rendered extremely doubtful from the purely Danish suffix "by" and the entirely English way of spelling "cross," viz., "Crosse." Then, too, the fact that we find eight or ten towns called "Crosby" and all located in the north of England, in Scotland, and in the Isle of Man, must surely indicate that some of these towns were of an origin prior to that of the Normans; for mention is made of a Crosby† in Lancashire in the reign of Henry III. And it is hardly to be supposed that all these towns were founded after the arrival of William the Conqueror, and all in that part of England furthest away from the influence of the Normans, even in Scotland, whither William drove many of his enemies as exiles in their flight.‡ The campaign of 1068, in which William impressed his personality on the north of England, was absolutely on his part a campaign of vengeance§ for the slaughter of his garrison in York,‖ and he so devastated the country as far as the

---

* "English Surnames," p. 31.   † Testa de Nevill, 1220 A.D.
‡ Green's History of the English People, vol. 1, p. 125.   § *Ibid.*, p. 124.
‖ Interesting to us, as we find later that the American line of Crosbys came from Yorkshire.

Tees "that no hold might remain for future landings of the *Danes*. Crops, cattle, the very implements of husbandry were so mercilessly destroyed that a famine which followed is said to have swept off more than a hundred thousand victims. Half a century later indeed the land still lay bare of culture and deserted of men for sixty miles northward of York." (Green.) So we can hardly imagine an unfriendly people giving expression to their gratitude after such an experience, naming several of their towns at that time by a name distinctly Norman in its origin. In brief, we should expect to find any towns named Crosby, had that name been of Norman origin, located in the south of England, where Norman influence was most felt, and not in the north, where, as we have seen, those were driven who still adhered to the cause of Saxon England.[*] But is it not more logical to suppose that "Crosby" was the name of towns in the north of England before the Normans came at all, and that the name not only meant "the town of the cross," but, in meaning that, it held a special significance? For we read how Oswald of Northumbria kneels before the cross at Hexham,[†] showing that the establishment of crosses was not general at that time, and therefore still more to be supposed that towns which theretofore had set up the symbol of Christianity were sufficiently proud of their progress and enlightenment in the midst of pagan surroundings to proclaim themselves residents of "the town of the cross," or "Crosby." And this, it would seem, must dispose of any argument that admits of any other origin than the Danish origin we first mentioned.

[*] Knight's History of England, vol. 1, p. 196.   [†] *Ibid.*, p. 173.

And of these towns so named there appear to have been ten, as follows:—

1. CROSBY in Lincolnshire.
2. CROSBY GARRET in Westmoreland.
3. CROSBY RAVENSWORTH in Westmoreland.
4. CROSBY in Cumberland.
5. CROSBY (possibly Crosby Cannonby), also in Cumberland.
6. GREAT CROSBY in Lancashire.
7. LITTLE CROSBY, also in Lancashire.
8. CROSBY in Yorkshire.
9. CROSBY in the Isle of Man.
10. CROSBY in Ayrshire in Scotland.

This list of towns and hamlets called "Crosby" is given here simply to identify their location in the north of England in the light of the probable origin of the name, and not because any of them have any special interest to the student of the Crosby family in America, for it does not appear that the ancestors of Thomas Crosby of Yorkshire, the founder of the family in America which we are writing of, were in any way connected with any town named "Crosby," except so far back as that time, previously indicated, when the surname "Crosby" might have attached itself to a family living in a hamlet so named.

Crosby in Lincolnshire * is located between the rivers Ankholm and Trent, south of the Humber, and is so small a place that it does not even appear in that very complete atlas of English counties by Philips.† It has some historical interest, however, being mentioned as far back as the reign of Henry VIII., at which time it was spoken of as "a

---
* Mentioned in Testa de Nevill, 1220.
† Philips's Handy Atlas of the Counties of England. London, 1888.

dependency of Thorneholme (and thus of Thornton Abbey) and of the Gaykewell Monastery, and situated on the Deaconate of Manlake." *

Crosby Garret rises to the importance of a place on the maps, as does Crosby Ravensworth, which is six miles northwest of it. These two places are in the southeast part of Westmoreland between Kirkby Stephen and Appleby. "Crosby Garret (also called Crosby Gerard, Crosby Gerrard, Crosbygere and Crossebyger) is in Westmoreland, about sixteen miles east of Ulleswater. It is probably the same with 'Parva Crossebygg, in Westmoreland,' of Edward II.'s reign, 1310. It is mentioned in Richard II.'s reign, 1380, and afterward." †

There is a small place on the coast of Cumberland called "Crosby," but very insignificant in importance. The principal place of this name in Cumberland is just north of Carlisle. "Crosby (called Crosseby, Crosseby juxta Eden, Crosseby in Allerdale, and perhaps Crosby Cannonby, and in Edward I.'s time 'Alta Cresseby,' 1300) is a barony, four miles north of Carlisle, in Cumberland. I find it first mentioned about 1300, in the 'Placite de quo warrante' of Edward I." †

Ernest Howard Crosby, in his pamphlet on the Crosby family, says, "The parish of Crosby-upon-Eden, near Carlisle, in Cumberland, containing the villages of High Crosby and Low Crosby, which is supposed to have derived its name from the ancient cross to which the inhabitants resorted for prayer before the church was built on its site in the reign of Henry I." ("The Crosby Family of New York," by Ernest Howard Crosby, p. 1.)

---

* "A Crosby Family," p. 3, by Nathan Crosby. (These references to "A Crosby Family" are given only on their face value, and have not been confirmed by the author of this work, as it was not considered of sufficient importance to do so. They are credited to the researches of a Chancellor Crosby, who is said to have made them about 1855.—ED.)

† *Ibid.*, p. 3.

Crosby Station in the Isle of Man is in Glenfaba, a few miles west of Douglas. The Crosbys located in Yorkshire and in Ayrshire in Scotland are of even less importance.

But the towns of Great and Little Crosby in Lancashire are the most important of those bearing that name. They are really suburbs of Liverpool, and are a few miles north of that city, on Crosby Channel, near Crosby Lighthouse. These towns of Crosby in Lancashire, sometimes called "Crosby Magna" and "Crosby Parva," are of especial importance because mentioned in the Testa de Nevill* of Henry III.'s reign, 1220. And, being of such early mention and relative importance, it has led those who have heretofore made a study of the Crosby family to suppose that Simon Crosby, known as "the Emigrant," came from Lancashire, in the absence of any definite information as to

---

* These records of the reign of Henry III. were ordered printed in the time of George III. as per report of the sub-committee of the House of Commons, as follows: "In the King's Remembrance Office of the Court of Exchequer are preserved two ancient books called the Testa de Nevill or Liber Feodorum. The entries, which are specially called Testa de Nevill, are evidently quotations; they have in all probability been copied from a Roll bearing that name, a part of which is still extant at the Chapter House of Westminster, containing ten Counties; the Roll appears to be of the age of Edward I. and agrees with the entries in these books.

"John Calley } Sub-Comm."
"W. Illingworth }

A copy of this book is kept at the Patent Room of the Boston Public Library. Fortunately, one of the counties preserved was that of Lancashire, and it there appears, on page 402, under the entries for the County of Lancashire,—"Ričs Walensis tenet una caruc' de $\hat{d}$ ne Rege pro x sel' in villa de Litherland Simo' de Crosseby tens dimid' caruc' de $\hat{d}$ ne Rege in Crosseby pro x sel'" (Richard Walensis is possessed under tenure from the King one carucate in the town of Litherland for ten solidi and Simon de Crosseby holds a part of a carucate from our lord the King in Crosseby for ten solidi). From which it might appear that land was worth more in Crosby than in Litherland. A carucate "in the mediæval manor, [was] the land which could be tilled in a year by one plow with its eight oxen. The carucate was used as a unit of measure, but varied in different localities from 120 to 180 acres." (New International Encyclopædia.) A solidus was worth about three dollars, so that land was not worth then what it is to-day. These references show that Simon de Crosseby held directly from the King and not from any feudal over-lord, which is a distinction. After the conquest by William I. there was a general redivision of land in England, a great deal being given to Norman feudal lords who came with William, and it is quite likely that some such passed into the hands of a Norman adherent of William, who took his surname from the town of Crosseby, as the use of surnames was at that time just becoming to be recognized as necessary. So, in brief, it is quite likely that Odo de Crossbey may have been the father of Simon de Crosseby, and may have been of Norman descent, but by no means that the name of Crosby as a name is of Norman origin. In these Testa de Nevill there are several other entries of persons holding land in Crosseby in Lancashire, as well as one entry of land held in Crosseby in Lincolnshire.—Ed.

where he did come from. But the wish must have been father of the thought, for we are unable to find any connection between the family which settled on the shores of New England in the early part of the seventeenth century and the family of Crosbys which were known to have come from Lancashire, some of which achieved some reputation in the affairs of the country afterwards. And, from what we have already said, it is open to a good deal of question if the Crosbys we are concerned with were in any way connected with Crosby in Lancashire, for we find them living in Yorkshire as far back as our records go, and very likely they were there for a still longer time previous to the time to which we are able to go back, and may have got their name from the town of Crosby in Yorkshire or have come to that county from any of the other Crosbys in the north of England. And so, while all this history of the Crosby family is interesting to the student of the subject, the matter is so enshrouded with mystery and uncertainty that the probability is that it will never be known exactly where the family we are interested in got its name nor at what time. These are the sorts of thing that crystallize and take form out of apparent nebulous mists of antiquity, and are only valuable as a thing to dream and speculate upon.

Before leaving this subject we must give a little attention to Sir John Crosby and Crosby Hall of London, more because of the name they bear than because of any proved connection with the American family of Crosby.

For many years there has been a rumor or tradition among the Crosbys of America that Simon the Emigrant must have been descended or connected with Sir John Crosby of London, builder of the famous Crosby Hall; in this case, again, the wish being father of the thought.

In 1466, one John Crosby, a wealthy London merchant,

built in Bishopsgate Street an exceedingly handsome house, which eventually became known as Crosby Hall, and which was considered to be one of the finest examples of Gothic domestic architecture belonging to that period*; which, because of its beauty, historical interest, and that protecting fate which sometimes preserves things for us in spite of the ruthless onward rush of progress and civilization, came down to modern times, when its fame was increased by the excellence of the chops served in it. Neither the date of his birth nor his birthplace, so far as we have been able to discover, is known.† The report that he was a foundling and derived his name from having been found near a cross is, of course, absurd.

Sir John Crosby, Knt., was born about 1410, son of John Crosby of London living 1406 and 1415, grandson of John Crosby of London living 1390, and great-grandson of Sir John Crosby, Knt. who was an alderman of London, lord of the manor of Hanworth, and died before 1375.

He inherited from his ancestors the manor of Hanworth, and, embarking in trade, in 1452 became a freeman of the Grocers' Company, and soon amassed a large fortune as a wool-dealer and import grocer.‡

His life in London was an active one, occupied much with public affairs and public charities. In 1440 he was elected sheriff of London, being already an alderman. Whether he was knighted for resisting the attack of the Bastard Falconbridge as some seem to think,§ and hence received the honor for gallantry in the field, or whether it was upon the occasion of his going forth to meet Edward IV. in 1461 between Shoreditch and Islington, upon the entry of that monarch into London, and upon which occasion he attended in his capacity of alderman, is possibly uncertain; suffice it

---

* "Crosby Hall," printed by Marchant Singer & Co. London, 1876.

† Report of E. S. Carlos, 1832, on "The Preservation of Crosby Hall."

‡ Stowe—Survey, ed. 1603, p. 174.

§ "Crosby Hall," *supra*, and "The Crosby Family of New York," E. H. Crosby, p. 2.

to say that he was knighted as the reward for a public duty well done. In 1472 he was appointed one of the commissioners for settling the differences between Edward IV. and the Duke of Burgundy, having by that time built Crosby Hall, and become himself one of the foremost men in London.* He then became a member of Parliament for London, and received further commissions from his sovereign, showing in what high regard he was held.

With these introductory remarks concerning the history of the discovery of the Crosbys in England and the probable origin of the family name, I wish to refer again to the long years of careful and painstaking effort in a most tiring field of research that have been given to the preparation of this work by the author.

SUMNER CROSBY.

BROOKLINE, MASS., August, 1914.

* Stowe Chronology, p. 789.

SIMON CROSBY THE EMIGRANT

Chapter I.

THE ENGLISH ANCESTRY OF SIMON CROSBY THE EMIGRANT.

An Account of the Crosby Family of Stillingfleet, Alne, and Holme-on-Spalding-Moor, of York County, England.

The year 1440, back to which time this history of the Crosby family carries in an unbroken line the Crosbys descended from Simon the Emigrant, where once more the line is lost in the mists of the past, is not easy to visualize unless we take time enough to consider the many great changes that have taken place in the long years that divide us from those days; and it is worth while to stop a moment and try to orient our attitude towards those days, before we begin a detailed account of the Crosbys then bearing the name, whose life in Yorkshire now yields a fascination to the present-day student of the Crosby genealogy.

America was unknown; the great Reformation was not an established fact; the mists of the Dark Ages with all their superstitions hung heavy over the civilized world, or at best were only beginning to break. Henry VII. and the great Tudor family which gave to England her sea power were still below the horizon. Means of communication were of a most primitive nature. Indeed, it is not necessary to relate all the changes that have taken place in these intervening years. But it is well to recall that it was in some such dark and nearly primitive existence that there lived in the north of England a man called Crosby, the first definitely established of the family that gave rise to most of that name now living in America. It may be, and it is hoped, that some later genealogist may penetrate successfully into the mysteries of a still further past, but 1440 is as far as we can now go.

To be sure, in the broad flight of time through the ages, 474 years is but a moment, but in the history of the Christian era it forms some considerable part.

There are two kinds of pride of ancestry,—the false pride, which finds itself living in the borrowed exploits of the past, failing to meet the necessities of the present, and the legitimate pride in an unbroken line of men and women whose achievements have been a guarantee of their preservation from oblivion, and hopeful augury for the future.

Beset by many difficulties, and with only a slight clue to go on, Mr. J. Gardner Bartlett was able to uncover the bulk of the material that comprises this chapter.

We have accepted John Crosby and the probable date of his birth, 1440, as the point of demarcation for our history of the Crosby family, fully aware of the fact that a great deal of uncertainty surrounds the absolute connection of the first two generations here given. But, after a careful consideration of the facts presented, it has seemed as if the preponderance of probability rested in favor of the establishment of the links as here set forth. We have already called attention to the haziness of the times we refer to, all the more hazy as relating to a family not very prominent in public affairs, and therefore all the more remarkable that even so much circumstantial evidence should be connected therewith. Mr. Bartlett believes the proof conclusive, and, while we do not share fully such a cheerful optimism, we set forth the facts for what they are worth, believing that, on the whole, the line here given may fairly be said to be unbroken.

Holme-on-Spalding-Moor, in York County, England, is an extensive parish located about fifteen miles southeast of the city of York, and lies in the midst of a great flat plain of clayey soil which is bounded easterly by a range of hills called the Wolds. The parish is somewhat circular in form, with a diameter of about five miles, and is bounded

INTERIOR OF CHURCH AT HOLME ON SPALDING MOOR.

on the north by the parishes of Seaton Ross, Everingham, Harswell, and Shipton, on the east by the parishes of Market Weighton, North Cliff (formerly part of Sancton), South Cliff (formerly part of North Cave), and Hotham, on the south by the modern parishes of Bishopsoil and Wallingfen (formerly parts of Eastrington), and on the west by the parishes of Spaldington, Gribthorpe, and Foggathorpe, formerly townships and chapelries of the parish of Bubwith. The railroad station is on the northwesterly border of the parish, nearly two miles from the village and church. In the southern part of the parish are the hamlets of Tollingham, Bursea, and Hasholme. Agriculture and grazing have always been the only occupations of importance. In 1900 the population was about 1,700; in 1600 it was probably nearly 1,000. About twenty miles to the southeast is the seaport of Hull, located near the mouth of the river Humber.

In the northern part of the parish, a small oval-shaped hill rises about one hundred and fifty feet above the level of the plain, and is of such regular outline as even to suggest artificial construction. On its summit stands the ancient parish church, an edifice of stone, comprising chancel, nave, aisles, and a handsome tower at the westerly end, from the top of which a fine view can be had for many miles, the lofty spires of York Minster being discernible some fifteen miles to the northwest.

In past centuries a regular system of beacons was established around the coast regions of England, the firing of which was a signal for mustering the militia to repel a hostile invasion. These beacons were located on the tops of hills, and the favorable situation of the hill in Holme-on-Spalding-Moor caused its use for that purpose from time immemorial. On two occasions were especially elaborate plans made for utilizing these beacons,—in 1588, when the Spanish Armada threatened England, and in 1805, when Napoleon was preparing to invade the country. The beacon erected on Holme Hill on the latter occasion remained standing some forty years. It consisted of a heavy wooden column about twenty feet high, with two iron cross-arms at the top, the outer ends of which supported iron grates for holding tar-barrels.

Except for the above-mentioned hill, the rest of the parish is a low level plain dotted over with farm-houses, and with a small village near the hill. Most of the land has been drained and cultivated since about 1775, previously much of it being swampy moor. In ancient times, so difficult was the crossing of these dreary wastes that the Constable family, lords of the manor, established and maintained on the westerly edge of the moor a cell for two monks, whose employment was to guide strangers over it, one acting as conductor while the other prayed for the safety of the travellers, the monks alternating at the two offices.

From as early as A.D. 1300 the manor was part of the extensive possessions of the ancient knightly family of Constable of Flamborough, County York; but in 1537, Sir Robert Constable, Knt. (1478-1537), the then head of the family, was executed for complicity in the Pilgrimage of Grace, an unsuccessful rebellion in the north of England against the sequestration of the monasteries by Henry VIII., and the Constable family estates, comprising some thirty-five manors, passed to the Crown, by attainder for treason. In 1563, however, Queen Elizabeth restored his ancestral estates to Sir Robert Constable, Knt. (1528-1591), grandson of the executed one. He and his two sons joined, in 1585, in selling some of the lands in the manor of Holme to the Lambert, Tomlinson alias Millington, Barker, Sotheron, and other Holme families, previously tenants of the manor (Feet of Fines, Yorkshire, Michaelmas 28 and 29 Elizabeth). This Sir Robert Constable had two sons,—Sir Robert Constable, his heir (1552-1600), who married Anne Hussey, and Francis Constable, who died without issue. The last of this family, Sir William Constable, Knt. (1577-1655), son and heir of the last-named Robert, became financially involved, mortgaged his estates, and was finally obliged to sell the manor of Holme, in 1633, to Sir Marmaduke

Langdale, later created Baron Langdale, whose descendant, Mrs. Frederick D. Harford, is the present (1913) possessor of the manor. (See Allen's History of Yorkshire, vol. 3, pp. 388–392; and Constable pedigree in Foster's "Pedigrees of the County Families of Yorkshire," vol. 3.)*

1. JOHN CROSBY, birthplace unknown; born about 1440; married before 1470. Name of wife, place of birth and death unknown. Children:—

    i. John², b. about 1470.
    ii. Emma², living 1502.
   iii. Agnes², living 1502.
   iv. Robert², b. about 1475.
    v. Richard², b. about 1478.
   vi. William², b. about 1480.
  vii. MILES², b. about 1483.

John¹ Crosby died in 1502.

The will of John Crosby of Styllyngfleyte, dated 20 Apr. 1502. To be buried in the choir of the parish church of Styllyngfleyte. To the church of Styllyngfleyte 10s. and to the church of Alne 5s. For masses in the church of Styllyngfleyte £4. To the four orders of Brothers of York 2s. To my son John 6s. 8d. To my son Richard ten sheep, two calves, and 20s. To my daughters Emme and Agnes 6s. 8d. each. To my son Robert 20s. To my son Miles the remainder of all the years which I have in a house called Gyhowse lying in Flawath, with the appurtenances. To John Crosby, son of Robert Crosby, a house called Boyhowse lying in Flawath, with appurtenances. All residue of goods to my sons William and Miles, they to be executors. Witness, John Myln, chaplain. Proved 8 June 1502 by William Crosby one of the executors named, power reserved for the other. (Prerogative and Exchequer of York Wills, vol. 6, fol. 29. Translated from the Latin.)

The church of Stillingfleet is an ancient stone edifice showing features of the Norman, Early English, and Decorated Gothic styles, and comprises chancel, nave, aisles, north transept, and a square tower with embattled parapet, located at the westerly end of the nave.

The parish of Alne is divided into five townships or villages of Aldwark, Flawith, Thorlthorpe, Tollerton, and Youl-

---

* We are indebted to Mr. Harford and Mrs. Harford, Lady of the manor of Holme, for their kind permission of a thorough examination of the muniments of the manor, by which much valuable and interesting matter was obtained.

ton. This parish was a probate peculiar under the Dean and Chapter of York Cathedral (still in existence).

It is possible that the John Croseby, yeoman, who became a freeman of the city of York in 1458, may be identical with John[1] Crosby of Stillingfleet and Alne; but the only authentic information secured of the latter is derived from his will, a full abstract of which, translated from the Latin, is given above. It is likely that his elder sons, John, Richard, and Robert, had been deeded lands by their father during his lifetime. It should be borne in mind that bequests of that period should be multiplied by at least ten, to give an equivalent in modern value of money.

John[1] Crosby was a substantial yeoman of superior position, as is proved by the large amount he left for masses, and the fact that his will directs he be buried in the *choir* of the church. The yeomanry were almost always buried in the churchyard, only the very wealthiest of that class and the clergy and gentry securing sepulture within the church itself; and, of the burials in the church, interment in the choir or chancel was of special distinction.

Of the ancestry of John[1] Crosby nothing has been discovered, but there can be no doubt that one of his ancestors, over a century before his birth, took his name from one of the Crosby places in Northern England, and most likely from Crosby in Yorkshire, only eighteen miles north of Alne.

The life of John[1] Crosby was passed during the reigns of Henry VI., Edward IV., Edward V., Richard III., and Henry VII. In his early manhood commenced the civil wars of succession, commonly called the Wars of the Roses, which raged intermittently for a quarter of a century, and during which battles of Northampton and Wakefield (1460), Mortimer's Cross and Towton (1461), Hexam (1464), Barnet and Tewksbury (1471), and Bosworth (1485) nearly extinguished the ancient feudal nobility of England.

John[2] Crosby (John[1]), born about 1470, evidently succeeded as eldest son to his father's lands, etc., in Stillingfleet, according to the custom of the manor, where he appears as a witness to the will of John Grene of Stillingfleet, dated

27 July 1506. (P. and E. York Wills, vol. 7, fol. 7.) Soon after this time he evidently disposed of his interests in Stillingfleet and removed from there, as in subsidies and many other records examined no Crosby ever again appears in that parish. To what place he removed has not been absolutely proved; but, after prolonged researches and considerations on all the Yorkshire Crosbys, it seems very probable he was identical with a John Crosbye who was a witness in a court case between Sir Marmaduke Constable, Knt., and Sir John Salvayne, Knt., in regard to lands in Holme-on-Spalding-Moor, in 1511 (Assize Rolls, East Riding of Yorkshire, 3 Henry VIII.); and it also seems very likely that some of the Crosbys of the next generation who appear in Holme-on-Spalding-Moor in and after 1523 were his children.

Robert² Crosby (John¹), born about 1475, was a legatee of his father's will in 1502, and a legatee and executor of the will of his brother William in 1512. He resided in the parish of Alne, where he appears on a subsidy of 15 Henry VI. (1523). No will or administration of his estate has been found, nor has the name of his wife been ascertained.

Richard² Crosby (John¹), born about 1478, was a yeoman of Alne, where he died about 1559. His will, dated 30 Jan. 1558, gives to his wife (unnamed) a stagg (stallion), to son Robert two stotts (bullocks), to sons William, John and Rauf three ewes and three lambs each, and to son Thomas a quye (cow). All residue to wife, and said sons, executors, all of whom proved the will 24 Apr. 1559. (Dean and Chapter of York Wills, vol. 5, fol. 5.) The name of his wife has not been ascertained.

William² Crosby (John¹), born about 1480, was an administrator of his father's will in 1502; became a parish priest at York, where he died in the summer of 1512. The nuncupative will of William Crosby, Priest of the College of St. William, York, dated 9 June 1512.

Fifty pounds of wax to be burned at my burial before the altar of Holy Innocents in York Cathedral. To said college a bovate of land at Tollerton (in Alne) to my brother Robert Crosby an acre of land in said Tollerton and to his son William a dwelling house in Alne. Residue of goods to Sir Robert Flesher, Sir Lawrence Park and my brothers Robert and Richard Crosby, executors. Witnesses John Baroon, parson at York Cathedral, Robert Moreland, Chaplain and others. Proved 4 Aug. 1512. (Dean and Chapter of York Wills, vol. 2, fol. 100. Translated from the Latin.)

2. MILES² CROSBY, born about 1483; married —— ——. Children:—

  i. THOMAS³, b. about 1510.
  ii. William³. Time and place of death unknown.

MILES² CROSBY (John¹) was appointed one of the executors of his father's will in 1502; but, being under age at the time of the latter's death, the instrument was proved only by his elder brother, William² Crosby. By this will Miles² Crosby received the remainder of the term of the lease of a house called "Gyhowse," in Flawith in Alne; how many years he remained on this lease has not been ascertained. No further mention of Miles² Crosby appears in Alne, so it is evident he removed from there. Absolute proof as to where he went has not been secured; but a very extensive search throughout Yorkshire has disclosed but a single later mention of any Miles Crosby of his generation, one of the name appearing in a muster-roll of 1538 at Shipton (a parish adjoining Holme-on-Spalding-Moor on the north), and was probably identical with Miles², formerly of Alne. In 30 Henry VIII. (1538), a muster was ordered taken in Yorkshire of all able-bodied males between the ages of sixteen and sixty years; in the lists appear forty-two males in Stillingfleet, fifty-three in Alne, thirty-four in Wheldrake, sixty in Aughton, forty-eight in Thorgunby, eighty-two in Bubwith, fifty-two in Holme-on-Spalding-Moor, nearly nineteen hundred in the city of York, etc., etc.; so the lists are quite extensive of the names of the male residents of Yorkshire at that time. In the lists for Shipton at that time appear: Archer, *Miles Crosbe, a bowe;* Archer, Thomas Crosbe, a bowe; Archer, Wyllam Crosbe, a bowe. (Muster for Harthill Wapentake, Yorkshire, 30 Henry VIII.) It may be reasonably concluded that those names represent

Miles² Crosby and his two sons. No will of Miles² Crosby can be found. It appears that his descendants through his son Thomas³ Crosby, for at least five successive generations, without exception adopted the custom of naming the eldest son in each generation for the child's grandfather.

3. THOMAS³ CROSBY, born about 1510; married, about 1542, WIDOW JANNETT BELL (widow of John Bell). She died 1568/9. Children:—

   i. Miles⁴, b. about 1543.
  ii. ANTHONY⁴, b. about 1545.
 iii. Ralph⁴, b. about 1547.
 iv. Nicholas⁴, b. about 1550.

Thomas Crosby died in 1558/9.

Thomas³ Crosby (Miles², John¹) is first found on a record as an archer with a bow at Shipton (a parish adjoining Holme-on-Spalding-Moor on the north), in a muster-roll of 30 Henry VIII. (1538), on which roll also appear Miles Crosby and William Crosby, probably his father and brother, as previously stated.

In 36 Henry VIII. (1544) Thomas³ Crosby was assessed 12 pence on goods valued at £6. (Lay Subsidy, Yorkshire 303–322.)

Among the muniments of Holme Manor are documents of a suit in 1620/1 by Sir William Constable, hereditary lord of the manor, against Marmaduke Dolman for having his servants dwelling at Thex cottage pasture large droves of cattle on Holme commons, Constable claiming that according to immemorial custom of the manor only tenants of messuages * (in distinction from cottages), who resided there most of the year, were entitled to rights in the commons. Among the documents appears the statement:—

"Robert Patchett's wife, daughter to Chr: Ellithorpe wch Chr: lived at Thomas Crosbye's former farm, employed

---

* In the manor of Holme "those are called messuages whereunto an oxgang or more of land belongs; other dwellings are called cottages. An oxgang in this manor is twenty-six acres of arrable land and meadow" (Depositions in this suit).

one (William) Crake as an overseer for him of his goods in Morgan Inge, the said Crake being a very poor man and had a small stocke." This Christopher Ellithorpe, second son of Thomas Ellithorpe of Thex, was born about 1530, and died in 1586. According to various depositions, William Crake took the cottage at Thex about 1565; and it is evident that the Thomas Crosby above mentioned was this Thomas³ Crosby who was buried at Holme-on-Spalding-Moor, 16 Mar. 1558/9. No will or administration on his estate can be found.

Thomas³ Crosby was born about the beginning of the reign of Henry VIII. and his life continued through the reigns of Edward VI. and Mary, and extended into a few months of the reign of Elizabeth. During his life took place the rapid growth of Protestantism under Henry VIII. and Edward VI. (1509–53), the fiery ordeals of over three hundred of its martyrs under Mary (1553–58), who attempted to crush the reformed faith, and its final triumphant establishment under Elizabeth in 1558.

Thomas³ Crosby married, about 1542, Jannett Bell, widow of John Bell. The will of John Bell of Bursay in Holme-on-Spalding-Moor, dated 7 Aug. 1537, names mother Jannett Bell, wife Jannett Bell, brother Thomas Bell, sisters Phillippa Thornton and Julia Wright, and sons John and Thomas Bell. Residuary legatees and executors, wife Jannett and sons John and Thomas Bell. Witnesses, Thomas Savage, Christofer Spofforth, John Davie, John Millington. Proved by the widow Jannett, 3 Oct. 1537, the other executors being minors. (P. and E. York Wills, vol. 2, fol. 252.)

After the death of Thomas³ Crosby, his widow Jannett removed from the hamlet of Bursea in the parish of Holme-on-Spalding-Moor into the adjoining township or manor of Gribthorpe in the parish of Bubwith. This parish comprised no less than nine townships or manors, viz., Bubwith, Menthorpe, Breighton, Gunby, Willitoft, Harlthorpe, Faggathorpe, Gribthorpe, and Spaldington, several of which had chapels under Bubwith parish church. For several centuries the knightly family of Vavasour were the lords of most of these manors. Bubwith Church is picturesquely located on the east bank of the river Derwent, and is an ancient stone fabric dedicated to All Saints, consisting of chancel, nave, side aisles, and square embattled tower at the westerly end, the chancel being the most ancient part of the edifice and of the Early English period. The parish is part of an extensive low and flat plain.

Jannett, the widow of Thomas³ Crosby, survived her husband about ten years, and, dying in 1568 or 1569, left a will, a complete copy of which is appended.

> In the name of God Amen, the fyft day of November in the yeare of our Lord god a thousand fyve hundrethe threscore and eight, I Janett Crosbye of Gripthorpe, of hole mynd and ꝑfytt memorye make this my last will and testament in this worlde in forme hereafter followinge:
> First I bequeathe my soull to almyghtie god my creator and redemer beseeching him most hartilie to have mercie upon me, and my bodye to be buryed wᵗhin the ꝑishe churche yeard of Bubwithe. Itm I gyve to the verye nedye poure folkes of this ꝑishe one mett rye to be devyded amongs them. Itm I give to John* my sonne iiiᵗʰ youngest children one gymber sheringe. Itm I gyve to Myles my sonne my lease and good will of my farmehold after my decease. Itm I gyve to Katheren Myllington one gymber sheringe. Itm I gyve to Nicholas Crosbye my sonne one chist wᶜʰ was his fathers and my best brasse pott, willinge that he shall gyve to Anthony his brother v s. Itm I gyve to Myles my sonne one quarter wheate, wishinge him to be goode to his other brethren. Itm I gyve to Rauf my sone one yearinge whye. Itm I gyve to Rauf, Anthony, and Nicholas, my sonnes, half one Close at Harlthorpe called the Whyn Close, that is to say Nicholas to occupie the one half and Anthony and Rauf the other half duringe the terme of the Lease. The rest of my goods not legat, my detts paid my bodye buryed and this my last will fullfilled, I gyve to Myles, Anthonye, Rauf, and Nicholas my sonnes, whom I mak my executors. Thes witness, Thomas Blansharde, John Gower, John Webster, Clarke, and John Willmson, with other mo. Prob. 9 May 1569 by Miles and Ralph, sones of the deceased, executors named in the will, power reserved for son Nicholas, coexecutor, when he shall demand it. (Prerogative and Exchequer of York Wills, vol. 18, fol. 49.) The name of Anthony Crosby was accidentally omitted in record of probate.

Thomas³ Crosby, in giving to his eldest son Miles⁴ the name of the child's grandfather, started a custom in this branch of the family which continued without exception for five generations.

*I.e., John Bell.

Children of Thomas[3] and Jannett (Bell) Crosby.

i. Miles[4] Crosby, b. about 1543, named for his grandfather, succeeded, according to his mother's will in 1568, to the lease of her farm in Gribthorpe in Bubwith, which he lived to enjoy but a few years, dying in 1573, at the early age of about thirty years.

The will of Miles Crosbie of Gribthorpe in Bubwith, co. York, husbandman, dated 6 Jan. 1573–4. To be buried in the churchyard there. To my wife Alison and to my children the lease of my farmhold. To my brother Nicholas my raiment. To my daughter Ann a table. Residue of goods to wife Alison and daughter Anne, they to be executors; and if my wife have another child, said child to share with them. Witnesses, Thomas Blanchard, John Gower. Proved 1 Apr. 1574 by the widow Alice, power reserved for the other executor. (P. and E. York Wills, vol. 19, fol. 613.)

ii. Anthony[4] Crosby, b. about 1545.
iii. *Ralph*[4] Crosby, b. about 1547; resided in Bubwith, probably with his elder brother Miles, and d. in the spring of 1570, unmarried, aged about twenty-three years.

The will of *Rauffe Crosbie* of Gribthorpe yeoman, dated 25 Apr. 1570. To be buried in the churchyard of Bubwith. To Elizabeth Harison a mare. To the "childringe" of John Bell* of Harlthorpe £5. To Elizabeth Fletcher, Agnes Stelle of Seaton and Elizabeth Blande 5s each. To my brother Nycholas one "gymber bridringe" [a year yearling ewe]. All residue of goods to Myles Crosbie, Anthonie Crosbe and Nycholas Crosbe, my bredringe, they to be executors. Witnesses, Henry Ramsay, William Garver. Proved 9 July 1570 by Miles and Anthony Crosby brothers of deceased, power reserved for Nycholas Crosbie, a minor. (P. and E. York Wills, vol. 19, fol. 178.)

iv. *Nicholas*[4] Crosby, b. about 1550, was living, a minor, in 1570, as above stated. His further history has not been traced.

4. Anthony[4] Crosby, born about 1545, in Holme-on-Spalding-Moor; married, about 1570, Alison ———, parentage unknown. Children:—

i. Ellen[5] Crosby, b. about 1571; m., about 1586, George Westobie of Weldrake, County York. His widow, Ellen (Crosby) Westobie, is made administratrix of his estate (Administration Act Books, Hartwell Deanery, P. and E., Court of York). The will of the father (Anthony[4] Crosby) names the five children of Ellen[5] and George Westobie as "my grandchildren."
ii. Thomas[5] Crosby, b. in Holme-on-Spalding-Moor about 1575.

Anthony Crosby died in 1599. See will.

* Half-brother of the testator.

Anthony[4] Crosby (Thomas[3], Miles[2], John[1]), when a youth, removed with his mother from Bursea in Holme-on-Spalding-Moor into the adjoining township or manor of Gribthorpe in the parish of Bubwith, where she secured the lease of a farm, and she also had a lease of Whyn Close in the adjoining manor of Harlthorpe. By her will in 1568, her son Miles[4] Crosby succeeded to the Gribthorpe farm, and Anthony[4] was bequeathed an interest in Whyn Close in Harlthorpe, where he probably settled. On 7 Apr. 1580 as "Anthony Crosbye" he was a witness to the will of Robert Riche, the elder, of Lathorne in Angleton (a parish adjoining Harlthorpe on the north); and as "Anthony Crossebye" he appears as a witness to the will of Robarte Essingwood of Harethorpe, dated 24 Jan. 1590/1. (P. and E. York Wills, vol. 21, fol. 446, and vol. 24, fol. 547.)

Anthony[4] Crosby was a yeoman, and evidently a man of energy and thrift, as he acquired means to become a landowner, purchasing by fine* in 1592 a commodious hundred-acre farm in Holme-on-Spalding-Moor, as appears by the following document:—

Final concord made in the Queens Court at Hartford Castle on the morrow of All Saints, 34 Elizabeth (2 Nov. 1592) between Anthony Crosby, plaintiff, and Thomas Lambert and his wife Jane, Francis Lambert, Philip Lambert, John Lambert, and George Lambert, deforciants, of one messuage, one toft (ruined building), one garden, sixty acres of arable land, thirty acres of meadow, ten acres of pasture, and commons rights in pasture for all beasts, with all appurtenances, in Holme in Spaldyngmore, of which by plea of covenant the said Thomas, Jane, Francis, Philip, John, and George recognize the aforesaid premises to be the right of said Anthony, and they remise, quit claim, and warrant for themselves and their heirs to the said Anthony and his heirs against themselves and their heirs forever. For which acknowledgement, quit claim, warranty, etc., the said Anthony gave the said Thomas, Jane, Francis, Philip, John, and George, £40 sterling. (Feet of Fines, Yorkshire, Michaelmas Term, part 1, 34 and 35 Elizabeth (1592).)

* For over five centuries a custom existed in England of conveying lands by "fine." The process consisted in the grantee (plaintiff) bringing a friendly lawsuit against the grantor (deforciant) for the premises to be conveyed, the deforciant acknowledged the right of the plaintiff to the premises, for a consideration, and the record of the suit was enrolled in court archives called "Feet of Fines," the fine being the court fees.

As the above document gives no names or bounds of the premises conveyed, their exact location has not been determined. The Lambert grantors were sons of Richard Lambert of Holme-on-Spalding-Moor, who died in 1573. The £40 consideration named was nominal, and does not represent the actual full price paid for the property.

Besides the above-mentioned farm in Holme-on-Spalding-Moor, Anthony[4] Crosby also acquired a close called Leonard Scayles Close in Wheldrake (a parish about eight miles northwest of Holme), in which parish he was residing at the time of his death, in 1599. His will mentions a man-servant and a maid-servant, so he evidently was a farmer in prosperous and comfortable circumstances. Born at the very end of the reign of Henry VIII., his life was passed during the reigns of Edward VI. (1547–53), Mary (1553–58), and Elizabeth (1558–1603). The latter reign, under the stimulating influence of freedom from Rome and the establishment of the Reformation, became an era of sudden and remarkable advancement for England. The destruction of the Spanish Armada in 1588 first made England the mistress of the seas, and, followed by reverses to the Spanish arms on the Continent, established the country as a world power and started her greatness as a mercantile nation and world-wide colonizer. Besides this great advance in political and commercial supremacy, and in the intelligence, enterprise, wealth, and culture of the population, the period is also famed as the golden age of English literature, made illustrious by Shakespeare, Bacon, Spenser, Jonson, Raleigh, and Sidney. The country being freed from the thraldom of Rome, the cheapening of printing and increasing circulation of the Bible among the people gave rise to religious agitations and dissensions among the Protestants, resulting in the Puritan movement, which led a generation later to the settlement of New England, in which Anthony[4] Crosby's son Thomas[5], grandson Simon[6], and great-grandson Anthony[7] participated, thus transferring the family to the New World.

Shortly before his decease, in 1599, Anthony[4] Crosby

made a will, the original document itself being still preserved in the Probate Registry at York, of which a complete copy is appended:—

In dei noie Amenn, I Anthonye Crosbye of Wheldrake in the dyocesse of Yorke, sicke of bodye yet of sound and pfecte memorye and understandinge, the almightye god be therefore praysed, doe make my last wyll and testament in maner as followeth. Firstly I commend my soule unto the handes of almightye god who by his sonne Jesus Christ hatth created and redeemed me, and my bodye to be buryed in the Church or Churchyard of Wheldrake, as myne executors shall directe. Nextlye I geve and bequeathe unto Thomas Crosbye my sonne all and singular my landes whatsoever lyinge and being in Holme in Spaldingmore and in the libertyes thereof, to him and his heyres for ever. Also I geve unto the said Thomas my sonne j yoke of my best Oxen which he wyll chuse and my base wayne with yoakes and teames to serve four oxen. Also I give to Alysonn Crosbye my wife my close in Wheldrake called Leonard Scayles close for ev; also I give to the said Alysonn my wife two of my best kyne. Also I give to the said Thomas Crosbye my sonne my yonge blacke mayre, my bridle, and my sadle. Also I give to Luke Westobye, Willm Westobye, John Westobye, Thomas Westobye, and Richard Westobye, children of George Westobye of Wheldrake, Tenn pounds to be in equall ptes devided amonge them whenn they comme to the full age of one and twentye yeares, or to be bound apprentices to some good trade or occupaconn, so that myne executors maye thenn be lawfullye dischardged and acquitted thereof. Also I geve to Richard Jacksonn my servnte twentye pence so y he be diligent and trustie to his service this yeare followinge, otherwise to succease. Also I give to Isabell Stevensonn my mayd servnte twentie pence. Also I give to poore people of Wheldrake ten shillinges to be distributed amonge them, after the discretionn of Georg Howsemann there curate and Robte Wynterburne. The reste of my goodes and cattells unbequeathed I give to Alysonn Crosbye my wife and Thomas Crosbye my sonne, they dischardging my debtes and funerall expences, whome I make executors of this my laste [torn] and testamente.

Witnesses hereof and at the sealing, John Blansherd, Robte. Winterburne, Richard Butler, George Howseman. Prob. 7 March 1599–1600 by the executors. (Copied from Original Will in Prerogative and Exchequer Court of York; also registered in vol. 28, fol. 65.)

Anthony[4] Crosby married, about 1570, *Alison* ——. Her parentage has not been determined, but perhaps she was a Blanchard of Bubwith. A John Blansherd was a witness to the will of Anthony[4] Crosby in 1599. The will of John Blancharde of Bubwith, dated 20 Oct. 1571, mentions a wife but no children, gave small bequests to nearly a score of persons, and left all residue to "Thomas Blancherde and his brother John Blancherde, Elizabeth Blancherde, Janet Blancherde, Willm Howdell, Alison Crosbie, Robt.

Thorpe, Agnes Thorpe, Alexander Elerthorpe, and Janet Elerthorpe"; no relationships are stated, but it is likely these residuary legatees were nephews and nieces of the testator. (P. and E. York Wills, vol. 19, fol. 450.)

As the early registers of Bubwith and Wheldrake are lost, the records of baptisms of the children of Anthony[4] and Alison Crosby are not to be found; and his will reveals but two.

Anthony[4] Crosby was the father of Thomas[5] Crosby, and grandfather of Simon[6] Crosby, who came to New England, both of whom were in Cambridge, Mass., prior to 1640.

As the two ministers who influenced the coming to New England of Thomas[5] Crosby and his son Simon[6] Crosby were Rev. Thomas Shepard and Rev. Ezekiel Rogers, a short note of them seems appropriate here.

Rev. Thomas Shepard was born in Towcester, Northamptonshire, 5 Nov. 1605 (the day of Guy Fawkes's "Gunpowder Plot"), son of William and —— (Bland) Shepard. His parents and connections were Puritans, and at the age of fifteen years he entered that famous Puritan institution, Emmanuel College, Cambridge University, where he received the degrees of B.A. in 1623 and M.A. in 1627. In the summer of that year he located at Earles Colne, County Essex, where he preached for three and a half years and secured a large following; but in December, 1630, he was silenced by Archbishop Laud and obliged to flee for safety; and by the solicitation of his friend Rev. Ezekiel Rogers, rector of Rowley in Yorkshire, he took refuge in the household of Sir Richard Darley, Knt., at Buttercrambe in the parish of Bossall, County York (about twenty-five miles northwest of Rowley), where he remained for a year and preached successfully to assemblages gathered from the surrounding country for miles about. In 1632 he went to Heddon in Northumberland, about five miles from Newcastle-on-Tyne, and remained in that vicinity about two years, continuing to preach, and gathering another following from that region. His friends urging him to remove to New England, in June, 1634, he went by ship from Newcastle-on-Tyne to Ipswich,

County Suffolk, whence in December he started in the ship *Hope* for New England, but the ship was disabled and soon put back. Mr. Shepard then went to London, whence on 10 Aug. 1635, accompanied by many of his adherents, he sailed for New England in the ship *Defence*, arriving at Boston, 3 Oct. 1635. A few days later he removed to Cambridge, where many of his old friends had settled, and where a church was organized of which he was ordained pastor; and he continued in that office until his decease, 25 Aug. 1649. He was married three times. He was made "freeman" on same date with Simon[6] Crosby, 3 Mar. 1635/6.

Rev. Ezekiel Rogers was a member of a distinguished ministerial Puritan family and was born about 1589, son of Rev. Richard Rogers, lecturer at Wethersfield, County Essex. He was educated at Christ's College, Cambridge University, receiving the degrees of B.A. in 1605 and M.A. in 1608. After serving several years as chaplain to Sir Francis Barrington, Bart., of Hatfield Broad Oak, County Essex, the latter appointed him in 1620 rector of Rowley in Yorkshire, where for nearly a score of years he labored with zeal and acquired a great influence among the people in Yorkshire and Lincolnshire living within a radius of some forty miles from his parish. His non-conformist doctrines finally got him into difficulties; in May, 1638, he resigned his living; and in the autumn of that year, with a company of some sixty families from Yorkshire and Lincolnshire, he sailed from England and arrived at Boston in December, 1638. During the winter this band of colonists remained in and around Boston, and a removal to New Haven, Conn., was considered; but they finally decided to start a new plantation by themselves, and accordingly bought a large tract of land on the Merrimack River, and in April, 1639, started a new settlement, which was named "Rowley," after the old home in England of their venerated pastor. On 3 Dec. 1639 a church was formally organized, of which Mr. Rogers was installed pastor, and he remained in this service until his decease, 23 Jan. 1660/1, aged about seventy years. He was married three times, but all his children died in infancy.

As Holme-on-Spalding-Moor is located midway and directly between Rowley and Buttercrambe, it is evident that Thomas[5] Crosby and his son Simon[6] Crosby fell under the influence of Rogers and Shepard, and, imbued with the Puritans' fervid faith and strong convictions, joined the throng who relinquished their beloved ancestral homes, endured the perils and discomforts of the Atlantic, and braved the hardships and dangers of pioneer life in a wilderness infested with hostile savages, to establish a nation in the New World.

And so we will leave these four generations of Crosbys, surrounded as they are with much of the mist of the past. They were yeomen of the better class, filling their allotted niches in destiny, and in their way doing their part. No romance nor deeds of valor caused them to adorn the pages of history, but each in his simple way filled out his sphere of action, until the time came when religious oppression at home, and opportunity to seek other lands, led the more untrammelled spirits to remove to a new world; and the next chapter will deal with the elder of those two men, father and son, who within a few years of each other departed for America, which in those days must have seemed a venturesome trip indeed.

Chapter II.

THOMAS CROSBY, FATHER OF SIMON THE EMIGRANT.

Thomas Crosby of Cambridge and Rowley, Mass., seems to have escaped a large share of the attention and curiosity directed towards the early pioneers of New England. Nor is this to be wondered at, for no certain record of just when he came to America is available, and he was identified directly with no one of his name, for the only one of his children who came to America had preceded him, actuated probably more by a spirit of adventure and possibly of necessity than had been the case with Thomas Crosby. And Thomas Crosby had hardly rejoined his son in the new country before the latter was taken off by death, his widow remarrying and of course taking Thomas Crosby's grandchildren with her.* And so he seems to have completed his life in America, first in Cambridge and then in Rowley, quietly caring for his property and perhaps doing his share for the public good, none the less effectively if quietly.

And so it is in father and son we have the two connecting links between England and America, and this very wealth of links proved to be to all past searchers in the annals of the Crosby family their chief stumbling-block, for it must be very apparent to the most casual observer that, where the representatives of two connecting generations had come to this country and because of unavoidable circumstances their connection with each other unsuspected, a considerable increase was added to the difficulty of bridging across to England. All the more so as these very men were quite unsuspicious of the fact they would some day be the subject of genealogical investigation.

* With the exception of Anthony[7] Crosby, see later.

5. THOMAS[5] CROSBY, born in Holme-on-Spalding-Moor, County York, England, about 1575; married in Holme-on-Spalding-Moor, England, 19 Oct. 1600, to *Jane Sotheron* (*Parish Register at Holme*), bapt. 4 Mar. 1581 (*Parish Register at Holme*), died in Rowley, Mass., 1662. (Essex Institute Records, Salem, Mass.) Thomas[5] Crosby died in May, 1661. Children:—

 i. Anthony[6], b. about 1602, in Holme; d. June, 1632, in Holme.
 ii. Thomas[6], b. about 1604, in Holme; d. Dec., 1658, in Holme.
 iii. William[6], b. about 1606, in Holme; d. June, 1636, in Holme.
 iv. SIMON[6], b. about 1608, in Holme; d. Sept., 1639, in Cambridge, Mass.

THOMAS[5] CROSBY (Anthony[4], Thomas[3], Miles[2], John[1]) was born in Bubwith, County York, about 1575, but no record of his baptism is to be found, as the early registers of that parish are lost. The first record found of him is in 1599 as executor of his father's will, by which he inherited half the latter's goods and the hundred-acre freehold farm in Holme-on-Spalding-Moor which in 1592 had been bought of the Lambert family. In 1600 Thomas[5] Crosby settled on this estate and in the same year enhanced his fortune by marriage to *Jane*[5] *Sotheron*, daughter of *William*[4] and *Constance* (*Lambert*) *Sotheron*, her father being the wealthiest resident of the parish, as is proved by a subsidy in 1609, in which he paid double the tax of any one else, and (except Gabriel St. Quentin) his two sons-in-law Thomas[5] Crosby and William Millington ranked next in wealth. Only about one-tenth of all heads of families had sufficient estates to be subject to this subsidy; so, of over one hundred and fifty households in Holme-on-Spalding-Moor, but nineteen were assessed. As indication of the substantial position of the Crosby and allied families of Sotheron, Lambert, Brigham, Watson, and Millington, reference is made to Lay Subsidy, Holme Beacon, East Riding of Yorkshire, 7 James I. (1609), East Riding of Yorkshire, 204–401, where a full copy may be found.

Thomas[5] Crosby was a witness to the will of William

Emyson of Holme-on-Spalding-Moor, dated 24 Jan. 1601/2; and was a creditor for 25s. of the estate of William Wright of same, whose will was dated 18 Aug. 1620. (P. and E. York Wills, vol. 28, fol. 657, and vol. 40, fol. 463.)

After Thomas[5] Crosby had emigrated to New England, in 1641 Peter Millington of Holme-on-Spalding-Moor brought a suit in chancery against his cousin Marmaduke Millington and others, concerning lands there formerly of William Millington to whom complainant was eldest son and heir. In the depositions on this case the following mentions of Thomas[5] Crosby appear:—

John Southerne of Holme in Spaldingmore, aged fifty-two years, deposed that among the lands owned by William Millington were Closes called Crosby Close purchased of one Crosby and Brigham Close purchased by one Brigham, which Closes were anciently called Low Wood Closes or the Burne Closes.

John Carlin of Whalsey, co. York, aged about thirty years, deposed that his father Thomas Carlin was a tenant of some of the premises in question, and that one Thomas Crosbye refused to purchase the same at the price asked by Mr. Constable, Crosby saying "it was tooe Deare."

Robert Strother of Everingham, co. York, yeoman, aged fifty-four years, deposed that the premises in question were valued by a commission consisting of Robert Stapleton Esq., Marmaduke Dolman Esq., Henry Acrod, and Thomas Crosbye, gent., at £160; and that later Mr. Constable offered to sell them to the said Thomas Crosbie, one of the commissioners, at the same price at which John Atkinson had them, but said Crosbie declined the same.

(Chancery Depositions, Elizabeth, James I., and Charles I. (1558–1649), M–41–5.)

In 1628 Thomas[5] Crosby and his eldest son, Anthony[6] Crosby, brought a suit in the common law in the Court of Kings Bench against one Bartholomew Steere, to recover on certain bonds. Steere replied with a counter suit in equity against the Crosbys in the Court of Chancery, and, dying before the suits were finished, in 1631 his nephew and heir John Steere was sued in the matter by the Crosbys, in the Court of Chancery. The bills of complaint by plaintiffs and answers by defendants in these counter chancery suits are not now to be found; but the depositions in the last suit are preserved, from which the following facts can be gathered; viz., John Dales of South Dalton, County York (who married, about 1613, Anne Sotheron, a younger sister of Jane Sotheron, wife of Thomas[5] Crosby), inherited certain copyhold lands there, which on 26 Aug. 1624 he sold to Bartholomew Steere; and at the same time said Steere gave bonds in £280 to Thomas[5] and Anthony[6] Crosby that before 25 June 1625 he would pay to them £140 to be turned over to Anne Dales, wife of said John Dales, in consideration of rights of dower in the premises. John Dales died about 1625, and Bartholomew Steere failed to pay to the Crosbys the £140 for the benefit of the widow Anne Dales, so the Crosbys sued him for the bonds in the Court of Kings Bench, and in 1628 Steere replied with a counter suit in chancery. Before these suits were finished, Bartholomew Steere died, and his estate was claimed by his nephew John Steere, and by his kinswoman the wife of Thomas Greenberry. The latter secured appointment as administrator on the estate of Bartholomew Steere, and as such paid over to the Crosbys £20 worth of corn as part payment on account of the bonds, for which the Crosbys gave him a receipt. Later, John Steere succeeded in establishing his claim as heir to the premises, and, as he refused to pay the remaining £120 due, claiming the settlement made by Greenberry was in full, in 1631 he was sued in chancery by the Crosbys for the recovery of same. The decree on this case has not been found. (Chancery Depositions, Elizabeth, James I., Charles I. (1558–1649), C–31–16.)

About 1625 Sir William Constable, the last of the Constable family to possess the manor of Holme, became financially involved, mortgaged his estates, and was finally obliged in 1633 to sell the manor of Holme to Sir Marmaduke Langdale. Thomas[5] Crosby and his son Simon[6] Crosby were participants in a part of this tragedy of the ruin and extinguishment of an ancient and knightly landed family, as is revealed by an original indenture still preserved in the muniment chest of the manor of Holme, an abstract of which is herewith appended:—

This indenture made 24 Mar. 1633/4, between Sir William Constable of Flamborough, Bart., Thomas Crosby and his son Simon Crosby of Holme-on-Spalding-Moor, yeoman, of the one part, and Sir Marmaduke Langdale of North Dalton, Knt., and Richard Meadley of Sancton, gent., of the other part, all of the County of York, witnesseth; that whereas on 17 Sept. 1632, the said Sir William Constable conveyed to the said Thomas and Simon Crosby five messuages with all rights and appurtenances in Holme, in the occupation of William Hewley, John Varnill, George Atkinson, William Johnson, and Thomas Ashland, for term of three hundred years, with proviso that if said Sir William Constable should pay to said Thomas and Simon Crosby £400 within seven years after above date, with interest of £32 per year, then the mortgage should terminate and the premises revert to said Constable; now this indenture witnesseth that the said Thomas Crosby and his said son Simon Crosby, with the assent of said Sir William Constable, in consideration of a "competent sum" of money, hereby do convey to said Sir Marmaduke Langdale and Richard Meadley, all their term and interest whatsoever in the above premises. (Signed by) WILLIAM CONSTABLE,

Thomas Crosbye   Simon Crosby

Witnesses: THO: FUGILL, CHRISTOPHER JACKSON.

This and other documents to be found in the Proprietors' Records of Cambridge, Mass., establish the fact that Thomas Crosby was comfortably well off at the time of his coming, a fact merely to be noted for what it is worth, as indication that other than the spirit of adventure actuated his removal to America. While no proof exists as to the exact date of his arrival in this country, it may fairly well be supposed he came over with the flock in charge of Rev. Ezekiel Rogers, with whose destinies he later cast his lot in Rowley, Mass.

That he was not only sufficiently well off to be comfortably independent, but also was able to utilize his funds for the public good, is shown by his connection with the first printing-press ever brought to America and there set up, for which enterprise he advanced what at that time was a considerable sum of money. Mention is made of this printing-press in nearly all the histories of printing in America, but we will refer here to the Jewett Family of America (Year Book of 1911, p. 27):—

The ship "John of London" on her eventful voyage from Hull to Boston brought the first printing press set up in the colonies. . . . That the printing press was brought over at that time is unquestioned. It was the enterprise of the Rev. Joseph Glover, rector, it is said, of Sutton, Surrey, and Glover's contract with Stephen Daye, who came out as foreman, made with Daye at Cambridge, 7 June, 1638, provided that Daye was to go to New England at Glover's expense in the ship "John of London." Glover died on the voyage, and Daye set up the press at Newtowne, now Cambridge. This press is often referred to as having been "brought over for Harvard College," but as Harvard College did not exist until 1639, when it received the name in consideration of seven hundred pounds given by the Rev. John Harvard; and as the printing press did not go there it was evidently never intended for Harvard.

. . . So far as known the only member of Rogers's original company who did not settle at Rowley was Thomas Crosby, who had an interest in the printing press, and who remained at Newtowne with Daye. Whether the interest was acquired after the death of Glover, or was an original one, is not known.

It is known that Simon[6] Crosby preceded his father in emigrating to New England, the former coming in the spring of 1635; and, although the exact time of the emigration of Thomas[5] Crosby has not been absolutely proven, he certainly came before 1640, and probably was a member of the company who came with Rev. Ezekiel Rogers in the autumn of 1638. On his arrival in New England, Thomas[5] Crosby probably went to live in the household of his son Simon[6], who had settled in Cambridge, Mass. The following record, dated 16 Apr. 1640, furnishes the earliest mention of Thomas[5] Crosby in New England:—

Be it known to all men by these p'sents that I Steven Day of Cambridge in the Colony of ye Massachusetts Bay do freely & voluntarily binde over my fyve lots (lyeing in the new field beyond the water) wch are the twenty-fourth, twenty-fifth, twenty-sixth, twenty-seventh, &

twenty-ninth, of wch lots in all is sixty Acres and upwards of ground: wch ground I say I do freely bind over to Thomas Crosby Senior, of the same towne & Colony above mentioned, for his Counter security for fifty & seven pounds wch the said Thomas lent me for one whole yeare, paying him use for it according as the Church or any honest man shall see fitt, reserving to myselfe free liberty to take of all wood and timber as is uppon the ground, and to this Act I binde myselfe my heires Executors & Administrators, & hereunto set my hand this 16th of the 2° month 1640. Steven Day. John Edwards: Matthew Day:

This was the transaction in connection with the Steven Day of the printing-press.

The Proprietors' Records of Cambridge have the following mentions of Thomas[5] Crosby:—

20 July 1645. Thomas Crosby bought of Cary Lathum seaven Acr of land more or lesse wth a Dwellinge house & out-houses uppon it, wth all the rights & priveledges thereunto belonging, John Bridge Nor-West, highway to Windmill-hill southeast, his owne land southwest, Elizabeth Greene, William Wilcocke, Robert Parker, Roger Bancroft, & the highway to Watertown northeast. (Cambridge Proprietors' Records, printed volume, pp. 119 and 131.) (This estate was situated on the westerly side of the present Ash Street, at the corner of Brattle Street.)

12 of (10) 1648. Andrew Stevenson bought of Thomas Crosbye one dwellinge house, within the Towne, wth about halfe a rood* of ground wth the purtenes thereto belonging sometyme in the possession of Marke Pierce; Edward Collins North & East, Crooked street West, Back-lane south. (*Ibid.*, p. 137.) (This estate was located on the northeasterly corner of the present Holyoke and Mount Auburn Streets.)

It seems likely that Thomas Crosby resided in the household of his daughter-in-law, the widow of Simon[6] Crosby, until she was married in 1645 to her second husband, Rev. William Tompson of Braintree, Mass., whither she then went to reside, taking her children with her; and about this time Thomas[5] Crosby bought for a home the Cary Latham homestead, on the present Ash Street, as previously mentioned. Here he resided a few years, but the death of his pastor, Rev. Thomas Shepard, his friendship for Rev. Ezekiel Rogers, and his large circle of Old England friends living at Rowley, Mass., evidently induced his

* A rood is one-fourth of an acre.

removal thither, where he remained the rest of his life, disposing of his remaining Cambridge property as follows: On 10 Oct. 1649 Thomas Crosby of Rowley, County Essex, acknowledged that for a valuable consideration he had divers years past sold to Edmund Frost of Cambridge, County Middlesex, three acres of land* there, bounded by land of said Crosby east, Charles River and John Bridge southwest, Roger Bancroft northwest, and Richard Eccles and Nathaniel Greene north, together with the privileges of commonage pertaining to the house some time on said land and originally occupied by John Masters, deceased, said Frost to build and maintain a fence against said Crosby's land; also about four acres of marsh bounded by Herbert Pelham, Esq., west, and Charles River east. Witnesses: Joseph Juitt, Richard Eccles. On 12 Feb. 1662/3 Edmund Frost acknowledged the covenant as to a fence in above deed. Witnesses, Joel Jacoomys, Caleb Chesheteamuck,† Thomas Danforth. Recorded 12 Jan. 1669/70. (Middlesex County Deeds, vol. 3, fol. 424.) On 14 July 1657 Thomas Crosby of Rowley, County Essex, yeoman, acknowledged that in 1651 for £40 he sold by verbal agreement to Richard Eccles of Cambridge, County Middlesex, weaver, an old house with six acres of upland and meadow in said Cambridge, bounded by Thomas Longhorne east, Charles River south, John Bridge west, and John Hastings and Deacon Marrett north; also a lot of about seventy acres of remote wilderness land, lying in Cambridge Woods (Billerica). Witnesses, Samuel Platts, Benjamin Scott. Recorded 6 Dec. 1682. (Middlesex County Deeds, vol. 8, fol. 236.)

As a proprietor of Rowley, Thomas[5] Crosby received grants of twelve acres of land there in various of the later divisions (Rowley Town Records, printed volume, pp. 26, 31, 33, and 46). On 30 Apr. 1656 he bought of John

---

* This was part of the seven-acre homestead of Cary Latham, who acquired it by marriage to Elisabeth, daughter of John Masters.

† These two witnesses were Indian students at Harvard College, the latter of whom graduated in 1665, the only Indian who ever became an alumnus of the college.

Haseltine the latter's homestead in Rowley, consisting of dwelling-house, barn, orchard, and home-lot, lying as recorded in the town-book; together with the planting-lot, meadows, gates in the commons or ox-pasture, etc. Witnesses: John Tod, Robert Hesseltine. Acknowledged by John Hesseltine, 25 Feb. 1662/3. (Ipswich Court Deeds at Salem, vol. 2, fol. 124.) This homestead of John Haseltine is described as follows: Wethersfield Streete. To John Haseltine one Lott containing two Acres bounded on the South side by John Trumble and the East end by the streete (Rowley Town Records, printed volume, p. 4). John Haseltine had also received grants of about twenty-two acres of upland and meadow (*ibid.*, pp. 9, 13, 18, 21, 24, 27, 31, 33, 36, 41). These also passed to Thomas[5] Crosby by above deed.

Thomas[5] Crosby was about sixty-five years of age when he emigrated to New England. He never made application for admission as a freeman, held no public offices, and took no part in public affairs. He provided for his eldest surviving son, Thomas[6] Crosby, property in England, where this son remained; evidently advanced to his youngest son, Simon[6] Crosby, the latter's portion before he went to New England; and in his old age adopted and brought up his orphan grandchild, Anthony[7] Crosby (only surviving son of his second son, William[6] Crosby), whom he made his sole heir by the following deed of gift:—

This present wrighting wittnesseth yt we Thomas Crosbye and Jane Crosby of Rowley in the county of Essex, have of our free will and pleasure given & granted, alienated and disposed, and by these presents doe fully and freely give, grant, allienate, and dispose unto our well beloved grandchild Anthony Crosbye of the same towne and county, all & every part of our whole estate that we are possessed of and doth belong unto us or either of us, whether houses or lands, in ould England and in New England, bills, bonds, rents, and arrears, with all debts and demands that are anyways dew unto us or unto either of us, from any person or persons whatsoever, in New England or Old England, for him the sd Anthony to have, hould, possess, and enjoy all the whole outward estate which the Lord of his meere merce & good pleasure hath bestowed upon us, both houses and lands with all their appurtenances and priviledges belonging unto them, whether in Old England or New England, bills, bonds, rents, arrears of rents, debts, dews, and demands, giving and granting our full power to aske, demand, receive, and recover, by all lawful ways & means, of all and every person or persons, as fully and amply every waye as we ourselves or either of us might have done before we signed and sealed this our deed of gift, and the same soe recovered to have, hold, possess, & enjoy as his own proper right, and to his heirs and assignes forever, without any lett, hindrance, or molestation from any person or persons laying any claime thereunto, by, from or under us or either of us forever: provided always that we doe still reserve unto ourselves sufficient maintenance, to be alwayes alowed unto us by the above named Anthony Crosbye our grandchild, during our naturall life, or twenty pounds per annum to be payd unto us while we live together and to the survivor of us, at our choice, during the time of our naturall life as aforesaid. In witness of this our deed of gift (to be our full and free act and deed unto our aforesaid grandchild) we have hereunto sett our hands and seales this twelfth of February 1658 (1658/9).

Witnesses:	THOMAS CROSBY
Read, sealed and delivered in presence of	with a marke and a seale.*
THOMAS LEAVER	JANE CROSBY
JOHN LAMBERT.	with a marke and a seale.

This was acknowledged by Jane Crosby, the late wife of the sayd Thomas Crosbye, upon the 29th day of the second month called Aprill, 1662, before me Samuel Symonds.

(Ipswich Deeds at Salem, vol. 2, fol. 116.)

Having thus in his old age settled his affairs, Thomas[5] Crosby, progenitor of all the American Crosbys, passed a few declining years with his grandson, Dr. Anthony[7] Crosby of Rowley, Mass., where he died at the advanced age of over eighty-five years, and was buried 6 May 1661.

He married, in Holme-on-Spalding-Moor, County York, England, 19 Oct. 1600, *Jane*[5] *Sotheron*, baptized there 4 Mar. 1581/2, daughter of William[4] and Constance (Lambert) Sotheron. She came to New England, probably with her husband, and died in Rowley, Mass., at the age of eighty years, being buried 2 May 1662.

The registers of Holme-on-Spalding-Moor commence in Jan. 1558/9 and run to Jan. 1600/1, with gaps in this period, caused by leaves being cut out, from 1564 to 1573 and for parts of the periods 1584 to 1586 and 1593 to 1598. From Jan. 1600/1 to Aug. 1628 no register now exists, but transcripts for 1600, 1623, and 1627 are preserved at York. From 1628 registers exist to the present time.

* His autograph signature, with that of his son Simon[6] Crosby, is signed to the Constable document.

On account of the loss of the registers from 1601 to 1628, the records of baptisms of the children of Thomas[5] and Jane (Sotheron) Crosby do not exist; but they are named in the will of their grandmother Constance Sotheron, dated 14 Nov. 1622. (Prerogative and Exchequer of York Wills, vol. 37, fol. 252.) Children, born in Holme-on-Spalding-Moor:—

i. Anthony[6], b. about 1602, named for his grandfather. He was a legatee of 10s. in the will of his grandfather William Sotheron, dated 2 Dec. 1616, and of £10 in the will of his grandmother Constance Sotheron, dated 14 Nov. 1622 (P. and E. York Wills, vol. 35, fol. 492, and vol. 37, fol. 252). From 1628 to 1631 he was associated with his father in the law suits with Bartholomew and John Steere, as previously related. (See *ante*, pp. 21, 22.) He d. unmarried, and was bur. at Holme-on-Spalding-Moor, 23 June 1632, aged about thirty years.
ii. Thomas[6], b. about 1604.
iii. William[6], b. about 1606.
iv. Simon[6], b. about 1608.

THOMAS[6] CROSBY (*Thomas*[5], *Anthony*[4], *Thomas*[3], *Miles*[2], John[1]), born in Holme-on-Spalding-Moor about 1604, second but eldest surviving son of his father, was given 10s. by the will of his grandfather William Sotheron, dated 2 Dec. 1616, and £10 and all her ploughing-gear by the will of his grandmother Constance Sotheron, dated 14 Nov. 1622 (P. and E. York Wills, vol. 33, fol. 492, and vol. 37, fol. 252). On a subsidy of 16 Charles I. (1640), fifteen persons were taxed in Holme-on-Spalding-Moor, of whom Thomas Crosbie and his uncle John Sotheron each paid 37s. 4d. on goods valued at £7 each, these two being the wealthiest men in the town, each of their estates being more than double that of any one else (Lay Subsidy, Yorkshire, 205-463). The will of Robert Brigham of Holme-on-Spalding-Moor, dated 5 Sept. 1640, mentions land sold by him to Thomas Crosby of Holme (P. and E. York Wills, Original Will, 1640).

Although his father, Thomas[5] Crosby, his brother Simon[6] Crosby, and his nephew Anthony[7] Crosby all went to New

England, Thomas[6] Crosby alone remained at Holme-on-Spalding-Moor until his death, 28 Dec. 1658. Doubtless he was given estates there by his father, but to what extent has not been learned. As he had no sons the Crosby name in this family line became extinct in England; and to his two daughters, who married into families of the armorial landed gentry, he left his estate by a will, a full copy of which is appended:—

In the Name of God Amen, I Thomas Crosby of Holme on Spaldinge Moore in the Countye of Yorke, being sick and weake of body but of pfect memory, Gods holy name be praysed for the same, doe constitute and ordayne this my last will and testament in manner and forme following, first I give and bequeath my soule unto God my creator firmly trusting in him and hopeing for Salvation through the death and passion of Jesus Christ my most gracious Redeemer and Saviour onely, and my body to be buried with decent christian buriall att the discretion of my Executor. Imprimis I give and demise to my daughter Prudence Bower and to the heires of her body lawfully begotten or to be begotten, the messuage, tenement, or house wherein I now dwell with all houses, buildings, Stables, Barnes, orchards, gardens, Closes, Lands, pfitts, Comodityes, hereditaments and Appurtenances whatsoever to the sayd Messuage house or tenement belonging or in any wise apperteyninge part thereof, being now in my owne occupation, and the other part thereof in the occupation of one William Yeoman of Holme aforesaid. Alsoe I give to my sayd daughter Prudence and to the heires of her body lawfully begotten or to be begotten All those two closes called Pigh hills, all those two Closes Called Sadler Closes, all that Close Called Chantry Close, with their and every of their appurtenances, And for want of heires of the body of the said Prudence I give the said Messuage, house, or tenement wherein I now dwell and all other the Closes and premises with the appurtenances before mentioned, to my daughter Jane Belt wife of Jesper Belt of Pocklington and to the heirs and assigns of the sayd Jane for ever. And all the rest and residue of my Lands, tenements, and hereditaments whatsoever, as well in my owne occupation as in the occupation of any other pson or psons whatsoever, I give unto my sayd Daughter Jane Belt and to her heirs and assigns for ever. Item I give unto my sayd loveing wife Prudence Crosby forty pounds by yeare dureing her naturall life, to be payd out of the house wherein I now dwell and out of the lands and Closes wth the appurtenances that are in the possession of me or my assignee, in full satisfaction of her dower or thirds forth of my estate, reall and psonal, and I give all the household goods belonging in the dwellinghouse, and one Cow which shee will chuse. Item I give to Thomas Crosby my Nephew, the sonne of my brother Symon Crosby deceased, Tenn pounds. Item I give unto Symon Crosby, the sonne of my brother aforesaid, Tenn pounds. Item I give unto Joseph Crosby, another of the sonnes of the sayd Symon Crosby, Tenn pounds. Item I give unto Robert Belt my Grandchild my gray fillye. Item I give unto Sarah Belt my Grandchild Tenn pounds. Item I give unto Thomasin Bower my grandchilde Tenn pounds. Item whereas as there is in my hands Twenty one pounds belonging to the Stock of the paore of

Holme Above-sayd, I give to be added to it Nine pounds to be payd att Christmas after my decease. Nevertheless my mynde and will is that neyther of my sayd daughters or any clayminge under them or eyther of them shall have or receive any benefitt or pfitt by or out of my said tenements or lands or any part thereof, eyther in my owne occupation or in the occupation of my assignes, untill my debts and legacies be fully payd and discharged, but that the rents, issues, and pfitts thereof (save the sayd forty pounds by yeare to my wife aforesayd) shall be received by my Executor hereafter named for and towards the payment and satisfaction of soe much of my debts and legacies as my psonall estate will not extend to pay. And after my debts and legacies fully satisfied and payd forth of my psonal estate and out of the rents and pfitts of my sayd lands as aforesayd, Then the sayd Messuage, house, or tenement, Lands, and premises with the appurtenances, to be holden and enjoyed according to the severall uses, Limitations, and purposes hereinbefore limited, expressed, and declared. All the rest of my goods, Chattels and psonall Estate I give unto my sonne Jesper Belt whom I make my sole Executor of this my last will and Testament. In Witness whereof I have sett my hand and seale the twenty fifth day of November in the yeare of our Lord God one thousand six hundred fifty eight. Tho: Crosbye. Sealed signed and delivered in the psence of us, Richard Goodland, his I marke, Christopher Haiton, his X marke, Richard Barker, his O marke.

Proved at York on the 19 day of April 1669 by Jane Belt, widow of Jasper Belt the executor named in the Will. (Prerogative and Exchequer of York Wills, vol. 50, fol. 330.)

Concerning the will, it is noteworthy that it was made 25 Nov. 1658 and the testator died a month later, 28 Dec. 1658; but it was not proved until over *ten years* later, 19 Apr. 1669. *Also it appears that the testator gave bequests to his nephews Thomas[7], Simon[7], and Joseph[7] Crosby* (sons of his youngest brother Simon[6] Crosby of Cambridge, Mass.), but makes no mention of his nephew Dr. Anthony[7] Crosby of Rowley, Mass. (son of his second brother, William[6] Crosby), who was his male heir-at-law from a primogeniture standpoint. Further, less than three months after Thomas[6] Crosby made this will, his father, Thomas[5] Crosby of Rowley, Mass., on 12 Feb. 1658/9 made his deed of gift of all his estate both in Old England and New England to his grandchild Dr. Anthony[7] Crosby (see *ante*, pp. 27, 28); and in 1662 the latter made a voyage to England evidently in regard to his inheritance. It is possible that when Thomas[5] Crosby emigrated to New England he left his son Thomas[6] in occupation of certain of his lands, but did not deed them to him; and, as the latter left no sons, the old man may have desired them to go to his male heir, his grandson Dr. Anthony[7] Crosby. If so, there may have been some litigation which delayed the proving of the will of Thomas[6] Crosby for ten years.

Thomas[6] Crosby married, about 1633, *Prudence* ——, who survived him. Children:—

    i. *Jane*[7], b. about 1634; m., in Holme-on-Spalding-Moor, 11 Jan. 1654/5, *Jasper Belt* of Pocklington, County York, bapt. at All Hallows, York, 20 July 1625, sixth son of Sir Robert Belt, Knt., of York City and Bossall, County York, and Lord Mayor of York in 1628 and 1640. Jasper Belt was given by his father estates in Pocklington, County York, where he resided, and d. in 1661; and his widow, Jane, d. there 20 May 1703. The communion chalice of Pocklington Church bears this inscription: "The Gift of Mrs. Jane Belt, For the Use of the Church of Pocklington"; and in a shield is engraved the Belt arms, viz.: *Argent, a chevron gules charged with a cross pattee fitches and two mullets or*, between three torteaux (Yorkshire Archæological Journal, vol. 14, p. 97). Children (*Belt*), b. in Pocklington:—

        1. *Robert*[8], b. about 1657, d. in Bossall, 25 Mar. 1690, where a mural inscription to him remains in the church. By the death without surviving issue of all the elder brothers of his father, this Robert Belt eventually became sole heir to the Bossall estates of his grandfather Sir Robert Belt, Knt. He married and left descendants.

        2. *Sarah*,[8] b. about 1659, d. 23 Apr. 1690; m. her cousin *William Bower* of Bridlington, County York.

    ii. *Prudence*[7], b. about 1636; m., 7 June 1655, *William Bower* of Bridlington, County York, and had issue.

    iii. *Katherine*[7], bur. at Holme-on-Spalding-Moor, 2 May 1640.

WILLIAM[6] CROSBY (*Thomas*[5], *Anthony*[4], *Thomas*[3], *Miles*[2], *John*[1]), born in Holme-on-Spalding-Moor about 1606, received a legacy of 10s. in the will of his grandfather William Sotheron, dated 2 Dec. 1616, and £5 in the will of his grandmother Constance Sotheron, dated 14 Nov. 1622 (P. and E. York Wills, vol. 35, fol. 492, and vol. 37, fol. 252). No will or administration on his estate can be found, and, except the records of his marriage and children, no further information of him has been discovered; and it is probable that he died about 1640.

He married, in Seaton, County York, 2 Apr. 1633, *Anne Wright*, whose parentage has not been discovered; she was buried at Holme-on-Spalding-Moor, 22 June 1636. Children:—

i. *Thomas*[7], named for his grandfather, bapt. in Seaton, 18 Dec. and bur. there 20 Dec. 1633.

ii. *Dr. Anthony*[7], bapt. in Holme-on-Spalding-Moor, 5 Oct. 1635, being left an orphan in childhood, was adopted by his grandfather Thomas[6] Crosby, by whom he was brought to New England, where the earliest mention found of him is when a boy of sixteen years in 1651 the town of Rowley, Mass., paid "Anthony Crosby and John Trumble for goiing with hoggs to the neck, £0–1–4" (Rowley Town Records, printed volume, p. 73). He studied medicine, probably with Dr. John Alcock * of Boston, was made sole heir of his grandfather Thomas[6] Crosby of Rowley, to whose estate there he succeeded, and practised his profession in Rowley and the surrounding towns.

On 18 Jan. 1661/2, Anthony Crosbye of Rowley, chirurgeon, being about to make a voyage to England, appointed his loving friend Robert Lord, senior, of Ipswich, his attorney, to complete some land transactions in negotiation with John Pickard of Rowley (Ipswich Deeds at Salem, vol. 2, fol. 119). On 19 Mar. 1661/2, Robert Lord of Ipswich, attorney to Mr. Anthony Crosby of Rowley, conveyed to John Pickard a farm of thirty-seven acres in Rowley, called the Manning Farm; and John Pickard of Rowley, in consideration of above, conveyed to Mr. Anthony Crosbye twenty bushels of wheat and seven hundred acres of village land, being upland and meadow (*Ibid.*, vol. 2, fols. 64 and 65). Dr. Crosby evidently went to England to claim and settle the property left to him there by his grandfather; but what he accomplished has not been learned. He was back in New England a year later, when on 6 May 1663 he acknowledged at Salem before William Hathorne, Assistant, two deeds of 13 Jan. 1661/2, in which he and his wife, Prudence, had conveyed for £6–10–0 to Ezekiel Northend and Henry Riley

---

* Dr. John Alcock of Boston, son of Dr. George Alcock of Roxbury, graduated at Harvard College in 1646. On 29 Jan. 1657/8, John Alcocke, Anthonie Crosbie, John Lewis, and Samuel Mayo witnessed a retraction of slander on John Saffin of Boston, published by Joseph Green of Weymouth (Recorded in Plymouth Colony Deeds, vol. 2, fol. 201). Alcock, Lewis, and Mayo were then all residents of Boston, and doubtless Crosby was studying and living with Alcock.

of Rowley certain rights in ox-pastures there (*Ibid.*, vol. 2, fols. 151 and 152).

On 25 Sept. 1666, John Todd of Rowley obtained a judgment against Anthony Crosby for £150 in a controversy on land matters, and secured on execution a moiety in the latter's seven hundred acres of village lands. Several years later Dr. Crosby got a review of this case, but Todd again secured a verdict in Sept. 1672. (Ipswich Deeds at Salem, vol. 3, fols. 59, 221, 235, 251, 276.)

The following amusing depositions are of value in confirming the age of Anthony[7] Crosby: On 28 Nov. 1671, Anthony Crosbie, aged about thirty-five years, deposed that, being in company with Robert Marshall at Boston, the latter stated that Capt. Welsh was an atheist, believing there was neither God or devil, hell or heaven; and, being questioned as to his own views, the said Marshall stated he was of the same mind, but dared not speak what he thought in this country. (Suffolk County Court Files, No. 162102.)

In a suit brought by William and Anne Edmonds against Henry Greene for a claim of curing a sore leg of one of the latter's children, on 27 Mar. 1660, Anthony Crosbie, aged about twenty-three years, deposed he heard Goody Edmonds say the child's illness was the King's Evil and she had cured it. Afterwards, Greene brought the child to Rowley for examination by deponent, and, according to deponent's best skill, he thought the bone was not sufficiently scaled. (Essex County Court Files, Sept. 1660.)

The Puritan asceticism of the times is revealed in the following record: Court held at Ipswich, 2 May 1661. Nathaniell Tredwell and Mr. Crosbye, upon their presentments for smoking a tobacco pipe in the street, were fined. (Essex County Court Files, May 1661.)

Dr. Anthony[7] Crosby died in Rowley, intestate, and was buried there 16 Jan. 1672/3. The inventory of his estate, taken 19 Feb. 1672/3 by Richard Swan, Abraham Jewett, Samuel Brocklebank, and Ezekiel Northend, and presented by his widow, Prudence, on 25 Mar. 1673, showed goods of £102-2-6, debts due to estate of £73-14-2, and real estate of £347-10-0, a total of £523-6-8; debts due from estate £143-3-5; leaving a net estate of £380-3-3 (Essex County Probate Records, File No. 6589).

He married, in Rowley, Mass., 28 Dec. 1659, *Prudence Wade*, born in Ipswich, Mass., about 1638, daughter of Jonathan and Susanna Wade. Her father was a merchant of wealth and distinction, and the family were allied with the best blood in the Colony: one of her sisters married a son of Dep'ty Gov. Samuel Symonds, and the other married Samuel Rogers of the celebrated ministerial Rogers family of Ipswich; one of her brothers married a daughter of Gov. Thomas Dudley, and the other married a daughter of Gov. Simon Bradstreet. After the death of Dr. Anthony[7] Crosby, his widow, Prudence, married (2), as his second wife, 9 July 1673, *Rev. Seaborn Cotton* of Hampton, N.H., a graduate of Harvard College in 1651, eldest son of Rev. John Cotton of Boston, the most eminent of all the Puritan divines who emigrated to New England. Mr. Cotton died 20 Apr. 1686, and his widow, Prudence, married for a third husband, in 1689, Lieut. *John Hammond* of Watertown, Mass., she being his third wife. She died in Watertown, 1 Sept. 1711, in her seventy-fourth year, according to her gravestone there. Children of Dr. Anthony[7] and Prudence (Wade) Crosby, born in Rowley, Mass.:—

1. *Thomas*[8], b. 4 Mar. 1660/1, settled in Hampton, N.H., where he was employed as a school-teacher for several years. He m., about 1686, *Deborah* ——. Children, b. in Hampton, N.H.: *Hannah*[9], b. 27 Dec. 1687; *Abigail*[9], b. 2 June 1689; *Prudence*[9], b. 8 Mar. 1691/2; *Jonathan*[9], b. 8 May 1694, d. young; *Mehetabel*[9], b. 5 Jan. 1695/6; *Elizabeth*[9], b. 26 Apr. 1699; *Jonathan*[9], b. 24 Jan. 1700/1; *Samuel*[9], b. 22 Nov. 1703.
2. *Jonathan*[8], b. 26 Jan. 1663/4; bur. 27 May 1664.
3. *Jonathan*[8], b. 28 Oct. 1665, removed to York, Me. Further history untraced.
4. *Nathaniel*[8], b. 5 Feb. 1666/7; d. young.
5. *Nathaniel*[8], b. 27 Sept. 1668, resided in Rowley, Mass., where he d. 7 Mar. 1699/1700. He m., 13 Dec. 1693, *Elizabeth Bennett*.

As to Jane Sotheron, the plucky wife of Thomas[6] Crosby, who accompanied her husband to face the almost unknown perils of New England, and who removed with him to Rowley, Mass., where she survived him but one year, it seems worth while here to give briefly some account of her family.

1. WILLIAM[1] SOTHERON, born about 1440, is the earliest member of this family at Holme-on-Spalding-Moor, County York, from whom a direct line can be traced; and for a continuous period of nearly three centuries they seem to have been the wealthiest family of the parish, except the Constables and later the Langdales, who were the lords and proprietors of the manor. During the fifteenth, sixteenth, and seventeenth centuries the Sotherons were substantial yeomen, farming extensive estates which they held by leases from the manor of Holme; and as early as 1585 they began to be also freehold owners of lands there which they acquire by purchase.

The will of William Sothern of Holme-on-Spalding-Moor, dated 2 Apr. 1509, is in Latin and may be found in the Prerogative and Exchequer of York Wills, vol. 8, fol. 10. In it he mentions his son Robert, who represented the line of Jane Sotheron in the second generation. He m., about 1467, ALICE ———, who survived him. Children, born in Holme-on-Spalding-Moor:—

i. Agnes[2], b. about 1468; m., about 1490, Thomas Millington alias Tomlinson,* of Holme-on-Spalding-Moor. His will, dated 14 May 1508, was proved 12 July 1508 (P. and E. York Wills, vol. 7, fol. 44). Six children.
ii. ROBERT[2], b. about 1470.
iii. John[2].
iv. Christopher[2].
v. "Sir" Thomas[2] was a priest at Beverly, County York, and d. unmarried in 1550. His will, dated 28 July 1550, proved 15 Apr. 1551, mentions a large number of nephews, nieces, grand-nephews, and grand-nieces, named Sotheron, Tomlinson, etc. (P. and E. York Wills, vol. 13, fol. 710).
vi. William[2] was a yeoman of Holme-on-Spalding-Moor, where he d. in 1517. His will, dated 10 May 1517, was proved 26 June 1517 (P. and E. York Wills, vol. 9, fol. 47). The name of his wife has not been found. Four children.

* This family for a century and a half are variously called Millington, Tomlinson, Millington alias Tomlinson, and Tomlinson alias Millington.

2. ROBERT² SOTHERON (*William¹*), born in Holme-on-Spalding-Moor about 1470, resided there until his death in 1524. He was a witness to the will of John Watson of Holme-on-Spalding-Moor, dated 3 Aug. 1521; and was appointed a supervisor of the will, dated 18 Feb. 1521/2 of Agnes Wright of Spawdyngton [Spaldington in Bubwith] (P. and E. York Wills, vol. 9, fols. 212 and 224). In a subsidy of 15 Henry VIII. (1523), Robert Sothern was assessed for goods of 60*s.*, paying a tax of 18*d.*, the largest in the parish (Lay Subsidies, Yorkshire, 203–183).

Robert² Sotheron was a substantial and prosperous yeoman, and left a will, a full copy of which may be found in P. and E. York Wills, vol. 9, fol. 303. Children of Robert² and Alice Sotheron, born in Holme-on-Spalding-Moor:—

 i. Thomas³, b. about 1495.
 ii. Beatrix³, m. —— Wright.
 iii. Margaret³, m. —— Simpson.
 iv. JOHN³, b. about 1500.
 v. William³ resided in Holme-on-Spalding-Moor, and was administrator of his brother Robert, 24 Nov. 1562. (See below.)
 vi. Robert³, b. about 1505, was the principal legatee of the wills of his parents. In a rental roll of Holme Manor in 1528 he is listed for tenements in the Monks held of the Prior and Convent of Selby, and for his common rights pays 5*s.* yearly. (Rentals and Surveys, Public Record Office, Roll 735.) He d. in 1562, administration on his estate being given on 24 Nov. of that year to his brother William Sotheron. (Admon. Act Book, P. and E. Court of York, Harthill Deanery.)

3. JOHN³ SOTHERON (*Robert²*, *William¹*), born in Holme-on-Spalding-Moor about 1500, is mentioned in a rental roll of Holme Manor of about 1535 as holding a messuage, a croft, an oxgang of land, three flatts, and two acres of meadow, paying yearly therefor 20*s.* 2*d.* (Holme Manor Muniments). In a subsidy of 36 Henry VIII. (1544), John Sothrone was rated for goods of £6, his tax being 12*d.* (Lay Subsidies, Yorkshire, 203–222). He died late in 1547, leaving a will, which may be found in P. and E. York Wills, vol. 13, fol. 374.

He married, about 1538, PHILLIPPA ——; she married second, about 1550, Wilfred Millington alias Tomlinson, who was buried at Holme-on-Spalding-Moor, 16 Nov. 1562, administration on his estate being given to his widow, Phillippa, 24 Nov. 1562 (Admon. Act Book, P. and E. Court of York, Harthill Deanery). Phillippa Sotheron-Tomlinson alias Millington died in 1585. Children of John[3] and Phillippa Sotheron, born in Holme-on-Spalding-Moor:

    i. Margaret[4], b. about 1539; d. young.
    ii. Janet[4], b. about 1541; d. young.
    iii. Alison[4], b. about 1543; m., about 1561, John Bell of Everingham, County York. Five children.
    iv. WILLIAM[4], b. about 1545.

4. WILLIAM[4] SOTHERON (*John*[3], *Robert*[2], *William*[1]), born in Holme-on-Spalding-Moor about 1545, being an only son, inherited an extensive estate and became the most prominent and the wealthiest resident of his native parish in his generation (except the Constable family, the lords of the manor).

William Sotheron was a witness to the wills of John Ellithorpe dated 2 June 1589, Margaret Madson in July 1591, and Henry Watson dated 19 Apr. 1597, all of Holme-on-Spalding-Moor; and he was appointed guardian of her daughter Jane by the will of Sisley Cowper, widow, of Holme-on-Spalding-Moor, dated 29 Jan. 1609/10. (P. and E. York Wills, vol. 24, fols. 60 and 676; vol. 26, fol. 552; and vol. 31, fol. 256.)

On 16 May 1607, Thomas Millington of Holme-on-Spalding-Moor, County York, gent., sued William Sotheran and the latter's son-in-law William Millington in regard to a bond and mortgage to John Sotheran, an infant, son and heir of said William Sotheran. Also in May 1616 Marmaduke Millington of Holme-on-Spalding-Moor, gent., sued William Sotheran and William Millington of same, as to the same lands there, formerly of his father, Thomas Millington. (Chancery Proceedings, James I., M–18–11 and M–20–22.)

Among the freehold estates in Holme-on-Spalding-Moor secured by William Sotheron appear the following acquisitions by "fine"*:—

In Michaelmas term 28 and 29 Elizabeth (1586), William Sotheron [and nine others], plaintiffs, against Robert Constable, sen., Esq., Robert Constable, jun., gent., and wife Ann, and Francis Constable, gent., deforciants, on nine messuages with lands in Holme-on-Spaldingmore; also in Michaelmas term 39 and 40 Elizabeth (1597), William Sotheran and John Sotheran [his son], plaintiffs, against Richard Horsman and his wife Barbara and Henry Millington alias Tomlinson and his wife Agnes, deforciants, on two messuages with lands in Holme in Spaldingmore; also in Trinity term, 43 Elizabeth (1601), William Sotheron, plaintiff, against Richard Horsman and William Bedall, deforciants, on a messuage and a cottage with lands in Holme in Spaldingmore. (Yorkshire Archæological Association, Record Series, vol. 7, p. 63, and vol. 8, pp. 82 and 169.)

William[4] Sotheron died in 1619, leaving a will, of which a full copy is appended:—

In the name of God Amen the second day of December Anno Dmi 1616 I Willm Sotheron of Holme in Spaldingmore sicke in bodye but perfect of memorie and of good Remembrance praysed be god, doe make constitute and ordayne this my last will and Testament in manner and forme followeinge. First I doe give and bequeath my soule to god almightie, my maker, redeemer, and saviour, by whose mercye I trust to be saved, and my bodye to be buried in the parish church or churchyeard of Holme in Spaldingmore afforesayd. Itm I doe give unto the poore people of Holme in Spaldingmore xl s. to be distributed by the hands of John Millington and John Sotheron my sonne at my buriall. Itm I do give unto the sayd poore people of Holme in Spaldingmore vi s. viii d. to be taken forth of the yearely rent of one cottage lyeinge and beinge in the uppend of Holme, now or late in the occupacon of Willm Slingsbie, to be distributed by the heyres or assignes of the sayd Cottage to the afforesayd poore people yerely and everie yere soe long as the world doth contineu, always as uppon all Saints day. Itm I doe give unto my wife Constance Sotheron all my debts wch is oweing unto me whatsoever, whether they be uppon speacialtye or other wayes. Itm I doe give unto sayd wife Constance Sotheron my house wherein I doe nowe dwell w[th] all the houses and offices and buildings to the same belonginge w[t]hall the grounds adioyneinge to the same now in myne owne occupacon, vizts my hempe garth, my hey house, and hay house and close, two closes called Playsterer closes, to parcells of grounds called the Springes, one cottage w[th] a hempe garth adioyneinge to the same wch was late the lands of Henrie Millington, and three other Closes called Horseman Closses and one Close called Madson close wth th' appurtenncs, for and dueringe her naturall life. Itm I doe give unto Phillippe Sotheron my daughter one hundereth markes of lawfull English money to be payd unto her by my executor when as she cometh

* That is, by friendly lawsuit.

to the full age of twentie and one yeares or when as she shall be lawfullie married, in the full satisfacon of her child's portion. Itm. I doe give unto John Dayles twelve pence, in the full satisfacon of his wife's portion. Itm I doe give unto Symond Appleton xii d., in the full satisfacon of his wife's porcon. Itm I doe give unto Mr. Millington xii d., in the full satisfacon of his wife's porcon. Itm I doe give unto Thomas Crosbye thelder xii d, in full satisfacon of his wife's portion. Itm I doe give unto Phillippe Dales x s. Itm I doe give unto Robert Appleton x s. Itm I doe give unto Marye Appleton x s. Itm I doe give unto Anthonye Crosbye ten shillinges. Itm I doe give unto Thomas Crosbie the younger ten shillings. Itm I doe give unto Willm Crosbie ten shillings. I doe give unto Simond Crosbye x s. Itm I doe give unto Peter Millington the sonne of Willm Millington x s. Itm I doe give unto Phillippe Millington x s. Itm I doe give unto Anne Millington x s. Itm I doe give unto Marmaduke Millington the sonne of Willm Millington x s. Itm I doe give unto Edward Madson my servant two shillings. Itm I doe give unto Willm Wyllis my servant two shillings. Itm I doe give unto James Sotheron x s. Itm I doe give unto John Sotheron thelder the house wherein he nowe dwelleth wth the hempe garth adioyneinge to the same, for and dueringe his naturall life, yeildinge and payinge for the same to my sonne John Sotheron his heyres or assignes yearlie and ever yere the yearlye rent of twentye six shillings and eight pence. Itm I doe give unto my wife Constance Sotheron all my leases which is due unto me whether they be upon specialtye or otherwayes. Thee resydue of my goods which I have not given by will, my debts payd and my funerall expences discharged, I doe give it all unto Constance Sotheron my wife whom I doe make my full and whole executor and executrix of this my last will and testament to dispose the same to the glorie and prayse of Almightie god amen: these beinge witnesses, Anthonie Lambert and Marmaduke Hyde.

Prob. 12 Oct. 1619, by Constance Sotheron, widow and executrix. (P. and E. York Wills, vol. 35, fol. 492.)

William[4] Sotheron married in Holme-on-Spalding-Moor, 9 Nov. 1578, Constance Lambert, baptized there 12 Jan. 1560/1, daughter of William Lambert and grand-daughter of Richard Lambert; she died there in the winter of 1622, leaving the following will:—

In the name of God Amen this fowerteenthe Day of November and in the yeare of our Lord one thousand six hundred twenty and two, I Custance Sotherone of Holme in Spaldingmore within the Countie of Yorke, widdowe, sicke in bodie but of good and perfecte remembrance, praised be Allmightie god, doe make and ordeyne this my last will and testamente, recallinge all former wills, in manner and forme followeinge. First I give and bequeath my Soule to allmightie god my maker and to Jesus Christ in whom alone I putt my whole confidence, my redeemer, and my body to be buryed in the parish church or churchyeard of Holme afforesaid. Itm I give and bequeath to Mathewe Sotherone one farme in the waterend wherein John Lindsley now dwelleth, to him and his heires for ever. Itm I give and bequeath unto Anne Dayles my daughter one house w[th] app[r]tennes knowne by the name of Woodhouse, w[th] the wood close, and one other little close theirto adioyneinge, duringe her naturall life, payinge unto Jaine Sotheran and Isabell Sotheran, daughters of John Sotheran, the value of xl *s.* yearely. Provided allwaies that she shall not cutt downe any of the greater timber. And after the death of Anne to come to Mathewe Sotheran and his heirs forever. Itm I give and bequeath unto Robert Apleton, sonne of Symon Apleton of Newbald, one house wth the app$^{r.}$tennes in the waterend now in the occupacon of Robert Plaxten als Plasteer, payinge unto Mary Appleton his said sister the sume of forty pownds. Itm. I give and bequeath unto Phillipp Sotheran and her heirs for ever, my yongest daughter, one house in the moore end wth the app^{r}tennes theirto belongeing now in the tenure and occupacon of Alice Barley. Itm I give unto Anthony Crosbie, sonne of Thomas Crosbie, the sume of ten pounds. Itm. I give unto Thomas Crosbie, sonne of the said Thomas Crosbie, ten pownds wth all my ploughgeare cowpes, waines, and all other implem^{ts} unto the said things belongeinge as yocke and teames and such like things. Itm I give unto William Crosbie, sonne of the said Thomas Crosbie, the sume of five pownds. Itm I give unto Symon Crosbie, the yongest sonne of the said Thomas, thirteene pownds six shillings eight peence. Itm. I give unto Mary Appleton, daughter of Symon Apleton of Newbald, the sume of tenn pownds. I give and bequeath unto John Dayles, sonne of John Dayles, the sume of six pownds thirteene shillings eight pence, and fortie shillings to be paid yearly out of my lands att Holden duringe his life naturall, and one Cowe. Itm I give and bequeath unto Phillip Dayles, daughter of the said John Dayles, six pownds thirteene shillings and eight pence, and forty shillings to be paid yearely to her out of my lands at Holden duringe her life naturall, wth one Cowe. Itm I give and bequeath unto William Dayles, the yongest sonne of the said John Dayles, six pownds thirteene shillings eight pence, and one Cowe. Itm I give to the poore of Holme afforesaid xl *s.* to be distributed att my buryall. Itm I give and bequeath unto the said William Dayles, sonne of the said John Dayles, the whole and entire sume of xl *s.* to be paid yearely to him dureinge his naturall life out of my lands of Holden by my sonne John Sotheran, and the remainder theirof to redound to himselfe. Itm I give and bequeath unto Phillip Sotheran the rest of my goods ungiven and unbequeathed, and if the goods do not amounte to the full satisfieing of these my legacs allreadie given, my will is that the said Phillip Sotheran shall make them upp and pay them out of the rente of Barley wife's house wherein nowe she dwelleth. And I doe make the said Phillipp Sotheran my full and perfecte executrix of this my last will and testamente. In witnes whereof I have setto my hand and seale this day and yeare abovesaid. Sealled in the p^{r}sence of us viz: John Laycocke, Anthony Lambert, Anthony Crosbie.

Prob. 20 May 1623 by the executrix Phillipa Sotheran. (P. and E. York Wills, vol. 37, fol. 252.)

Children of William[4] and Constance (Lambert) Sotheron, born in Holme-on-Spalding-Moor:—

i. Isabel[5], bapt. 1 Feb. 1579/80; m., 18 Nov. 1598, Simon Appleton of Newbald, County York. Children (Appleton): *Robert[6], Mary[6]*.

ii. JANE[5], bapt. 4 Mar. 1581/2; m., 19 Oct. 1600, THOMAS[5] CROSBY, b. about 1575. They came to New England about 1639, resided in Cambridge, Mass., and later at Rowley, Mass., where he was bur. 6 May 1661, and she was bur. 2 May 1662. Children (Crosby): *Anthony*⁶, b. about 1602; *Thomas*⁶, b. about 1604; *William*⁶, b. about 1606; *Simon*⁶, b. about 1608. (See Crosby Line, *ante*, p. 20.)

iii. WILLIAM⁵, bapt. 27 Sept. 1584, bur. 25 Nov. 1584.

iv. ELIZABETH⁵, b. in 1586; m., in 1603, WILLIAM MILLINGTON of Holme-on-Spalding-Moor, bapt. 11 Mar. 1575/6, d. 1618. His will, dated 20 May 1618, was proved 12 Oct. 1618. (P. and E. York Wills, vol. 35, fol. 228.) Children (Millington): *Peter*⁶, *Phillippa*⁶, *Anne*⁶, *Marmaduke*⁶.

v. JOHN⁵, bapt. 8 Dec. 1588, only surviving son, was the wealthiest resident of Holme-on-Spalding-Moor of his generation, and d. in 1652. His will, dated 13 Dec. 1652, left to eldest son Thomas £200; to son Mathew a farm bought of Robert and Thomas Millington; to son Philip annuities of £18; to sons-in-law Thomas Thackwray, Thomas Smith, and Richard Browne. Grandchild Thomas Sotheron to have all other lands in Holme, and to be residuary legatee and executor. Witnesses: T. Millington, Tho: Crochie.* On 26 Apr. 1653, commission issued to Thomas Sotheron, father of the executor, during the minority of the latter. (P. C. C., 9 Aylett.) The name of his wife has not been learned. Children: *Thomas*⁶ (b. about 1615), *Matthew*⁶, *Isabel*⁶, *Jane*⁶ (m., 23 May 1637, THOMAS THACKWRAY), *Philip*⁶, *Anne*⁶ (m., 29 Jan. 1636/7, GEORGE HEWLEY).

vi. ANNE⁵, b. about 1592; m., about 1613, JOHN DAYLES. Children (Dayles): *Phillippa*⁶, *John*⁶, *William*⁶, *Peter*⁶ (d. young), *Constance*⁶ (d. young).

vii. PHILLIPPA⁵, b. about 1597; m., 29 Apr. 1624, REV. PETER HAMMOND of Harswell and Holme-on-Spalding-Moor.

* *Sic* in the registered copy of the will; perhaps an error for Crosbie.

Chapter III.

SIMON CROSBY THE EMIGRANT.

As we have seen, there were two connecting links in t Crosby family between Old and New England. The pi vious chapter dealt with the first and most obscure, and this will be taken up the subject of Simon Crosby who ha always been known as the Emigrant, and who in point o fact was the first Crosby to come to America.

There is always some romantic attachment by those who look back over their family line to that first early pioneer who braves the risks of a new and primitive existence, whether the motives of the pioneer himself be those actuated by what is commonly called principle or what is generally attributed to a lack of that subtle thing. In the case of Simon Crosby, endowed as he appears to have been, by his father's generosity, amply in property, and coming as he did to a country farther removed from England than the end of the earth is to-day, and accompanied by his wife and small baby, it is fairly to be supposed he came to America in search of that religious freedom which drove many from England in those days. Indeed, those who read this and other accounts of the Crosby family will hardly fail to have noticed that, although not a family seeking adventure or danger for its own sake, the spirit of free thinking and insisting upon the rights appertaining thereto has been a marked characteristic of the family in all generations; and, if they have not kept abreast of the greatest activities, they have at least generally kept up with all that form of what may more truly be called progress,—the ability of each individual to think for himself.

And so Simon Crosby the Emigrant, although living but a brief time after his arrival in America, and dying as a comparatively young man, was rather a unique exception in the ranks of the Crosbys, as we find them, for he was a man of action, and setting up the family banner in a new and strange land made it possible for those who succeeded him to live up to the progress that is demanded of all civilized people, namely, the right to live.

Added to these characteristics was that element of mystery that so long has surrounded his forebears, and which made it seem as if he had been set down from the sky. We are proud of Simon Crosby the Emigrant, with that sort of pride that goes out to the man of quiet achievement.

Simon[6] Crosby (Thomas[5], Anthony[4], Thomas[3], Miles[2], John[1]), born in Holme-on-Spalding-Moor, County York, England, about 1608, is first found mentioned as a legatee of 10s. in the will of his grandfather William Sotheron, dated 2 Dec. 1616; and six years later he received a bequest of £13–6–8 in the will of his grandmother Constance Sotheron, dated 14 Nov. 1622 (P. and E. York Wills, vol. 35, fol. 492, and vol. 37, fol. 252). On 17 Sept. 1632, he and his father Thomas[5] Crosby, took a mortgage for £400 on five messuages in Holme-on-Spalding-Moor, which mortgage they transferred on 24 Mar. 1633/4 to Sir Marmaduke Langdale and Richard Meadley, the original deed being still preserved at Holme (see Appendix B). The will of his brother Thomas[6] Crosby of Holme-on-Spalding-Moor, dated 25 Nov. 1658, gave £10 each to Thomas, Simon, and Joseph, "sons of my brother Symon disceased" (P. and E. York Wills, vol. 50, fol. 330).

The above records and his marriage and baptism of his eldest child are all the mentions that have been found of Simon[6] Crosby in England, except the sailing from London to New England, to be given later.

As Simon[6] Crosby grew to manhood, the wave of Puritanism was sweeping over England with steadily increasing force, and the preaching of Rev. Ezekiel Rogers, rector of Rowley, County York, but a dozen miles southeast of Holme, was securing many converts in that region. But the ministrations of Rev. Thomas Shepard in 1631 and 1632 at Buttercrambe, County York, about twelve miles northwest of Holme, evidently caused the momentous crisis in the life of Simon[6] Crosby which resulted in the establishing of the Crosby family in America. Thomas Shepard was then a young man of about Simon[6] Crosby's age, fired with youthful zeal, of forceful and magnetic personality, and eloquent and persuasive as an orator. Imbued with the fervid faith and strong convictions of the young preacher, Simon[6] Crosby decided to share the fortunes of a company of Shepard's followers gathered from his ministries in Essex, Yorkshire, and Northumberland, and formed to establish a home in the New World. As Simon[6] Crosby, on his appearance in New England, was possessed of substantial means, it is to be concluded he was advanced his patrimony by his father, who was a man of extensive estate. Early in April, 1635, he bade farewell to his ancestral home and kindred, and, with his young wife, an eight-weeks'-old son, and a few friends, started on the two-hundred-mile journey to London. By what means or route he travelled is not known, but it seems likely he would have adopted the most comfortable route by travelling by ship from Hull (a seaport about twenty miles southeast of Holme) direct to London. Arriving at the metropolis, he found several vessels about to sail for New England, and secured passage in the *Susan and Ellen*, Capt. Edward Payne master, embarking 18 Apr. 1635.

Twentieth-century travellers who have encountered Atlantic storms while crossing in six days in the fifty-thousand-ton leviathan steamers of the present time, can appreciate the undaunted resolution of those who, nearly three centuries ago, braved the perils and discomforts of a passage requiring ten weeks in the tiny sailing craft of about two hundred tons then in vogue. The writer has so often met with accounts of the *Susan and Ellen* in which *Simon[6] Crosby* and his family came to Massachusetts that she now believes the *Susan and Ellen* was practically a packet-ship between Old and New England.

In the library of the New England Historic Genealogical Society is a book entitled "The Original Lists of Persons of Quality, Emigrants, Religious Exiles, Political Rebels, serving men sold for a term of years, apprentices, children stolen, maidens pressed and others who went from Great Britain to the American States, 1600–1700; with the ages, the localities where they formerly lived in the Mother Country, the names of the ships in which they embarked, and other interesting particulars." This book is from MSS. preserved in the state paper department of Her Majesty's Public Record Offices, England. Edited by John Camden Hotten. A subdivision of the work (pages 33 to 145) has this title:—

> [Regi]ster of the names
> of all ye passinger w^{ch}
> Passed from ye port of
> London for *on* whole
> yeare Endinge at
> Xp*mas* 1635.

The ship *Susan and Ellen*, E. Payne master, made three voyages in that year. Her passenger lists are recorded on pages 59, 62, and 72. The record on page 62 contains the names of thirty-four passengers, and is headed as follows:—

"This under written names are to be transported to New England inbarqued in the *Susan & Ellin*, Edward Payne M^r the pties have brought Certificattes from ye Ministers & Justices of the Peace yt they are no Subsedy men; & are conformable to ye orders & discipline of the Church of England."

The names follow. The 20th, 21st, and 22d are:—

> Husbandman Symon Crosby   26
> Uxor Ann Crosby   25
> (Thomas Crosby, 8 weeks)   1 child.

In the time of the Stuarts, subsidy taxes, viz., taxes on persons without regard to property, were sometimes levied. These assessments were among the subjects of contention between Charles I. and Parliament which led to England's civil war.

SIMON CROSBY THE EMIGRANT

The writer understands the statement made, that the passengers of the *Susan and Ellen* were "no Subsidy men," to mean that they were not of those who had refused to pay the assessments, and were not leaving England with the expectation of escaping the tax.

On the arrival at Boston, in July, 1635, of the *Susan and Ellen*, and some other vessels with parties of Rev. Thomas Shepard's adherents, a favorable opportunity was embraced to secure houses already built, with cultivated gardens, at Cambridge, Mass., which had been established about three years before by a company under Rev. Thomas Hooker who were removing to Connecticut. Having brought with him ample means, Simon[6] Crosby bought of William Spencer a homestead in Cambridge, located at the corner of the present Brattle Street and Brattle Square, where the Brattle House stood, and other parcels of property, all as described in the Proprietors' Records of Cambridge, as follows:—

Simon Crosby: Bought on house & three Acars of Land of William Spencer: butelimg upon ye East: ye greate Creeke west: and North west upon ye hie waye goeing to Robert Homes: and one A Parsell of Mr. George Cooke one ye South.*

It. Boughte one Acar of Ground of Mr. George Cooke; Buteld: ye End to ye greate Creeke to ye east, ye west end of itt Anttonie Colebie ground: ye North upon y^t wch he boughte of William Spencer: ye South upon ye Oxe Marshe. [This lot was south of the first lot and adjoined it.]

It. Boughte of Antonie Coleby one house & to Acars of Land more or less, Buteld on y East with his one Land: Willi͡ɔ Spencsers upon ye west Mr Beniamime South upon ye Oxe marsh: and north upon Joshepp Isake:

It. four Acars of upland in ye necke bounding upon ye sea: Sebastian Brigham one ye East: Robert Homes upon ye west: ye hie.waie y^t goes to ye water banke on ye North: Mr Joshepp Cooke on ye South:

It. Bought three Acars of marsh ground lieing at ye Oyster Banke: Bounded m^r Joshepp Cooke one ye East; Robert Stedman upon the west: ye River South & ye upLand North:

It. Boughte Eighte Acars of Land in ye west feild, on End of it ye Cow comon one ye East ye other End to ye west on ye hie waye of

* Brattle Street was known as Creek Lane in those days, and was "part of the old path that led from Charlestown to Watertown before 1632" (Paige's History of Cambridge, Mass.).

Watertowne Line Gregorie Stone upon y'e' South, & John Gibson on y'e' North:

It. Given in the new feild nexte too Charlestowne Line: Sixe Acars by y'e' towne: Buteling upon John Cooper one y'e' South side: & Gregorie Stone upon y'e' North Side, and y'e' end of it upon y'e' South bounding upon Charlestowne Line. y'e' other end upon y'e' hie waye y't' goes to Minatomie west:

It Boughte of Thomas Marret; 1 Acar of Marsh: In y'e' Oxe marsh:

(Proprietors' Records of Cambridge, printed volume, pp. 67 and 68.)

Simon⁶ Crosby was admitted a freeman, 3 Mar. 1635/6, at the same time with Rev. Thomas Shepard (Records of Mass. Colony, vol. 1, p. 153).

There are so many who seemingly do not understand the nature of a "freeman's oath," although our early Colonial records make constant reference to it, and it was absolutely necessary that the male individual who emigrated to the New England shores should subscribe to it before he could become a member of the church or the body politic, that I insert a copy of it here.

Under the first charter of the Massachusetts Colony, none were regarded as "freemen," or members of the body politic, except such as were admitted by the General Court and took the oath of allegiance to the government then established. This custom continued in existence until, by the second charter, the Colony was transferred into a Province.

Being by the Almightys most wise disposition become a member of this body, consisting of the Governor, Deputy Governor, Assistants and Commonality of Massachusetts in New England do freely and sincerely acknowledge that I am justly and lawfully subject to the government of the same, and do accordingly submit my person and estate to be protected, ordered and governed by the laws and constitution thereof, and do faithfully promise to be from time to time obedient and conformable thereunto, and to the authority of the said Governor, Deputy Governor and Assistants, and to all such laws, orders, sentences, and decrees as shall be lawfully made and published by them and their successors. And I will always endeavor (as in duty I am bound) to advance the peace and welfare of this body or commonwealth, to my utmost skill and ability. And I will, to my best power and means, seek to divert or prevent whatsoever may tend to the ruin or damage thereof, or of any the said Governor, Deputy Governor, or Assistants, or of any of them, or their successors, and will give speedy notice to them, or some of them, of any sedition, or violence, treachery, or other hurt or evil, which I shall know, or hear or violently suspect to be plotted or intended against the said Commonwealth or the said Government established. And I will not at any time suffer or give consent to any council or attempt, that shall be offered, given or attempted for the impeachment of the said Government, or making any changes or alteration of the same, contrary to the laws or ordinances thereof; but I shall do my utmost endeavor to discover, oppose and hinder all and every such council and attempt. So help me God.

Although then a young man, Simon Crosby's capabilities were immediately recognized by his fellow-townsmen, by whom he was soon elected to public office. On 7 Nov. 1636 he was chosen one of the selectmen for the ensuing year, and on 26 Oct. 1638 re-elected to that office and also chosen constable, the duties of the latter at that period being of the nature of a town treasurer, assessor, and marshal. On 4 Sept. 1637 he was elected surveyor of highways. (Town Records of Cambridge, printed volume, pp. 23, 24, 29.) A career of usefulness and prominence was cut off by his early death in September, 1639, aged about thirty years, leaving a net estate of £454-4-4. The site of the church which he attended is at the corner of Mt. Auburn and Dunster Streets; he was probably buried in the old cemetery opposite Cambridge Common, and his minister, Rev. Thomas Shepard, doubtlessly conducted the funeral services.

Simon[6] Crosby was a fine representative of the best class of the English yeomanry who formed the bulk of the Puritan founders of New England. His father and paternal grandfather were prosperous land-owning farmers, and his mother's father, William Sotheron, was the wealthiest man in his town, a position the Sotheron family had held for several generations. The wife of Simon[6] Crosby was also of a substantial family, and her second husband, Rev. William Tompson, was a graduate of Oxford University, an accomplished scholar, and a clergyman of local distinction. The eldest son of Simon[6] Crosby acquired a liberal education, graduating at Harvard College, and the other two sons were men of leading position in their respective communities, and married daughters of Capt. Richard Brackett, a planter.

No move was made for a settlement of the estate of Simon[6] Crosby until six years after his decease, when a second marriage of his widow made it necessary. Accordingly, in 1645 she petitioned the General Court for power to administer his estate, have it inventoried, make sale of his lands, and legally distribute the property, which procedure was carried out as detailed by the following documents:—

To the Honoured Generall Court now Assembled at Boston the humble petition of Anne Thompson late the wife of Symon Crosbie.

First she humbly craves the favor of the Court to pardon her ignorance & excuse the penalty for not proveing her deceased husbands will in due season.

2 ly. That the Honoured Court will please to grant unto her the Administration of the goods & chattells of her deceased husband Symon Crosbie.

3 ly. That you will bee pleased to confirme the portions of the children according as they were agreed by the Reverend Mr. Shepheard & elders & deacons of Cambridge, or so farr forth as the Court shall think meete.

Lastly that shee may have power, or whomsoever shee shall appoint, to make sale of the house & land of her late husband, shee or they putting in security to the Court for payment of the childrens portions, & your petitioner shall ever pray ec.

Mr. Simonde is chosen to joine with some of their bretheren the Deputys as A Comittee to examine the matter of this peticon & Report of what they judge meete to be granted by this Courte. The magistrates have past this with Reference to the Consent of their bretheren the deputys heereto.

EDWARD RAWSON, Secrety.

Mr. John Glover & Richard Fackson are chosen to joyne in this Committee.

W^M TORREY, Clerk.

The Comittee having pused with this peticon the agreement made by Mr Shepheard, the elders, the two then deacons of Cambridge with Ann the wife of Mr. Tompson then the widdow of Simon Crosby annexed hereunto should be allowed. And that the howses & lands be granted

SIMON CROSBY THE EMIGRANT

to her to sell provided that she put into the Court at Cambridge good security to pay the childrens portions.

They alsoe thinke it meet that ye rest of ye particulars mentioned in this peticon be granted as they are desired.

The Magistrates Consent hereto

EDWARD RAWSON, Secrety.

The Deputies have voted this returne of the Committee to be the answer to this petition with the addition of the word (Cambridge) with reference to the consent of our honoured magistrates hereto.

WILLIAM TORREY, Clerk.

15th of ye 9th mounth.

An Invitorye of the goods and chattells of Simon Crosbye of Cambridge diceased prised by John Bridge, Richeard Jackeson.

HIS WEARINGE APPARRELL.

Imps. one stuketafitie suite 26 *s.* 8 *d.*	1– 6–8
It. one stufe suite 2^l–6–8^d.	2– 6–8
It. one cloth suite and Cote	2–10–0
It. one cloth cloake of lighte cooler	1– 0–0
It. twoo old suites one of clothe, one of stufe	1– 0–0
It. one old coate 5 *s.*	0– 5–0
It. old overworne clothes 10 *s.*	0–10–0
It. one new hatt littell worne	0–10–0
It. 3 old hatts 5 *s.*	0– 5–0
It. 3 doosen silver buttons	0– 9–0

LYNNINGE

It. 3 shirtes 2 *s.* 6 *d.* apece	0– 7–6
It. 3 bands 2 caps 1 girdell	0– 3–0
It. one payre of Gloves	0– 1–0
It. 3 payre of sheetes at 10 *s.* ap.	1–10–0
It. one p of sheetes	0–15–0
It. a payre sheetes more	0–10–0
It. 3 p of pillowberes att 4 *s.*	1–12–0
It. 3 towells att 18 *d.* apece	0– 4–6
It. one table cloth	0– 2–6
It. 6 wrought napkines	0– 8–0
It. one doosen napkines 8	0– 8–0
It. twoo corse napkins	0– 0–8
It. a payre of sheetes more	0–10–0
It. 3 payre of corse sheetes	0–12–0
It. a bed teekinge new	0–16–0

In ye hall house

It. one birded coverlett	1- 0-0
It. say curtaines & valants	1- 0-0
It. one other coverlett	0-10-0
It. one payre of blanketts	0-12-0
It. 5 yards whitte carsie	0-13-4
It. one fetherbed, a boulster, one pillow	2- 0-0
It. flocke pillow	0- 1-0
It. 2 fether pillows	0-10-0
It. 4 trinke quishions	0-12-0
It. an imbroidered quishone case	0- 6-8
It. one coverlett & twoo blancketts	0-12-0
It. one small truncke 4s.	0- 4-0
It. one cheste	0- 5-0
It. one deale box	0- 1-0
It. 4 small painted boxes	0- 4-0
It. twoo bybells one of Bezar	1- 0-0
It. twoo bookes, Dod on ye co‾ and, preston on faith	0- 5-0
It. one table cubbard	0-10-0
It. 14 dishes of old pewter aboute 24 1	1- 4-0
It. 5 saltes and 4 potts 2 candellstickes of pewter, one beere-boule & other pewter	1- 0-0
It. one brase morter one irone pestell	0- 1-6
It. one smoothing irone 10^d a small locke 3	0- 1-2
It. one fryinge pan, pewter dishes more & old peces	0- 4-0
It. one greate fowlinge pece & a muskett	1- 5-0
It. one carbine with ye furniture	1- 4-0
It. firepan, toungs & gridirone	0- 4-0
It. one payre cobirones	0- 3-0
It. one irone trevett & one p hangs	0- 5-0
It. a brasse pan	0-15-0
It. two small brase kettells	0- 7-0
It. one skillett & an old chafinge dishe, an littell of kettell	0- 3-6
It. 2 brasse potts & potthoockes	0-14-0
It. an old fryinge pan	0- 0-8
It. one doossen olcomie spoones	0- 3-4
It. 3 silver spoones	0-18-0
Ir. a greate old brase pott	0-13-4
It. a brasse bason	0- 2-0
It. an old brase candellsticke	0- 1-0
It. a powdringe tub	0- 2-0
It. a Rundelett & woden tunell	0- 2-0
It. one jug with some other earthen wares & implements	0- 3-6
It. a littell square table, three old chaires	0- 4-0
It. a payre of bootes and spurs	0- 8-0
It. a p of shoes old ones	0- 2-0

SIMON CROSBY THE EMIGRANT 53

In yᵉ Chamb.

It. one baskett 2 sines	0– 3–0
It. one saddell	0– 6–8
It. one old cheste att yᵉ old mans	0– 8–0

In yᵉ siller.

It. a parcell of old irone	0– 6–8
It. 2 old Hachetts	0– 3–0
It. a beere barrell	0– 2–0
It. one churne	0– 4–0
It. one pistole	0– 5–0
It. a payre of taylors sheres a saw rifte	0– 1–8
It. a booke of Mr. Daniell Rogers	0– 4–0
It. a tray	0– 2–6
It. a booke of Saintes conventione	0– 1–6
It. 2 hammers	0– 1–6
It. one saw	0– 4–0
It. one spitt & curtaine	0– 3–0
It. corne hanginge by 20 bushell	5– 0–0
It. corne hanginge by yᵉ barne 30 bush	7–10–0
It. pease 4 bushell	1–12–0
It. wheate wee conceive Aboute 4 bush	1–12–0
It. Rie About 10 bushells	3– 6–8
It. Aboute 2 bushells of barlie	0–12–0
It. an old carte & an old plow, two yokes, a cheane & shakell	2– 0–0
It. twoo payre of steeres	60– 0–0
It. three young steres	23– 0–0
It. one red heifer	13–10–0
It. a white heifer	
It. 3 cows	60– 0–0
It. 4 stere calfes	13– 0–0
It. all yᵉ hay	15– 0–0

Hogs.

It. one hog 2 shotes 2 pigs	3– 0–0
It. one old swine with pig att [illeg.]	2–13–4
It. one swine in coate	1–11–0

Lands and Houses.

The new frame & barne & 7 acres of land with Colbies old house	140– 0–0
The 8 acers by Stones	40– 0–0
The 6 acers in yᵉ new lots by Charlestowne	12– 0–0
An acer of marshe in yᵉ oxe marshe	4– 0–0
4 Acres of plantinge ground in ye necke 2 broke up & 2 unbroken	11– 0–0
It. 10 Acers in Rokye meadow	10– 0–0
It. salte marshe	[£471– 3–0]
Debts due from him to others	16–18–8
[Net estate	£454– 4–4]

The 22 of the 7th month 1645

The elders and deacons of the church of Cambridge agree with An Crosbye widow for her (then) 3 sonnes to have yelded them for portions of their fathers estate as followeth namely, to Thomas Crosby the eldest 70 li, to Simon 50 li to Joseph 50 li to be payd them at their Ages of 20 yers [illeg.]. And if the eldest be brought up to learninge at the college, if the charge bee to heavy for the parents to bear nor is not otherwise borne, for that the benefit of the portion is too short to suffice, then 20 li of his portion is to bee taken for sustyening him in his learninge [illeg.]   50 li [illeg.] to ech alike.

The parents are to hold the childrens mayntaynance receiving the proffits of their portions towards the same for it is considered the 2 children at least [illeg.] will be like to dispose [a line illegible].

Also it is agreed the houses and lands that said Simon Crosbyes the late father deceased Held, bee ingaged for the performance of their legacies.

If it should be thought best to sell or charge any of the houses or lands it is not to be done without the consent of the parties above mentioned.

I Ann Crosby do hereto agree and confirme it by putinge to my hand the 21 of the 7th month 1645

by me   Ann Crosby

Witness, Benjamin Scott, Jane holmes.

Itm. the houses and lands now valued [a few words illegible].	
It. the houses and barn & 7 acres of land about them valued at	120 li
It. 8 acres of land at Goodman Stones at	28 li
It. 6 acres at goodman Coopers	24 li
It. one acre in the cow marsh	3 li
4 acres ye plantinge ground in the neck	5 li
10 acres of medow in Rocky medow	10 li
salt marsh [illegible] 4 acres	4 li

I William Tompson give leave to Anne Tompson my dear wiffe free leave to dispose of thirtie pounds of her estate as shee herself pleaseth. (Mass. State Archives, vol. 15B, pp. 181, 182.)

In accordance with the above authority of the General Court, the real estate of Simon[6] Crosby was sold through the agency of Joseph Jewett of Rowley, Mass., as appears by the following documents:—

On 8 Oct. 1652, William Tompson and Anne his wife (the latter being formerly widow and administratrix of Simon Crosbey late of Cambridge, deceased) by authority of the General Court convey to Joseph Juite of Rowley all the lands and houses late of said Simon Crosbey, being a messuage with six acres of land, also two acres of marsh, also six acres in Rockie Meadow, also four acres in Rockie Meadow, also one acre in the ox marsh, also six acres of pasture and eight other acres of upland, and also one hundred and twenty acres of remote waste lands in the limits of Cambridge granted to the dwelling house of said Crosby, said Joseph Juite having given good security into court for the portions of the children of said Simon Crosby. Witnesses: Hugh Mason, Edw: Michelson. Acknowledged 8 Oct. 1652. Recorded 29 Dec. 1652. (Middlesex Co. Deeds, vol. 1, fol. 44.)

On 5 Apr. 1653, Joseph Juite of Rowley bound over to the Middlesex Court £300 worth of land in Rowley, to be set out by Edward Michelson and John Pickerne [Pickard] before the end of next month, upon condition that the estate of Simon Crosby deceased now delivered into his hands to improve by his relict Anne Tompson and her husband Mr. William Tompson, shall be by him again repaid to the children of the said Simon Crosby deceased, as the order of the General Court made to the said Anne Tompson for the sale of her late husband's lands doth truly contain and intend. (Middlesex Court Records, vol. 1, fol. 35.)

On 8 Oct. 1652, Joseph Juitt of Rowley for valuable consideration sold to Thomas Longhorne* of Cambridge, butcher, the mansion house in Cambridge sometime of Simon Crosby with six acres of land, also one acre in the ox marsh, together with the rights and priviledges in the town commons. Witnesses, Abraham Jewett, Thomas Nelson. Recorded 9 Dec. 1669. (Middlesex Co. Deeds, vol. 3, fol. 368.)

On 5 Apr. 1653, Joseph Juite of Rowley for valuable consideration sold to Ellis Barron of Watertown six acres in Rockie Meadow and four acres in Birching Meadow, which land was granted by the town of Cambridge to Simon Crosby deceased. Witnesses, Jnº Shearman, Henry Bright. Recorded 1 Apr. 1656. (Middlesex Co. Deeds, vol. 1, fol. 163.)

On 15 Mar. 1653/4, Joseph Juite of Rowley, yeoman, for valuable consideration sold to John Cooper of Cambridge, yeoman, six acres in Cambridge in the ox pasture field, granted by the town of Cambridge to Simon Crosby deceased. Witnesses, Thomas Danforth, Andrew Belcher, Thomas Longhorne. Recorded 29 Dec. 1657. (Middlesex Co. Deeds, vol. 2, fol. 50.)

The sale of the eight-acre lot is not recorded in Middlesex Deeds.

Thus by the sale of the real estate in Cambridge of Simon[6] **Crosby his descendants relinquished connection with that**

---

*He was brother of Richard Longhorne of Rowley, Mass., who married, in 1648, Mary Crosby, daughter of Robert and Constance (Brigham) Crosby. (See p. 65.)

town. His widow removed with the three children in 1645 to Braintree, where her second husband was pastor; and, as the children attained manhood, the eldest son, Thomas[7], became minister at Eastham, Mass., the second son, Simon[7], settled in Billerica, Mass., while the youngest son, Joseph[7], continued in Braintree, thus establishing three separate branches of the family about 1660, which continued in those regions for several generations.

Simon[6] Crosby married in Holme-on-Spalding-Moor, 21 Apr. 1634, ANNE BRIGHAM, born there about 1606,* daughter of Thomas and Isabel (Watson) Brigham (and younger sister of Constance Brigham, wife of Robert[6] Crosby, a fourth-cousin of Simon[6] Crosby, who also came to New England with her children and settled at Rowley, Mass.). As "Anne Brigham" she was an administratrix of the estate of her father, Thomas Brigham of Holme-on-Spalding-Moor, 19 Mar. 1632/3 (Administration Act Books, Harthill Deanery, P. and E. Court of York); and as "Anne Crosby my daughter" she is mentioned with a legacy of five shillings in the will of her mother, Isabel (Watson) Brigham, dated 8 June 1634, evidently having received her share of her parents' estate at marriage (P. and E. York Wills, vol. 42, fol. 281). She accompanied her husband to New England in 1635, and after his death at Cambridge, in September, 1639, continued a widow there about six years. Her lands are recorded on pages 90 and 91 (printed volume) of the Proprietors' Records of Cambridge, being those formerly of her husband, and, in addition, twenty acres of land granted to her on the south side of Charles River (now Brighton) which she sold to Nathaniel Sparhawke (Proprietors' Records of Cambridge, printed volume, p. 122; and Town Records of Cambridge, printed volume, pp. 40 and 69). Upon her second marriage in 1645, she secured administration on Simon[6] Crosby's estate to dispose and divide same with his children, as before

*According to her age on the sailing-list of the *Susan and Ellen* she was born about 1609; but according to the age given on her gravestone she was born about 1606. The latter is correct. Her grave is in the old Hancock burying-ground, Quincy, Mass. (formerly Braintree). On the gravestone she is named "The pious Mrs. Ann Tomson."

described. She married second, in 1645, as his second wife, REV. WILLIAM TOMPSON of Braintree, Mass., and died his widow, 11 Oct. 1675, aged sixty-nine years, according to her gravestone. Rev. William Tompson, by second wife, Mrs. Anne Crosby, had one child, Anne.

Rev. William Tompson, born in Lancashire, England, about 1598, matriculated at Brasenose College, Oxford University, 28 Jan. 1619/20, aged twenty-two, where he received the degree of B.A., 28 Feb. 1621/2. For some time he was curate at Winwick in his native county; but, being persecuted for non-conformity, he emigrated to New England in 1637, preached for a while at Kittery, Me., and on 19 Nov. 1639 was ordained as pastor of the church at Braintree, Mass. At a later date Mr. Henry Flynt was appointed "teacher." According to Cotton Mather, Mr. Tompson was a very powerful and successful preacher, and collaborated with Rev. Richard Mather in the publication of several books. In 1642 he went as a missionary preacher to Virginia, but returned to New England about two years later and resumed his labors at Braintree. In his later years he became afflicted with melancholia, and for seven years was in retirement. Says Mather: "He fell into the bath of the devil, a black melancholy, which for divers years almost wholly disabled him for the exercise of his ministry; . . . but the pastors and the faithful of the churches in the neighborhood kept resisting the devil in his cruel assaults upon Mr. Tompson, by continually drawing near to God with ardent supplications on his behalf: and by praying always, without fainting, without ceasing, they saw the devil at length flee from him, and God himself draw unto him, with unutterable joy. The end of that man was peace" ("Magnalia Christi Americana," vol. 1, p. 439). Mr. Tompson died in Braintree, 10 Dec. 1666, in his sixty-eighth year, leaving his widow in rather straitened circumstances on account of his long period of mental derangement. Children of Simon[6] and Anne (Brigham) Crosby:—

i. Rev. Thomas[7], bapt. in Holme-on-Spalding-Moor, 26 Feb. 1634/5, named for his grandfather, was brought to New England in infancy by his parents, and graduated at Harvard College in 1653. Two years later he was engaged at an annual salary of £50 to preach in the church at Eastham, Mass., and, although never ordained and settled as pastor, he continued as a minister there until 1670. Later he became a merchant at Harwich, Mass., and while on a business trip to Boston was found dead in bed there, 13 June 1702, aged sixty-seven years. His inventory totalled £1091-16-0, with debts of £717-16-0, leaving a net estate of £374-0-0. His heirs divided his property by agreement, 8 Aug. 1705. (Barnstable Co. Probate Records, vol. 2, fols. 148 and 201.) His descendants were numerous and of high respectability; continued on Cape Cod for many generations, and about 1780 some of them went to Yarmouth, Nova Scotia.

He m., about 1662, Sarah ———, and she m., about 1704, as his second wife, John[2] Miller, Esq., of Yarmouth, Mass., b. in England in Mar. 1631/2, son of Rev. John[1] and Lydia Miller.

Children of Rev. Thomas[7] and Sarah (———) Crosby, born in Eastham, Mass.:*—

1. Thomas[8], b. 7 Apr. 1663.
2. Simon[8], b. 5 July 1665.
3. Sarah[8], b. 24 Mar. 1666/7; d. 20 Mar. 1705/6; m., about 1693, Silas Sears of Yarmouth, Mass.
4. Joseph[8], b. 27 Jan. 1668/9.
5. (———)[8], b. 4 Dec. 1670, twin of John[8], died at birth.
6. John[8], b. 4 Dec. 1670; bur. 11 Feb. 1670/1.
7. William[8], b. in Mar. 1672/3.
8. Ebenezer[8], b. 28 Mar. 1675.
9. Anne[8], b. 14 Apr. 1678; m, William Luse.
10. Mercy[8], b. 14 Apr. 1678; living unmarried in 1702.
11. Increase[8], b. 14 Apr. 1678; d. young.
12. Eleazer[8], b. 31 Mar. 1680.

ii. Simon[7], b. at Cambridge, Mass., in Aug. 1637. Settled in Billerica, Mass.

iii. Joseph[7], b. at Cambridge, Mass., in Feb. 1638/9, when a child of about six years was taken by his mother to Braintree, Mass., on her second marriage to Rev. William Tompson, pastor of that town, by whom he was brought up. During King Philip's War, 1675-77, he served as a trooper under Capt. Thomas Prentice and Quartermaster Thomas Swift, and also in the

* See Freeman's "Cape Cod."

garrison at Canton (Bodge's "Soldiers in King Philip's War," pp. 83, 94, 364).

On 30 May 1690 he was admitted a freeman (Records of Mass. Colony, vol. 36, fol. 104), and during many years he was an active figure in the town affairs of Braintree, serving on several important committees from the year 1672, on 20 May 1689 was chosen, with Christopher Webb, a representative for the town at a convention held at Boston to arrange for a provisional government upon the deposition of Gov. Andros, and was elected Selectman in 1690 and Constable on 4 Mar. 1694/5 (Records of Braintree, printed volume, pp. 11, 12, 17-19, 22, 24, 25-27, 30).

On 15 Jan. 1666/7, Joseph Crosby, Samuel Bass, Edmund Quincy, Gregory Belcher, and William Savil for £1900-0-0 bought of the estate of William Tyng the "Salter Farm" in Braintree, an improved property of several hundred acres, which they divided by agreement among themselves, Quincy and Belcher each having an eighth interest, and Crosby, Bass, and Savil a quarter interest each (Suffolk County Deeds, vol. 5, fol. 229, and vol. 12, fol. 265). On 13 June 1686 Joseph Crosby was admitted to full communion in the Braintree church, and he d. 26 Nov. 1695, aged fifty-six years.

The wife of Simon[6] Crosby, as we have already seen, was Anne Brigham of Holme-on-Spalding-Moor. There seem to be two reasons which make it advisable to give here somewhat of a record of the Brigham family in England. The first of these reasons, and perhaps a sufficient one, is that she was the first woman bearing the name of Crosby to come to America, and to undergo, with her infant child, the hardships of those days. The second reason is, that she had a sister Constance residing at Rowley, who also had married a Crosby (a somewhat distant relative of her husband), but who had died before Constance Crosby left for America.

Whereas it is not strictly a part of the history of the Crosby family, with which this book is intended to deal, to take up the subject of the widow Constance Crosby of Rowley, inasmuch as she has always heretofore furnished a certain mystery to those who have delved at all into the annals of the family, it is thought best to explain who she was and something about her, which the discovery of original documents in England for the first time has rendered possible.

All that is thought necessary to state about the Brighams follows:—

1. THOMAS[1] BRIGHAM, born probably about 1475, is the earliest of the Brighams of Holme-on-Spalding-Moor of whom record has been found. As "Thomas Brigham senior" he appears on the rental roll of the manor of Holme in 1528, as holding one toft, an orchard, a barn, a close called Leyre Pytts, and half a bovate of land called Salvan Lands, etc., for which he paid yearly 14s. 8d. (Public Record Office, Rentals and Surveys, Roll 735). No will or administration on his estate is preserved; and the name of his wife has not been learned. He was probably the father of the following child:—

　i. THOMAS[2], b. about 1500.

2. THOMAS[2] BRIGHAM (*Thomas[1]*), born about 1500, appears as "Thomas Brigham junior" on the rental roll of the manor of Holme in 1528, holding a cottage formerly in the tenure of William Armytts, three butts of arable land in Tathom, a flatt of arable land of five acres above Rowley, etc.; yearly rental, 5s. 8d. (Public Record Office, Rentals and Surveys, Roll 735). He was buried at Holme-on-Spalding-Moor, 6 Mar. 1559/60. No will can be found.

He married, about 1525, ELIZABETH ———; she died in 1573, administration being given to [her son] Henry Brigham, 5 Dec. 1573 (Adm. Act Books, P. and E. Court of York, Harthill Deanery). Children:—

　i. THOMAS[3], b. about 1525.
　ii. HENRY[3], of Holme-on-Spalding-Moor and of Seaton.

3. THOMAS[3] BRIGHAM (*Thomas[2], Thomas[1]*), born about 1520, was a yeoman of Holme-on-Spalding-Moor, where he was buried 6 Feb. 1558/9, leaving a will (P. and E. York Wills, vol. 15, part 3, fol. 347).

Thomas³ Brigham married, in 1550, JENNETT MILLINGTON ALIAS TOMLINSON, born about 1526, daughter of William and Barbara, and grand-daughter of Thomas and Agnes (Sotheron), Millington alias Tomlinson, all of Holme-on-Spalding-Moor. Children, born in Holme-on-Spalding-Moor:—

i. THOMAS⁴, b. in 1550.
ii. PETER⁴, b. about 1552; bur. 15 Oct. 1590. He m. EVERILL HESSYE, who administered his estate, 30 Oct. 1590 (Adm. Act Books, P. and E. Court of York, Harthill Deanery). She was bur. 15 Dec. 1591, leaving will dated 14 Dec. 1591 (P. and E. York Wills, vol. 25, fol. 1154). No children.
iii. WILLIAM⁴, b. about 1554; bur. 1 Feb. 1590/1. He was married and had several children, all of whom d. young.
iv. JENNETT⁴, b. about 1555.
v. RICHARD⁴, b. about 1557; m. (1), 28 May 1581, ALISON BURLEY, who was bur. 21 Mar. 1586/7; m. (2), 10 June 1589, ELIZABETH WRIGHT, who was bur. 30 Jan. 1589/90; m. (3), 14 Nov. 1591, MARGARET WILSH. He d. about 1600, without issue.
vi. FRANCIS⁴ (posthumous), b. in 1559; living in 1584, but d. without issue.

4. THOMAS⁴ BRIGHAM (*Thomas³, Thomas², Thomas¹*), born in 1550, is mentioned in his father's will, dated 25 Oct. 1558; also in the will of his cousin Peter Tomlinson alias Millington, dated 21 Dec. 1584 (P. and E. York Wills, vol. 22, fol. 677). In his burial record, on 8 Nov. 1586, he is called a "webster" (cloth-worker). On 3 May 1587 administration on his estate was given to his widow, Gillian (Adm. Act Books, P. and E. Court of York, Harthill Deanery).

He married, about 1572, GILLIAN ——, who survived him. Children:—

i. ELIZABETH⁵, b. about 1572; m., 20 Sept. 1590, EDWARD PALMER, and had at least five children.
ii. JOHN⁵, b. about 1574; lived in Holme-on-Spalding-Moor and finally in the adjoining parish of Hotham, where he d. in 1621. He m., 30 Sept. 1599, CONSTANCE WATSON, bapt. 17 Aug. 1578,

daughter of James Watson, and sister of Isabel Watson, the wife of his brother Thomas⁵ Brigham. On 11 May 1621, administration on the estate of John Brigham of Hotham, deceased, was given to his widow, Custance Brigham (Adm. Act Books, P. and E. Court of York, Harthill Deanery). They had issue.

iii. THOMAS⁵, bapt. 21 May 1576.
iv. WILLIAM⁵, bapt. 17 June 1578; bur. 17 Aug. 1578.
v. RICHARD⁵, bapt. 16 Aug. 1579, was the chief legatee of the will of his great-uncle Henry³ Brigham of Seaton, dated 30 June 1606. His will, dated 1626, left all estate to his wife, sole executrix. Proved 4 May 1627. (P. and E. York Wills, vol. 39, fol. 170.) He left issue.
vi. ROBERT⁵, bapt. 20 May 1582, lived in Holme-on-Spalding-Moor, where he was bur. 8 Sept. 1640.

5. THOMAS⁵ BRIGHAM (*Thomas⁴, Thomas³, Thomas², Thomas¹*), baptized in Holme-on-Spalding-Moor, 21 May 1576, is mentioned with his two children in the will of his great-uncle Henry³ Brigham of Seaton, dated 30 June 1606.

On 19 Mar. 1632/3 administration on the estate of Thomas Brigham of Holme-on-Spalding-Moor, deceased, was given to [his daughters] Anna Brigham and Constance Brigham alias Crosby (Adm. Act Books, P. and E. Court of York, Harthill Deanery).

Thomas⁵ Brigham married, 4 Feb. 1600/1, MRS. ISABEL (WATSON) ELLITHORPE, baptized in Holme-on-Spalding-Moor, 21 Feb. 1560/1, daughter of James Watson.*

Mrs. Isabel (Watson-Ellithorpe) Brigham, widow of Thomas⁵ Brigham, was buried 25 June 1634, and left a will in which she mentions her two daughters, Anne and Constance, as follows (P. and E. York Wills, vol. 42, fol. 281):—

"Item I give to Constance Crosby my daughter Five shillings. Item I give to Anne Crosby my daughter Five shillings."

* His will, dated 10 July, 1615, proved 31 May, 1616, mentions his daughter Isabel, wife of Thomas Brigham (P. and E. York Wills, vol. 34, fol. 95).

Children of Thomas[5] and Isabel (Watson-Ellithorpe) Brigham, born in Holme-on-Spalding-Moor:—

i. CONSTANCE[6], b. about 1602, was an administratrix of the estate of her father in 1632. She m., about 1622, ROBERT CROSBY, bapt. 30 Oct. 1596, d. about 1640. She came to New England a widow, with her three daughters, was granted a house-lot at Rowley, Mass., before 1643, and was bur. there 25 Jan. 1683/4. Children (CROSBY):—

   1. JOHN[7], bapt. 25 Jan. 1623/4; d. young.
   2. JANE[7], bapt. 22 Apr. 1627; m., in Rowley, Mass., 29 Oct. 1644, JOHN PICKARD.
   3. MARY[7], bapt. 4 Dec. 1629; m., in Rowley, Mass., 16 Jan. 1647/8, RICHARD LONGHORNE.
   4. ROBERT[7], bapt. 22 July 1632; d. young.
   5. HANNAH[7], bapt. 31 Oct. 1634; m., in Rowley, Mass., 6 Dec. 1655, JOHN JOHNSON.

ii. ANNE[6], b. about 1606, was an administratrix of her father in 1632. She m. (1), in Holme-on-Spalding-Moor, 21 Apr. 1634, SIMON[6] CROSBY, b. about 1608, youngest son of Thomas[5] and Jane (Sotheron) Crosby. They came to New England in the spring of 1635 and settled at Cambridge, Mass., where he d. in Sept. 1639. She m. (2), in 1645, REV. WILLIAM TOMPSON of Braintree, Mass., where she d. 11 Oct. 1675. Children (CROSBY):—

   1. THOMAS[7], bapt. in Holme-on-Spalding-Moor, 26 Feb. 1634/5.
   2. SIMON[7], b. in Cambridge, Mass., in Aug. 1637.
   3. JOSEPH[7], b. in Cambridge, Mass., in Feb. 1638/9.

And so we see who the widow Constance Crosby of Rowley was, and thus it is that the mists of the past are slowly rolled back, little by little, as the result of lights which come from the most unexpected sources.

For the information of those who may not know so much about her, as well as those who have been particularly interested, we give the following:—

Widow Constance Crosby was born about 1602 in Holme-on-Spalding-Moor, County York, England, and was a sister to Anne Brigham, who in 1634 married, in Holme-on-Spalding-Moor, Simon[6] Crosby of Cambridge, Mass. As "Constance Brigham alias Crosby" she is named as an administratrix of the estate of her father, Thomas Brigham of Holme-on-Spalding-Moor, 19 Mar. 1632–3 (Administration Act Books, Harthill Deanery, P. and E. Court of York); and as "Constance Crosby my daughter" she is mentioned in the will of her mother, Isabel (Watson) Brigham of Holme-on-Spalding-Moor, dated 8 June 1634 (P. and E. York Wills, vol. 42, fol. 281).

Mrs. Constance Crosby and her children were in New England before 1643; but the exact time of their emigration is unknown, although it is likely they came with Rev. Ezekiel Rogers' company in the autumn of 1638. On 10 Jan. 1643/4 a survey was taken of the town of Rowley and a record made of all land holdings at that time. The homestead of Mrs. Crosby is thus described: "On Wethersfield Streete. To Custins Crosby one house-Lott, containing one acre and a halfe, bounded on the north side by a peece of ground unlaid out, and the end of the streete" (Rowley Town Records, p. 6). Richard Wicom had the adjoining lot on the south. She also had received various grants of upland and marsh, amounting to twenty-one acres (*ibid.*, pp. 7, 12, 14, 16, 21, 22, 26, 30, 31, 34, 38).

In 1650 "Wid. Crosby" had one calf; and in 1653 "Uxor Crosby" had two cows (*ibid.*, pp. 59, 84).

Furnished by George B. Blodgett, Esq., Historian of Rowley, Mass.:—

To this Honoured Court now sitting at Ipswich: 4–3–1674 Constance Crosbie Grandmother to this Orphan Sarah Longhorne understanding that Daniell Wickam is like to be perswaded to accept of Gardianship for her; I thinking that she had need of one that hath more experience to oversee her and for other Reasons, I am very unwilling and doe desire that such a thing may not be proceeded in or Granted till Thomas Longhorne of Cambridge her uncle Knowes and Gives his Consent; for he takes more care of the Children than I expected he would have don: not more at psent your poor and humble servant and Handmaide.

CUSTANCE CROSBIE.

(Essex County Court Files, vol. 21, fol. 45.)
In Clerk of Court's Office, Salem, Mass.

"Constance Crosbee buryed the twentyfifth day of January Anno 1683" (1683/4) (Records of Rowley). Children, born in Holme-on-Spalding-Moor, England:—

i. *John⁷*, bapt. 25 Jan. 1623/4; d. young.
ii. *Jane⁷*, bapt. 22 Apr. 1627; was brought to New England when a young girl, and m., in Rowley, Mass., 29 Oct. 1644, *John Pickard*. He was born in England about 1620, and was son, by a previous marriage, of Widow Anne Lume, who d. at Rowley, 19 Mar. 1661/2. He was a carpenter by occupation, succeeded to the homestead of his mother-in-law, and was bur. at Rowley, 24 Sept. 1683. His widow d. in Rowley, 20 Feb. 1715/6, aged eighty-nine years, according to her gravestone. They had eight children (Pickard): *Rebecca⁸, Mary⁸, John⁸, Sarah⁸, Anne⁸, Samuel⁸, Jane⁸, Hannah⁸*.
iii. *Mary⁷*, bapt. 4 Dec. 1629; was brought to New England in girlhood, and m., in Rowley, Mass., 16 Jan. 1647/8, *Richard Longhorne*, b. in England about 1617, as on 25 Mar. 1662 he deposed, aged about forty-five years (Essex County Court Papers, vol. 7, fol. 82). He d. in Haverhill, while there on business, 13 Feb. 1668/9. Papers filed with his will state that in his last illness Dr. Anthony Crosby went from Rowley to Haverhill to attend him, and the doctor witnessed his will. His wife was bur. at Rowley, 29 Nov. 1667. They had nine children (Longhorne): *Thomas⁸*, d. young; *Elizabeth⁸; Constance⁸; Samuel⁸*, d. young; *Thomas⁸*, d. young; *Sarah⁸; Bethia⁸; Richard⁸*, d. young; *Thomas⁸*, d. young.
iv. *Robert⁷*, bapt. 22 July 1632; no further record; probably d. young.
v. *Hannah⁷*, bapt. 31 Oct. 1634; was brought to New England in childhood, and m., in Rowley, Mass., 6 Dec. 1655, *Capt. John Johnson*, b. in England, who came to New England with Rev. Ezekiel Rogers's company in the autumn of 1638, as did his brother Robert Johnson. They first settled in 1639 in New Haven; but before 1650 John Johnson removed to Rowley, Mass., where he purchased the homestead of Richard Thorley, became captain of the local military company, and d. 29 Jan. 1685/6. His estate was settled by agreement by his heirs (Essex County Probate Records, vol. 8, fol. 41). His widow, Hannah, d. 25 Dec. 1717, aged eighty-three years, according to her gravestone. They had five children (Johnson): *Hannah⁸; Elizabeth⁸; John⁸*, d. young; *John⁸*, d. young; *Samuel⁸*.

Chapter IV.

SIMON CROSBY OF BILLERICA.

Simon[7] Crosby (Simon[6], Thomas[5], Anthony[4], Thomas[3], Miles[2], John[1]) was born in Cambridge, Mass., in August, 1637, and died in Billerica, Mass., on 22 Jan. 1725/6. He was married in Braintree, on 15 July 1659, by Major Humphrey Atherton of Dorchester, to Rachel Brackett, daughter of Deacon Richard Brackett and his wife Alice of Braintree. Rachel Brackett was born in Boston, 3 Nov. 1639, and probably died in Billerica, but the exact date of her death has not been found. She was living in 1726. Children:—

- Rachel[8], b. 24 Aug. 1660, Braintree; m., 4 Aug. 1685 in Billerica, to Ephraim Kidder, son of James and Anna (Moore) Kidder of Billerica. He d. in Billerica, 25 Sept. 1724, and she d. there on 14 Sept. 1721, leaving nine children: Ephraim[9], Joseph[9], Rachel[9], Alice[9], Hannah[9], Dorothy[9], Thomas[9], Benjamin[9], Richard[9].
- Simon[8], b. about 1663, probably in Billerica; m., before 1689, Hannah ——, and had seven children recorded there: Simon[9], Abigail[9], John[9], John[9], Samuel[9], Hannah[9], Mary[9]. His wife, Hannah, d. 6 May 1702, and he m., 16 Mar. 1702/3, for a second wife, Abigail, widow of John Parker and daughter of John Whittaker. Simon and Abigail had six children: James[9], Phineas[9], Solomon[9], Nathaniel[9], Rachel[9], and Benjamin[9]. Simon Crosby d. some time after Dec. 1717, and his widow, Abigail, d. in Billerica, 31 Mar. 1755.
- Thomas[8], b. 10 Mar. 1665/6 in Billerica, was mentioned in the will of his father in 1717 as one of the executors, but, when the will was proved, Josiah, the other executor, appears to attend to all the business, and calls himself "acting executor." On 26 Feb. 1724/5 Thomas is referred to as "now sick," and his brother Nathan is his attorney. The date of his death has not been found, but it was before 28 Oct. 1737, when his share of his father's estate is divided between the other heirs.
- *Joseph[8]*, b. 5 July 1669, Billerica; m. there, 4 Aug. 1691, Sarah French, daughter of Lieut. William and Mary French. The

mother of Sarah French was the daughter of Thomas Lathrop of Barnstable, and she m., for her first husband, John Stearns of Billerica.

Hannah[8], b. 30 Mar. 1672, Billerica; m. there, 8 Jan. 1694/5, Samuel Danforth, son of Jonathan and Elizabeth (Poulter) Danforth, and after his death, on 19 Apr. 1742, she m. second, on 4 June 1743, Enoch Kidder. She d. 3 Oct. 1752 in Billerica, aged eighty. She had by Samuel Danforth: Elizabeth[9], Hannah[9], Samuel[9], Rachel[9], Lydia[9], Abigail[9], and Jonathan[9].

Nathan[8], b. 9 Feb. 1674/5, Billerica; m. there, Sept. 28, 1706, Sarah Shed, daughter of John and Sarah (Chamberlain) Shed; and d. 11 Apr. 1749. Sarah Shed was b. in Billerica, 3 Nov. 1678, and d. there 8 Mar. 1746/7. They had Sarah[9], Nathan[9], Rachel[9], Dorothy[9], Catherine[9], Oliver[9], and Mary[9].

Josiah[8], b. 11 Nov. 1677, Billerica; m. there, 2 Nov. 1703/4, Mary Manning, daughter of Ensign Samuel and his second wife, Abiall (Wight) Manning; and d. there before 7 Oct. 1745, when his will was proved. Mary Manning was b. in Billerica, 12 Sept. 1679, and d. after 1745. They had Josiah[9], Eliphalet[9], Elizabeth[9], Anna[9], Isaac[9], Ephraim[9], Mary[9], Elizabeth[9], Jane[9], Joanna[9], Jonathan[9], and Esther[9].

Mary[8], b. 23 Nov. 1680, Billerica; m. there, 7 Aug. 1701, John Blanchard, son of Samuel and Mary (Sweetser) Blanchard; and d. 7 May 1748. John Blanchard was b. 3 July 1677, in Charlestown, and d. 10 Apr. 1750, Billerica. They had Mary[9], Hannah[9], Rachel[9], Abigail[9], Sarah[9], Sarah[9], John[9], John[9], Samuel[9], David[9], Benjamin[9], and Simon[9].

Sarah[8], b. 27 July 1684, Billerica; m. there, 26 Oct. 1710, Capt. William Rawson of Braintree, son of William and Anne (Glover) Rawson, and grandson of Edward Rawson, first secretary of Massachusetts Bay Colony; and d. after 1733. Capt. William Rawson was b. in Braintree, 2 Dec. 1682, graduated from Harvard College in 1703, and after his marriage settled in Mendon. He kept the first grammar school in Mendon, and was prominent in town affairs, and d. there in Oct. 1769. Their children, all b. in Mendon, were: William[9], Perne[9], Anna[9], Sarah[9], Rachel[9], Anna[9], Perne[9], Thomas[9]. (See Rawson Genealogy, p. 15.)

It is not at all unlikely that the Mendelian law of heredity transmitted from Simon the Emigrant to his son Simon a part, if not all, of that restless, intrepid disposition that must seek new fields of endeavor and new scenes of activity. In some people there seems to be born to a greater degree than in others the inherent principle, which, whether you call it the free will of Schopenhauer or by any other term, is nothing more or less than the desire to carve out for one's self one's own destiny, and this seemed to exist in Simon Crosby of Billerica. For here again we find a man who perhaps was not pushed by the necessities of the struggle for existence so much as by the need of freedom for action. It was, of course, possibly not such a venturesome thing to remove from Braintree to what is now known as Billerica as it had been in the previous generation to brave the dangers of a long trip over the seas and the rigors of an unknown country and climate; but it is of the same quality of personality from which such an action is derived. Nor was it in the years around 1660 an easy or pleasant move to contemplate a change from the quasi-civilized community of Braintree to that part of the outlying country that went by the cheerful and inviting name of "The Wilderness," for as such was known all that part of the country in which Billerica came to be established. But it took more than an uninviting name to deter such a man of action as Simon Crosby proved himself to be from putting into action the contemplation of the move he thought necessary. Like his father the Emigrant, Simon Crosby was a younger son; and it is quite within the realm of possibility to conceive that this fact, as is often the case, furnished a compensating inward urge to the execution of such a change. Like his father, also, Simon Crosby had assumed the added duties and responsibilities of establishing himself as the head of a prospective family, and, indeed, again like his father, had achieved the distinction of having one child born in Braintree, the precursor of the others who were to follow. For in those days the duties and obligations attending the necessity of populating a sparsely settled community were understood and willingly faced. Perhaps it was a better constitution or perhaps it was only destiny, but at all events Simon Crosby of Billerica, unlike his father, lived to an advanced age.

Just as it is difficult to visualize conditions which the early Crosbys of Holme-on-Spalding-Moor were forced to

CROSBY HOME IN BILLERICA, MASS.

face, so is it only by the exercise of a duly trained power of imagination that we can try to think of Braintree or the more settled portions of the colonies in the middle of the seventeenth century, to say nothing of that strange and almost unexplored country called "The Wilderness." Simon the Emigrant, to be sure, came far, but he fell heir to an established community; even the houses had been erected in Newtowne, although shortly thereafter abandoned *en masse* by the settlers. Far different was it with Simon the son of the Emigrant. To-day it is only a short spin in an automobile from what was Newtowne, along smooth roads, girt on either side by pleasant gardens and apple orchards, to the town of Billerica, never out of sight of a dwelling and other constant reminders of the habitation of man. But in those days it was like taking a journey far afield in a land inhabited by Indians, along all too uncertain by-ways, through forests and untilled pasture lands.

It is not possible now to ascertain just when Simon Crosby took up his abode in Billerica, but we know from the records of that town that he became a land owner there in 1660, and it is very likely that he soon thereafter removed there, at least as soon as he had made ready for habitation the log cabin which was to house his wife and oldest child, Rachel. The foundations of this original log dwelling may still be seen to-day. Seventeen years later, in 1678, this log house gave way to a more modern and comfortable dwelling, which remained in a good state of preservation and occupied by an unbroken line of Crosbys until in 1877 it was destroyed by fire. A picture of this home of so many Crosbys is inserted in this volume.

Simon Crosby was born in 1637, two years after the arrival of his father in Newtowne and one year before what was probably the date of the arrival of his grandfather Thomas Crosby in Newtowne. As his father died in 1639, it is impossible he could have any recollection of him, but lived with his mother and his grandfather and his two brothers in the Crosby house in Creek Lane, or what is now Brattle Street, Cambridge.

At the age of eight, Simon Crosby found what perhaps was to him a startling change in life, for his mother, Ann Crosby, accepted the pleadings of the Rev. William Tompson to become a mother to the motherless Tompson children and to remove to Braintree, where he was the minister. And so the old home, or rather the only home that Simon Crosby had known, was broken up, and he had to cast about him for new playmates in the strange town of Braintree. But, if the change seemed strange to him, it had its compensating influence, for the Rev. William Tompson was a different sort of a man from the Crosbys, and exerted a different though perhaps not more useful influence upon the community. For Mr. Tompson was a man of thought rather than of action, and what value there is attaching to an education in schools and a university he had and was able to bring into the life of the boy Simon, although what its effect may have been on him is uncertain, for he, like his progenitors, proved to be a man of action; still it must have unconsciously stimulated him in some way and left its impression on his later years of great activity and service to the community in which he lived. And so, from 1645 until soon after 1660, Simon Crosby found a different side to life, and perhaps benefited by the broader atmosphere he lived in, for Rev. William Tompson was in his way a broad and useful man in his sphere of life, universally respected and, what is more important, generally loved.

The first eight years that Simon Crosby spent in Cambridge saw some important changes in that place, namely, the foundation of Harvard College, and the establishment of Stephen Daye's printing-press, and already the beginning of those milder influences which were later to work their impressions upon that community in the New World. Simon Crosby's grandfather, who was the head of the family, was a man, as we have seen, of considerable property, and the most important men in the community were undoubtedly frequent visitors to the house in Creek Lane.

Simon Crosby's life from the age of eight to the age of twenty-one in the home of his stepfather, Rev. William

Tompson, was undoubtedly the life of the average boy during those years and times. He secured what education he could or had inclination for, and fulfilled such duties as were allotted to him until, in July, 1659, he assumed the larger duties as head of his own family, when he married Rachel Brackett, the daughter of Deacon Richard Brackett, one of the most signally serviceable men to the town of Braintree.

That Simon Crosby was most fortunate in the choice of his lifelong helpmeet is continually evidenced by a study of his life and of hers. In his last will and testament, Simon Crosby refers to her as his "dear and beloved wife Rachel Crosbey," and indeed such evidence is not needed to tell us of the great help and comfort she was to her husband through long years of trials and hardships. For life in those days was not easy, but always the brave woman who faced "The Wilderness" cheerfully and gladly did her part to soften its asperities and to bring that gladness into life which means everything to a man. In all they had nine children, which was no small burden for Rachel Crosby to carry.

Just how or when the town of Billerica came to be settled is not known, but it is definitely known that Simon Crosby was not among the very first dozen or so families that settled there, for he was not then of a sufficient age. Billerica is in Middlesex County, Massachusetts, and takes its name from Billericay, Essex County, England, whence some of the first settlers are supposed to have come and to have given the name to the new settlement in "The Wilderness," particularly one Ralph Hill, Sr. It is not here the purpose to say much about Billerica, for those who are interested are referred to Hazen's excellent "History of Billerica," where all that is of particular interest may be found. Its origin is somewhat enveloped in mystery beyond the fact that it is known that a certain unrest existed among the followers of Rev. Thomas Shepard, and the religious and attending political differences of opinion that had been rife in the old country were more or less transplanted to the new country, for conditions are subjectively created by men, and the freedom of action and thought of a new land did not work to eradicate the differences thus created. The history of Anne Hutchinson and all the attending controversies are too well known to need mention here, but the possibility that further settlers might leave Cambridge and follow in the path already blazed by Rev. Thomas Hooker, especially as that gentleman was doing his utmost to get Mr. Shepard to follow him, led the authorities to open up a new tract of country, which we have already referred to as "The Wilderness," a country in the opposite direction from that into which Hooker had penetrated. Those more restless spirits of Cambridge whom a removal to a new country had not satisfied, set up the cry of a lack of room, and with some foundation in fact, for Newtowne was rather restricted in territory, owing to the contours of the country. In those days property was counted by acreage in land, there being little money in circulation. This was a situation of much seriousness that faced the authorities. But, fortunately for them, if there was a scarcity of coin, there was not a scarcity of available land, such as it was, and to that the authorities turned as the solution for the problem.

There was a vast territory known in the records as "The Wilderness," entirely inhabited by Indians. It contained rivers, ponds, and dense forests. This property was known as Shawsheen, so named by a tribe of Indians bearing that name. This wilderness was deeded to Governor John Winthrop and his wife, to Deputy Governor Thomas Dudley, to the church and town of Cambridge and to individuals living there, and thus came into existence what has since become Billerica, Mass. The town was slow in its settlement between 1650 and 1660. There was little to attract an outsider to become a pioneer in that wilderness. There were no roads, no houses, no communication with the outside world, and no fields ready to plant the grain in for their subsistence. It was poverty all about them, a lack of all those things which make life comfortable and endurable. If we look back upon it and reflect on those dozen families representative of large ability and great worth, it seems all but incredible that such records are facts.

Thus it was that most of the first settlers were from Cambridge. In the earliest records we find the names of Jonathan Danforth, Ralph Hill, Sr., Lieut. William French, and others who left their stamp upon that community. But among them the name of Simon Crosby does not appear, and indeed it was not until 1660 that we find the selectmen of Billerica convening to see if they shall validate the private sale of one William Brown of his property to Simon Crosby. For it was a condition of the deed of grant to the first settlers that they should within a given time improve their property, and it appears that William Brown had neglected to do so, possibly finding room enough for himself in Newtowne or not caring to face life in a new place. But in any event the idea of his disposing of his property in a rather irregular way to another person seems to have aroused some questions in the minds of the selectmen of Billerica, not as to whether Simon Crosby was a fit person to appear among them, but as to whether Mr. William Brown was to escape so easily. Fortunately, these resistances did not amount to anything, and it was decided to confirm the purchase; and so it was that Simon Crosby became a land owner in Billerica.

After the original settlement of Billerica by those who received their deeds from the government there were later additions to the new community, and among them were five families from Braintree, of which Simon Crosby's small family was one. The others were the twin brothers John and Peter Brackett and their families, and Samuel Kingsley and Joseph Tompson, a son of Rev. William Tompson, who, as well as Simon Crosby, had all three married daughters of Deacon Richard Brackett. That so many Bracketts both male and female should form a coterie to establish themselves in Billerica was probably due to the fact that Deacon Richard Brackett, although not among the original grantees of Billerica, soon afterwards acquired property there, and, although he probably never lived there himself, so full are the records of Braintree of his services to that town, it is more than likely he turned the attention of the next generation of Bracketts to the new town in the wilderness, of the future of which he may well have been most optimistic. But the optimism of Capt. Richard Brackett, if it existed as we imagine, did not lessen any the rigors or dangers of life in the newly settled district.

The part of Billerica that was acquired by Simon Crosby, as shown on the ancient map of Billerica,* lay near Nutting's Pond on Bare Hill, about one and a half miles from Billerica Common, on which stood the first meeting-house; and this farm remained continuously in the Crosby family from 1660 to 1913.

And so Simon Crosby in 1659 married Rachel Brackett, a brief account of whose family will be found at the end of this chapter; and not long after the birth of their first child, Rachel, they left Braintree behind them to carve a career in a new land. Rev. William Tompson was a graduate of Oxford University, and his two sons, William and Benjamin, were graduates of Harvard as well as Simon Crosby's older brother Thomas. It was therefore much of a change from that environment to go to the wilderness, the scene later of three Indian massacres, although, fortunately for Simon and Rachel Crosby, they suffered no ill consequences, for their home was in the nature of a blockhouse and was known as a garrison-house.

The influence of Rachel Brackett upon the life of Simon Crosby was not only that of great helpfulness, owing to her sterling character, but she was as well a woman of education and breadth of understanding. She thus brought into his life much that unconsciously affected him and sustained him on a side that might otherwise have become impoverished, and whatever value there is in heredity may ascribe no small share to Rachel Brackett as a means to understand the late generations of Crosbys.

They removed, as we have seen, about 1662 to Billerica,

* Hazen's History of Billerica, p. 16.

and settled on land near Nutting's Pond. The grant of land on which they settled was not an original grant to Simon[7] Crosby, but was the land granted as an "original proprietor" to William Brown and sold by him to Simon Crosby. The town records show that in 1660 a town meeting was held in the house of Lieut. William French to see if Simon Crosby should "enjoy this bargain," and this is the first record we have of Simon Crosby in Billerica. His house was on what is now Bedford Road. He is described in the records and writes of himself frequently as "Mr. Simon Crosby." His home is called "Crosby Place." He was admitted freeman, 24 Oct. 1668 (C. R. vol. 4, p. 624).

No sooner was Simon Crosby settled in the log house he had prepared for his family than his life of activity and usefulness in the new community began. In the list of inhabitants and proprietors taken 24 Dec. 1661 his name does not appear, but it does appear as having been chosen Surveyor of Highways 10 Feb. 1663. So as nearly as it can be fixed it must have been in 1662 that he went permanently to Billerica to live, for we know his first child, Rachel, was born in Braintree in 1660, and the second one, Simon, was born in Billerica in 1663.

We may suppose that these years 1660 and 1661 were occupied by Simon Crosby in building his log house and clearing some land for the planting of crops, for otherwise there was no food except the wild game and the fish with which the streams abounded. But it was necessary to have some degree of comfort for his young wife and child, and the building even of a small log house required some time.

The first town meeting was held on 5 Jan. 1660, and no Crosby attended, but in February of the same year Capt. Richard Brackett was granted twenty acres. So that it was probably early in 1660 that Simon Crosby's attention was turned by his father-in-law to the new settlement at Billerica, and Simon probably came there in the spring of that year to look over the ground, and perhaps discovered he could make a good bargain with William Brown for the land he had failed to improve. It must have come to the attention of the selectmen that William Brown had failed in his requirement, or perhaps he had notified the town authorities that he did not intend to improve his property, for on 6 Sept. 1660 it reads in the records:—

Will. Browne having forfeited his hous lott and acomidations into the hands of the Towne (according to the conditions on which he excepted of it) the Towne do receive it into their owne hands againe and doe wholy disalow of him disposinge of it without theire approbation and consente this is votted by the Towne on the affirmative.

It would seem the town was taking no chances; but in October they were forced to face this serious issue, and it appears in the records of the town as follows:—

At a meetinge at Lieftant ffrenchs a major prtt of ye Townsmen did agree yt Will. Browne shall wayt sum time for the disposing of his acomidations yt was granted him by the Towne in reference to the getting in his Charges yt he hath expended upon ye premises: by way of improvement of the same himselfe or by such other person as the Towne shall aprove'on: by his procuring or other ways procured by the Towne it was also yelded to the Saide Will Browne that it sholde be propounded to the towne and move to another vote whether Simon Crosby shall injoy the Bargain sould to him by the said Will Browne whether the saide Simon shall injoy the same not withstanding the vote yt is paste by the Towne alrady, or whether he shall not injoy it.

And so it finally came about that William Brown's name was erased from pages 47, 49, and 57 of the original first book of Billerica records and that of Simon Crosby substituted for it.

CROSBEE Wm. Browne	"Layd out to him three acres and a half more or less lying on both sides the river, his lott being 16 poles wide, bounded with James Kidder above and Wm. Tay below."
	Si Crosbe
	"Layd out to Wm. Tay" 4 a bounded with Wm. Browne above and Simon Bird below.
Wm. Browne CROSBEE.	"4 acres more or less 8 poles wide, bounded by James Patten above and Jacob Brown below."
	(Also this appears—"Laid out to Jacob Brown 4 a 8 poles

bounded by Wm Brown" (crossed out and Simon Crosbee written in) above and Thomas foster below.)

9-9-1659. "Laid out to Wm Brown 18 a 17 poles wide at ye head and 16 poles at ye foot, bounded with Samuel Kemp south and Jonathan Danforth north."

The above grants to William Brown are probably the land that Simon Crosby first bought in Billerica.

The first are not dated, but are undoubtedly earlier than Sept. 9, 1659.

These original purchases of land were not all that Simon Crosby secured in his early years in Billerica, for Book I. of the town records shows the following additional acquisitions in the form of land grants.

LAND GRANTS TO SIMON CROSBY IN BOOK I.

The town of Billerica has granted—

1660
1. 8 a lot 8/10 of single share, with priviledges.
2. 29 a, part of which was for his house lot—S of the township and of Dudley's farm, on E of country road to Shawshin on North of Bare Hill—W & S by highway 3 poles wide, N by highway & E by James Tomson and William Hamlet.
Above also includes 3¼ a of meadow.
3. 15 a E of Loes meadow,—N by highway between this lot and Jacob Brown, E by John Poulter, S&W by Samuel Kemp
4. 3½ a meadow on Shawshin river below Globe Hill on both sides of the river—S by James Kidder, N by William Tay, E&W by upland.
5. 4 a of meadow in the great meadow south of Prospect Hill—N by James Patterson and S by Jacob Brown "Crosse ye meadow."
6. 18 a in great common field east of Concord river below the bridge—W by river, S by Samuel Kemp and N by Jonathan Danforth.

1661
7. 46 a on east side of town in 2nd part of 2nd division in and about the "willow spangs" (with allowance for highway)—NW by Jonathan Danforth, N by James Kidder, Thomas Foster and James Patterson, W by Jonathan Danforth, E by John Poulter & SE by colledge farm line.

1663
8. 1 a 64 poles of meadow on west of concord river on south of fort wall—S by William Pattin, N by James Kidder, E&W by upland.

1663 9 mo.	9.	One small skirt of land by his house where it now stands which he hath taken wholly within his fence.
1664	10.	20 a. on left hand side of way as you go to Globe Hill, the 3rd lot in that common field—S by highway, E by Ralph Hill, W by Capt. Bracket, N by "heeth" meadow.
1665 25 10 mo.	11.	15 a of swamp by Nutting's pond.
1665. 29 11 mo.	12.	1 a. of swamp on north of former parcel of swamp & next adjoining it as payment "Which acre of land is granted to him for satisfaction in full for what service he did for the Town the last yeare assisting ye first Comitte about gratuitys."
	13.	17 a (& 1 a) in the swamp by Nuttings pond 1 acre more being added to the former grant to make his full proportion
1666 1 mo.	14.	¾ a & 8 poles on NE of Prospect Hill the 29th lot in order on E side of meadow—NW by Daniel Shed, SE by Nathaniel Hill, SW by George Farley.
1670 1 mo.	15.	4 a of swamps next his own formerly granted at Nuttings pond south by side of swamp next pond etc.
1677. Mar.	15.	15 a & 1 a in angle of meadow land at NE corner of Nuttings pond, granted for services to town
1685. 9 mo.	16.	4½ a of swamp in Mill swamp the last lot on E side of brook—above by John Brackett, W by ye brook and below by "ye great damm."
	17.	3½ a in Mill swamp on W side of brook & on N side of fox brook the 1st lot laid out in that place—by fox brook N, by upland S, by meadow of Lt. French E, by Edward Farmer, W.

These seventeen grants, together with his original purchase and that land he acquired through the drawing of lots, formed the bulk of his farm. On 28 Aug. 1661 Simon Crosby drew the last remaining lot in the drawing for meadow lots, and drew number 41; and again on 3 May 1663 he drew lot 8 of meadow land on the Concord River. Other drawings of lots were:—

25 Nov. 1663, lot 2 on north side of Content in the field;
25 Oct. 1665, 8 acres in swamp land by Nutting's Pond in last division;
8 Nov. 1665, lot 28 of meadow at Prospect Hill;
and on 29 Nov. 1665 he was paid, for his services in laying out land, one acre of swamp by Nutting's Pond.

Simon Crosby's earliest public service in Billerica seems

to have been in connection with laying out land, and, while he was not appointed Surveyor of Highways until 26 Jan. 1666, he was appointed on a committee to lay out land on 9 Dec. 1663, and, having together with William Tay made a request for land near their houses in September of the same year, it was probably because of that reason he was allotted land in payment of his services near Nutting's Pond, although we find that in September, 1666, his services were paid for in money at the rate of 4s. 6d. per day and a half of labor for the town.

In these years he was still living in his log house, which had already become what his later house became, a centre for meetings and much that was of public interest, for we have seen that it was at his house he was appointed on a committee of three to divide lands.

On 28 Jan. 1664 Simon Crosby extended his services as an inhabitant of Billerica from an interest in the division of lands to a greater activity in the capacity of constable, and thus began his wide field of usefulness to the community in which he lived.

In the years that now followed, Simon Crosby devoted himself to the gradual clearing of his farm and the usual rotation of crops, and to the strengthening of his home, for Billerica was not a very safe place in which to live, on account of threatened attacks by the Indians. In the history of King Philip's War by Bodge, we find on page 85 that Simon Crosby housed Lieut. Edward Oakes and some of his troopers, for which he put in a small bill. Perhaps it was because he was himself a trooper at Brookfield in the command of Captain Wheeler* that his home furnished entertainment for Lieut. Edward Oakes and his men in 1675, although Simon Crosby himself was not what would usually be designated as a military man.

In addition to the holding of the office of Constable, a very important office in those days, and by which title and with much apparent pride Simon Crosby sometimes signed himself, he was Deputy to the Massachusetts General

* Bodge, History of King Philip's War, page 114.

Court, February 1690, April 1691, 26 May to December 1697, and from 25 May to 10 Dec. 1698.

Like most of the men of his time, Simon Crosby took an interest in the affairs of the religious side of the community in which he lived. It was 9 Sept. 1659 that the first plans for a meeting-house for Billerica were drawn up, but, of course, Simon Crosby was not there. In 1668 he bought Mr. Kinsley's pew for £1 11s., and so became in his earliest years in Billerica definitely connected with the church, and in the same year he paid as his portion of the expense for the preaching of Rev. Samuel Whiting, £1 4s. 6d., it being necessary, apparently, to provide for their spiritual guidance by means of an assessment.

In 1693 the parish thought it was time to establish themselves in a new meeting-house, for they seemed to have outgrown the original place of worship; and so on the 8th of October of that year the town voted, in reference to a new meeting-house, their willingness and desire that Capt. Hill, Mr. Crosby, and Sergt. Richison should undertake the same, to begin and finish it, and should adopt as their model, in most respects, the meeting-house at Redding. The town also, as a practical earnest of their support, voted three hundred pounds for the project, and, being also at that time a selectman of Billerica, on 4 Dec. 1693, Simon Crosby was as well placed upon the committee of the Board of Selectmen for the new meeting-house. On 30 June 1696 he paid £2-0-10 towards the new meeting-house, and was assessed again in 1711, this time probably for repairs. It was in this latter year, also, we find that Simon Crosby changed his pew in the new church, for the following quaint entry in the town records states that the town granted "Liberty to build pues in ye vacant places in ye meeting house," and Simon Crosby was granted a place "on the north side between Mr. Whiting's and the old pue at the east end of the pulpit." It was also recorded on 31 June 1685 that Simon Crosby's wife "was seated in meeting, 2 in ye fore seat below."

As well as the office of Constable, which he held again in

Simon Crosbey Constable.

Age 42 years

THIS AUTOGRAPH SIGNATURE OF SIMON' CROSBY WAS APPENDED TO HIS DEPOSITION IN THE CASE OF WYMAN *VS.* FARMER MENTIONED ON PAGE 81

1677–8, and that of Deputy to the General Court, Simon Crosby devoted much time to public affairs as a Selectman of Billerica, and for twenty-eight years without a break he was a Selectman, namely, from 1671 to 1699, and again for a brief time in 1701. And during these years the Board of Selectmen met often at his home, especially during the years that he ran a tavern in his house; notably in 1689 there are constant references in the records of meetings at "Lanlord Crosbe's" house. For in 1678 Simon Crosby completed his new house, which was to replace the log house, and this new house was a very commodious affair for those times. In 1688, 1692, 1693, and 1694 there are several mentions of the meetings of the selectmen in his home. There are also some records of his being reimbursed for money expended on account of the town, as in March 1695/6 he was paid 8s. for money spent in 1694, etc.

Three interesting entries are given below that speak eloquently of the condition of the times. These are from the Court Records:—

8 Aug. 1678   Deposition of Simon Crosby in his own handwriting in the case of Wyman *vs.* Farmer. "Simon Crosbee aged about 42 years saith that about two years ago since he sold an ox to ffrancis Wyman of woburne for three pound five shilling in [probably June, writing is faded] or thereabouts, which ox Edward ffarmer received by [sge?] said Wyman's order and wrought him, witness his hand Simon Crosby."

25 Mar. 1684   Samuel Manning, Edward Farmer & Symon Crosby all of Bileriky with any others of the same company partners with them in their practice of setting potts & catching salmon at the fishing places belonging to the Indians at Pawtucket falls on the Merrimack river—were summoned in court.

15 June 1685   Simon Crossbee Senr & Joseph ffoster of Billerica testify that towards the latter part of last winter they being at Woburn saw Samuel Knight of Woburn sell 3 bearskins which he bought of Simon Blood of Concord for 14s. 6d.

From the above we can see that, wittingly or otherwise, Simon Crosby had a human side, for he seems to have been catching fish where he didn't belong. It is also somewhat of a relief to find him up before the court in 1688 for "retailing strong drink without a license."

Meanwhile, Simon Crosby's family was growing apace, and, possibly to help replenish the family larder, and perhaps because his home was on the main travelled road, he decided to take upon himself the added cares of a tavern. And on 27 Nov. 1672 he was granted permission "to keep a house of public entertainment." And thereafter up to 1693 he was referred to in the records as "Landlord"; as in 1685 he received one pound for entertainment which he furnished to the selectmen who often met there. But in 1686 he appeared to tire of his rôle of landlord, for it is recorded that "whereas Simon Crosbee who formerly hath kept a house of publick entertainment doth now refuse to hold it any longer." However, in 1688 the following records show he had returned to his previous occupation:—

"A list was taken of ye County Rate, we had then of Bro. Crosby in victualls and Drink of money 3s. 6d."
Ditto "We had of Bro. Crosbe 7 Suppers, 3s. 6d.
"   Drink 8d. Suppers 2s.
"   4 Suppers 16d. Drink 8d.
"   'Of our lanlord Crosbe' 7 meals 3s. Drink 1s. 6d."

As an interesting example of what was required of an inn-keeper of those days we insert here a copy of the bond given by Simon Crosby in 1690 by the filing of which he was entitled to become a licensed victualler. It will be observed there are some considerable differences in the requirements existing between those of the kepeer of a road-house in our times and the keeper of a tavern in 1690. If the selectmen of the town of Billerica could drop in of an evening in a modern road-house, with its crowds of automobilists and its exponents of modern dancing, it is to be presumed they might be somewhat confused in their attempt to readjust their perspective as to the change in conditions that has occurred.

MIDDX. MEMORANDUM— That on ye 28th. Day of May, Anno Domini sixteen hundred and ninety, and in ye second year of ye Reign of our Soveraign Lord and Lady Wm. & Mary by ye Grace of God of England Scotland France & Ireland King and Queen Defenders of ye faith &c. By vertue of ye order of ye County Court at Charlestowne by Adjournment from Cambridge Aprill 26th last past Simon Crosbee of Billerica in ye County aforesaid, became bound in ye Summ of Twenty pounds Current money of New England, which he doth acknowledge him selfe to ow and stand justly indebited to our Soveraign Lord and Lady King William & Queen Mary theire heirs and Successors, to be Levied on his goods & Chattells Lands and Tenements

The Condition of this recognisance is such, that whereas ye said Simon Crosbee above bound is admitted, and allowed by ye said County Court to keep a Common Publick house of entertainment and to use Common selling of wine, Beer, Ale Syder Rum Brandy and other Liquors for ye year ensueing in ye now dwelling house of said Simon Crosbee. If therefore ye said Simon Crosbee during ye time abovesaid, shall not permitt, suffer or have any playing at Cards Dice Tables Bowls, Billiards Nine Pins, or any other unlawfull game or games, in his said house yard, garden or Backside   Nor shall suffer to be or remaine in his house any person or persons not being of his own familie on Satturday nights after it is dark, or on ye Sabbath Daies, nor in ye time of Gods Publick Worship therein   Nor shall entertain as Lodgers in his house any strangers men or women above ye Space of forty eight hours, but whose names and sirnames he shall deliver to some one of ye Select Men, or Constables of ye Town, unless they be such as he verry well knoweth, and will answr for his or theire forth Coming, Nor shall sell any wine or Liquors in any wise to any Indians or Negros, Nor suffer any Children or Servants, or any other person to remain in his house Tipling or Drinking after Nine of ye Clock in ye Night time, Nor shall buy, or take to pawn, any stolen goods, nor willingly or knowingly harbour in his house or Barn or Stable, or other where any Rogues Vagabonds, Theives, Sturdy Beggars or masterless men or women or other notorious offenders whatsoever, Nor shall suffer any person or persons, to sell or utter any wine Beer Ale, Syder Brandy Rum or other Liquors by Deputation or by Colour of his Licence, nor shall entertain any person or persons of whom he shall be prohibited by Law, or by any of ye Magistrates of sd County, as persons of an Idle Conversation, and given to Tipling. Also shall keep ye true Assize & measure in his Potts, Bread and otherwise in uttering of wine Beer Ale, Syder Rum Brandy or other Liquors and ye same sell by sealed measure, and in his said house shall use and maintaine good order and Rule, and is and shall be well provided wth sufficient houseing and wth Two Beds at ye least for Entertainment of strangers & Travarllers and shall attend ye Laws and orders of Courts referring to that Imployment.   Then this present Recognizance to be void and of nowe effect, else to stand and be in full power force and vertue—

In wittness whereof he hath here unto sett his hand and Seal this day & year above written

Signed Sealed &c }
In Presence of

RICHARD AUSTIN Senr.   SIMON CROSBEY (Seal)
THIMO. PHILLIPS

Commonwealth of Massachusetts }
Middlesex ss. Registry of Probate

A true copy.

Attest,   W. E. ROGERS Register.

And as late as 1692 he renewed his license.

During his life in Billerica Simon Crosby was an active trader in real estate, as is shown by the record.* But in

*Jan 2 1664	S. C. of Billerica, planter, sells meadow land in Billerica granted him by town.
Dec 29 '64	Buys 43 a. in Bill. of John Parker
Jan 29 '64	Mort. " " "
May 3 '73	Buys 57 a. " " of John Kittredge
Jan 29 '74	Husbandman, mortages 100 a. in Bill. to Thos Russell.
May 31 '77	Buys 43 a. and 139 a. in Bill. of John Parker
Apr 8 '91	" 60 a. in Bill. the homestead of Nath. Tay.
Aug 23 '92	Sells to James Pollard land and dwelling house in Bill.
May 3 '95	" for love to s-in-law Ephraim Kidder and wife Rachel as part of her portion land and bldgs in Bill. also for 100 lbs in money.
July 1700	Sells to James Hosley 15 a. in Bill. for 24 lbs.
Mar 21 '01	Sells to son Joseph—Exchange of land 10 a. and 50 a. for 30 lbs.
Aug 6 '01	Sells to John Blanchard house and orchard in Bill.
Apr 2 '06	Sells to James Hosley land in Bill.
Nov 2 '06	Sells to T. Ivory of Charlestown small tenement in same, bought of John Blanchard.
Aug 6 '01	Buys of J. Blanchard land and bldgs. in Charlestown.

LAND GRANTS, No. 1, V. 2.

Simon Crosby, Sr.

Apr, 1707.	38½a.	(36) on Indian Hill. E. by road to Bacon's mill; S. by highway to Nutting's pond; N. by his own land; W. by Henry Jefts, and partly by Champney's land.
	(2½)	on S. of Nutting's meadow. N. by Joseph Foster; E. by Benj. Parker; S. by Isaac Stearns; W. by highway to Bacon's mill.
May, 1707.	14a., 64p.	West side of road to Bacon's mill, which is his 1st lot in 2nd draught in the pond squadron. N. by the way on the S. of Nutter's pond; E. by Caleb Farley; S. by Rubish meadow, & W. James Frost, Sr.
May 16, 1707	28a.	Upland and Swamp, S. of Nuttings pond. N. by pond and Nath Crosby; E. right of Thomas Stearns and Capt. Tompson; and S. by Deacon Frost and John Chamberlain; W. by John Shed. This was granted by the Pond Squadron May 8, 1707 for his 2nd lot which was 14 a. & 64 poles.
May, 1707.	16a.	South of Nutting's pond (which is instead of 14a 64 poles which is his 3rd lot in the 2nd draught in the pond squadron). N. by highway; S.

addition to his care for his personal interests he still had much time to devote to general public activities and service. We find he filled all sorts of positions and rendered various kinds of service to the town. He was Surveyor of Highways in 1677–8; on a committee to run line between Billerica and Chelmsford in 1669; on the committee for gratuities on land in 1670; on the Grand Jury in 1671; again on the committee to run bounds with Chelmsford in 1671; in 1672 he was commissioner for the county rate; in 1674–5 again on the committee for gratuities; in 1677 he was sent to the General Court to carry a petition about rates. From 1675 to 1678 he was one of a committee of three to examine the town accounts from time to time, from which we can infer that he had some experience in book-keeping, and in this latter year he was further intrusted with the buying of Cambridge lands for the town, as well as the collection of what was due of the college contributions to be sent to the college overseers, and so as tithing-man, Assessor, Surveyor of Fences and Highways, and in other capacities, he gave freely of his time to the public welfare, and at last approached the end of a life of singular usefulness. In 1717, being nearly at the age of eighty, he drew up his will, a document which we give below because to those who can read the human character perhaps in no better way can be made apparent the breadth and scope of vision of Simon Crosby of Billerica. The fair and just disposal of his property, of which a considerable portion occurred during his life, and the calm and dignified language of his will, show that Simon Crosby was no ordinary man.

In the Name of God amen I Simon Crosbey of Billerica, in the County of Middx., in his Majests. Province of the Massachuset Bay in New-

	by Nuttings pond; E. by Capt. Thompson and the Bacons; S. by Oakes' line, W. by right of Lt. French and Zechariah Shed and James Frost, Jr.
May 27 '09	Sells to grandson Simon Crosby of Bill. 90 a. in Bill. 46 granted him by Bill. 40 to John Poulter and 4a. to Capt. Brackett for 64 lbs.
Feb 1 '14	Sells to Mass. Commissioner.
Apr 29 '17	Sells to son Josiah 10 a. in Bill.
Apr 13 '16	Sells for love to son Josiah two parcels of land, one of 2 a. & 1 of 4 a.
" 10 "	Sells to son Josiah abt 16 a. in Bill.
" 30 '17	Sells to son Simon as part of his estate, 60 a. of land and 1/5 of woodland S. of Nutters (?) pond.

england,) this seventh day of June Anno Domini one thousand seven hundred and seventeen.) being weak in body but of perfect mind & understanding do make & ordain this my last Will and testament in manner and forme following, that is to say Principally & first of all I give and Recommend my Immortal soul into the hands of god that gave it, and my body to the Earth to a decent Burial at the discression of my Executors, and as for the worldy Estate wherewith it hath pleased god to bless me in this life, I give, demise and dispose of the same in the following manner and forme

Imps. I do give unto my dear and beloved wife Rachel Crosbey, the whol use & Improvement of my dwelling house and all the Rooms therein, and all the utensels & beding to be at her dispose during her natural life, and the one half of said utensels & beding to be at her dispose forever, and the use of the three gardains and the yard, & the house belonging to the yard and out of the orchard what fruit & cider may be needful, & a sufitiency to provide a maid or a nurs, according to her nesecity, and the use of a hors to cary her to meeting, or when she hath ocation to ride forth, and her choyce of two cows to be constantly provided for winter & sumers and six sheep to be kept & maintained by my execut so long as they shall se reson to keep sheep for themselves, and if they keep no sheep I order that they provide for their mother annually twelve pounds of merchantable wool, I, give unto my loveing wife, what swine I have to be at her dispose, and grant her liberty for the future to Rais what may be for her use; and a continual supply of corn & meal and mault & firewood for her cumfortable subcistance at all times, and further I do order my executors to pay unto my dear wife six pounds in money annually during her natural life.

Item as for my Eldest son Simon Crosbey I have allready given him his Double portion in my estate in full by a deed of gift of lands & medow, executed according to law to his satisfaction.

Item I give unto the Rest of my sons to each of them eighty pounds, and I give unto each of my daughters sixty pounds, accounting what each of them have had as part of their portions.

Item My son Thomas Crosbey hath Received of me in our way of trade twenty pounds.

Item My son Joseph Crosbey has Received in land and help about Building twenty pounds.

Item My son Nathan Crosbey hath Received in part of his portion twenty pounds in land and medow.

Item My son Josiah Crosbey hath Received in part of his portion in land thirty pounds.

Item My daughter Rachel Kidder the wife of Ephraim Kidder I have given unto her as part of her portion fifty pounds in the sale of that land that I sold unto my son in law Ephraim Kidder, and ten pounds besids which she is to Receive.

Item My daughter Hannah Danforth the wife of Samuel Danforth hath Received sixteen pounds.

Item My daughter Mary Blanchard the wife of John Blanchard hath Received fifteen pounds in his purchas and fifteen pounds in houshold stuff, in part of her portion thirty pounds.

SIMON CROSBY OF BILLERICA

Item   My daughter Sarah Rawson the wife of William Rawson of Braintry hath Received in part of her portion fifty & eight pounds, in houshold stuff, cattel and money.

Item   I do nominate, appoint and fully Inpower, my two sons Thomas and Josiah Crosbey to be my lawfull executors of this my last will. also I do give unto my grand son John Crosbey fifteen pounds and unto my grand daughter Rachel Danforth ten pounds in money to be paid by my executors after my decease, and in case my estate do amount to more than what I have given to my children my will is that after all debts and funeral charges be paid the Remainder shall be equally divided among my children.

In Witness that this is my last will and testament I have hereunto set my hand and seal the day and year above written In the third year of his Majestr. Reign.

Signed Sealed pronounced and declared by the said Simon Crosbey to be his last will and testament in the presence of us the subscribers.
Samll Fasset
John Duren: junr.
Jacob Danforth

Middx. County, Camb.   SIMON CROSBEY   (SEAL)
26th. February 1724/5
L S   This aforegoing last will & Testament of Simon Crosby was presented by Josiah Crosby one of ye Executrs. in ye sd will named for probate & Just Whiting Certifyed the Widow desired ye sd. will may be proved & came also. Nathan Crosby, James Crosby Son of Simon Crosby, Saml. Danforth, husband to Hannah and John Blanchard husband to Mary two daughters of sd. Testatr. Tho Kidder a son of Rachel a 3d. daughter Joseph Crosby, 3d. Son, the three Witnesses were sworn according to law sd. Josiah accepts his office, & room is left for Thomas ye other Ecr now Sick) & notice first to be given to ye other kindred. & this will is proved & approved & the sd. Testatrs. Estate & of this sd. will in any manner conserning is & ye admrn. comitted To ye sd. Josiah to fulfill ye. same. I order forthwith a Pfect Inventory to be taken (at kindrens choise) by Capt Saml. Hill, Enoch Kidder & Saml. Fasset of Billerica, to be sworn cor Just Whiting. Witness my hand & Seal of Court of pro

die supra   F. FOXCROFT Judge prob

Entred in the Registry of Probate for Middlesex Libr. 17 pae. 250, 1

PFRA. FOXCROFT Jun reg

Commonwealth of Massachusetts }
Middlesex ss.   Registry of Probate }

A true copy.

Attest,   W. E. ROGERS   Register.

SIMON CROSBY THE EMIGRANT

An Inventory of the Real and Personal estate of Mr. Simon Crosbey late of Billerica deceased, Testate Aprised by us the subscribers, March 18, 1724/5.

Imp The homstead on the west side of the Road containing seventy three acres of upland and medow with the buildings at four hundred and twenty Pounds	420 00 00
The homstead on the east side of the Road containing ten acres and three quarters of mowing land at one hundred and ten Pounds	110 00 00
Sixty nine acres of upland and swamp lying near Strong water Brook at sixty nine Pounds	69 00 00
one Parcel of land lying upon Rozen Plain containing a hundred and fourty acres at Eighty seven Pounds	87 00 00
sixty acres of land lying on the West side of Concord River at fifty Pounds	50 00 00
twenty five acres of wood land lying near flaggey medow in the Pond squadron at twenty five Pounds	25 00 00
	£761 — —

The Personal Estate.

one old hors at forty shillings, two oxen at thirteen Pounds	15 00 00
one Cow and Calf at five Pounds	05 00 00
two old Cows at seven Pound & ten shillings	07 10 00
one Bull and a heafer at five Pounds fifteen shillings	05 15 00
seven sheep at three Pounds & three shillings	03 03 00
his wearing apparrel at five Pounds eleven shillings	05 11 00
one Silver Cup at thre Pounds & ten shillings	03 10 00
the Peauter at two Pounds & two shillings	02 02 00
Beds, beding and linning twenty one Pounds four shillings	21 04 00
Iron ware and old Iron four Pounds & nineteen shillings	04 19 00
Brass ware two Pounds	02 00 00
Scales & weights a morter and Pestel at five shillings	00 05 00
one old gun and cutlash at eighteen shillings	00 18 00
Tables and Chairs and other utensils at three Pounds sixteen shillings	03 16 00
	£80"13"—

SAMUEL HILL
SAMUEL FASSET
ENOCH KIDDER

Billerica March ye 2 1725/6

These lines may certifie whome it doth concern that I have Received of my Son Josiah Crosby (Exetr. of his fathers will) the contents there in mentioned for the first year
I say Recd. by me for one year

Rachel Crosbey

Commonwealth of Massachusetts }
Middlesex ss. Registry of Probate }

    A true copy.
           Attest,   W. E. ROGERS.
                                                            Register.

AUTOGRAPH SIGNATURE OF RACHEL (BRACKETT) CROSBY, WIFE OF SIMON[7] CROSBY

Middx. ss. March. 18. 1724/5 The abovesaid Samuel Hill, Samuel Fasset & Enoch Kidder Personally appeared and made oath to the above apprisement
     before me OLIVER WHITING Juste of Peace.

Middsex. Camb. April 13 1725 Exhibd upon oath ℞ Josiah Crosbey the abovesaid deced's son and Execr. &c.
           F. FOXCROFT Jd. Prob.

Entred in the Registry of Prob: for Middlesex Libr 17 Pa. 264/5
          FRA FOXCROFT Jun. Rgr.

Commonwealth of Massachusetts }
Middlesex ss. Registry of Probate }
  A true copy.
    Attest, W. E ROGERS Register.

Simon Crosby died 22 Jan. 1725/6, at the age of eighty-eight. His life of usefulness and activity had finally come to an end. He was buried from his home in Billerica, and the body laid to rest in the Old South Burying-ground, about one mile from the centre of the town of Billerica, on the road to Concord, in which many of the Crosbys and their connections were interred.

Simon Crosby was survived by his widow, Rachel (Brackett) Crosby, but the date of her death is uncertain. Rachel Brackett's influence upon the life of her husband was considerable. She had whatever advantage lies in heredity and early environment, and joined with that her own powerful and useful personality. Her father was Capt. Richard Brackett of Braintree, sometimes called Deacon Brackett. The surname of the woman he married is not known, but her given name was Alice, as appears from his will. Richard Brackett was born in 1610, and died in Braintree, 5 Mar. 1690, at the age of eighty.

He came to New England as a member of the "Massachusetts Bay Company," with John Winthrop as Governor. He was one of the company who settled with Winthrop in Charlestown, and moved with this same company to Boston in the autumn of 1630, on the invitation of Rev. William Blackstone, "the hermit minister." Richard Brackett on

27 Aug. 1630 signed a covenant with John Winthrop *et als.* to establish the First Church in Boston. His home was on the site of the present Adams House in Boston. He lived there until 1641, during which time he was an active and useful citizen.

In 1637 Richard Brackett was appointed keeper of the prison with a salary of £13 6s. 8d. (Boston Records).

June 10, 1638: Richard Brackett may sell his house and garden next William Hudson the younger (*ibid.*).

June 6, 1639: Richard Brackett's salary raised to £20 as keeper of the prison (*ibid.*).

Richard Brackett was among the early settlers at Mt. Wollaston, named Braintree for Braintry in England.

On 26 June 1642 Richard Brackett was, with wife Alice, dismissed from the First Church in Boston, with letter to church at Mt. Wollaston (Braintry).

21 July 1642 Richard Brackett was ordained first deacon of this church, Rev. William Tompson pastor and Mr. Flynt teacher. A silver cup used at the communion service was evidently the gift of Deacon Richard Brackett and wife Alice, for it bears on its surface the engraved initials $\frac{B.}{R. \& A.}$, a custom then in use of engraving the initial of the family surname above and the initial of the Christian name below.

Captain Brackett's life was one of great usefulness, and the records attest to his constant activity. He was captain of the Braintree Military Company before 1655; Deputy from Braintree to the Massachusetts General Court from 1655 to 1665, 1667, 1671, 1672, 1674, and 1680; and on 15 Oct. 1679 he was appointed to join persons in marriage in the town of Braintree, and to administer oaths in civil cases. Bodge, in his book on King Philip's War (page 473), says:—

"About the opening of King Philip's War there were regiments or parts of regiments in each of the six counties. In the Suffolk Regiment, Major Thomas Clark; Richard Brackett is the Captain and Edmund Quincy Lieut. of the Braintree company."

But in 1684, being then seventy-three years of age, Richard Brackett decided to retire from further active military service, and on 15 October his request was granted, and Lieut. Edmund Quincy was appointed to succeed him.*

It was in such an atmosphere as this that Rachel Brackett lived up to the time of her marriage to Simon Crosby in 1659. That she was particularly close to her father is shown by the fact that he left her the family Bible.

* Mass. Bay Colony Records, vol. 5, p. 459.

Chapter V.

EARLY CROSBYS IN BILLERICA.

An Account of Joseph and William of the Eighth and Ninth Generations.

Joseph[8] Crosby (Simon[7], Simon[6], Thomas[5], Anthony[4], Thomas[3], Miles[2], John[1]) was born in Billerica, 5 July 1669; married there, 6 May 1691, Sarah French, daughter of Lieut. William and wife Mary French (who was a daughter of Thomas Lothrop of Barnstable and widow of John Stearns). Sarah French was born in Billerica, 29 Oct. 1671, and probably died there between 8 July 1727, when she releases her dower in some land (Middlesex Deeds, 26:529), and 29 Dec. 1727, when her husband deeds land to their daughter Hannah Watts. She does not sign the deed (30:9).

The date of Joseph[8] Crosby's death has not been found, but it was about 1736 or soon after. Children, born in Billerica:—

    Joseph[9], b. 2 Sept. 1692, m., before 1719, Hannah ———, and was living in Worcester before 1719, as they had a daughter Sarah[10] recorded there 5 May 1719. They also had recorded there Joseph[10], 16 Aug. 1731, and Catherine[10], 6 Nov. 1733. Administration was granted on the estate of Joseph Crosby of Worcester in 1744, and in 1746 guardians are appointed for Joseph[10] and Catherine[10] Crosby.

    Sarah[9], b. 12 June 1694, m. first, probably in Billerica, Thomas, son of Samuel and Mary (———) Hunt, who d. in Billerica, 16 Sept. 1709, and a daughter Sarah[10] was b. there 20 Nov. 1709. The widow, Sarah Hunt, m. second, on 11 Jan. 1715/6, in Andover, Ephraim, son of John and Sarah (Barker) Abbott, who was b. in Andover, 15 Aug. 1682, and d. there 8 June, 1748. She had by her second husband, Sarah[10], Ephraim[10], Mary[10], Joshua[10], Daniel[10], Elizabeth[10], Josiah[10], Ebenezer[10], Martha[10], Peter[10], and Martha[10], all born in Andover.

Rachel[9], b. 18 Apr. 1695, m., before 1719, Samuel Stearns, son of John and Elizabeth (Bigelow) Stearns, who was b. 8 Jan. 1693/4 in Billerica. They had Rachel[10], Elizabeth[10], Prudence[10], Samuel[10], Mary[10], and Benjamin[10].

Samuel Stearns d. before 1730, and the widow, Rachel, m. Thomas, son of William and Prudence (Putnam) Wyman, who was b. 23 Aug. 1687, and d. 21 Jan. 1760, in Pelham (?). He was in Jonathan Butterfield's Company, and served from 5 Oct. to 29 Nov. 1722.

Rachel Wyman d. 18 Jan. 1757, leaving children: Thomas[10], Lucy[10], Sybil[10], and Simon[10].

William[9], b. 13 Feb. 1697, m., before 1721, Hannah, daughter of Thomas Ross.

Mary[9], b. 12 Jan. 1699/00, m., in Dedham, 5 June 1718, Eleazer Ellis. Their children recorded in Dedham were Mary[10], Mehitable[10], Timothy[10], Hannah[10], Eleazer[10], Rachel[10], Eleazer[10], and William[10], the last one in 1738.

Thomas[9], b. 12 Oct. 1701, m. (published 24 June 1724, Chelmsford) Anna Parker (possibly daughter of Jonathan and Mary (Danforth) Parker, and b. 3 Apr. 1692, in Billerica). They had Thomas[10], Anna[10], and Jacob[10]. Anna, the mother, d. 20 Sept. 1729. He m. second, before 2 Mar. 1730/1, Susanna Brown, and they had Susanna[10], Sarah[10], Samuel[10], Elizabeth[10], and William[10].

Sergt. Thomas Crosby d. 7 Dec. 1745, his widow, Susanna, surviving him.

David[9], b. 27 Mar. 1703, m., before 1727, Sarah, daughter of Thomas and Hepsibah Foster, and removed to Shrewsbury about 1732. Sarah Foster was b. in Billerica, 30 June 1709, and she had children there: Hepsibah[10], David[10], and Sarah[10]. They also had recorded in Shrewsbury, Hannah[10], Solomon[10], Persis[10], Mary[10], John[10], Bulah[10], Relief[10], Prudence[10], and Rachel[10].

Prudence[9], b. 11 May 1705, m., in Needham, 20 Jan. 1725, Jeremiah Fisher, son of Capt. John and Rebecca (Ellis) Fisher, of Needham. He was b. 8 Sept. 1701; was Captain of the Needham militia, Selectman, Town Clerk and Justice of the Peace.

They had Jeremiah[10], Prudence[10], Rebecca[10], Hannah[10], Josiah[10], Joseph[10], Samuel[10], William[10], Jesse[10], Sarah[10], Elizabeth[10] and Timothy[10].

Hannah[9], b. 9 Mar. 1707, m. first, in Boston, 8 Nov. 1728, John "Peploe," who probably d. soon, as Hannah "Pepploe" and Samuel Watts, both of Boston, enter their intention of marriage, 6 May 1732. John and Hannah "Pepple" have a son John[10],

b. in Boston, 16 July 1729. Hannah is called Hannah Watts of Boston by her father in a court record, 1736.

Deborah[9], b. 13 July 1709, m., in Andover, 31 Mar. 1727, Peter Russell, probably son of Thomas and Phebe Russell, of Andover. Peter, b. 23 Apr. 1700, son of Thomas and Phebe Russell, is the only Peter of suitable age born in Andover. Peter and Deborah[9] Russell had recorded in Andover, Peletiah[10], Deborah[10], Rachel[10], Peter[10], Rebecca[10], and Phebe[10].

Robert[9], b. 20 July 1711, living in "Northtown" 31 Aug. 1736, and mentioned in court record. (Townsend was called Northtown at one time, and the northern end of Billerica was also called the North town.)

Peletiah[9], b. 5 Nov. 1713, and probably d. young, as he is not mentioned in the petition of 31 Aug. 1736.

The eighth and ninth generations of Crosbys of the line this book particularly deals with produced a different sort of man from those we have heretofore become acquainted with, and especially so from those of the fifth, sixth, and seventh generations. The law of average and compensation as well as the everlasting rotation of everything that exists must work as well in the field of genealogy as it does in every other field of study known to man. In those genealogies where we read of uninterrupted lines of successful achievements, unbroken by a single failure in life, the effect becomes most uncanny, and one is led to ask what the matter is. For just as forced and unnatural gayety merely betokens a secret gnawing at the heart, so constant success betokens some hidden failure somewhere, some lack of the power of adaptability to life as it exists. Then, too, the application of the law of Gregor Mendel to the evolution of species merely means that the dominant attributes that make for success are not transmitted to all the children of succeeding generations, either in their entirety or in part, but often lie dormant through a few generations, only to reappear often where least expected, but preserving their undiminished vigor at the time of their reappearance. As to what constitutes success in life there are as many opinions as there are people to furnish them. What is success for one would be a failure for another, and what the collectivity of the race has in the majority of instances considered to be success may some day, in a time of different standards of values, not be thought to have been a success at all.

We dwell a little upon this question before taking up the subject of Joseph[8] Crosby, because there is so little appearing about him in the records to furnish any material to go on. It is not the intention here either to furnish an excuse for him or a wish to feel that any excuse is necessary. As in the case of everybody else in the world, he was just what he was and nothing else. Too often in genealogies we find people judged by standards of comparison, one with another, individually or by generations. Such standards are not solidly constructed, for it is never a question if a person has achieved more than another, or been of greater service. The only question should be, has the individual achieved what he alone was destined to achieve? has he been able to adapt his destiny to the general destiny of everything that is? Success in life is, perhaps, largely a matter of the degree of adaptability a person can make to the circumstances surrounding them, and the seizing of such opportunities for usefulness to the community and to individuals as almost daily present themselves. And such usefulness quietly performed does not necessarily get into public records. Then, too, there are two distinct types of personality, those to whom the doing of things comes easy, and those to whom it does not. And, after all, it is not a matter of great importance whether Joseph Crosby made a success of his life or not, for that alone concerned him. His father, grandfather, and great-grandfather had been men of action, and of much action. It was time for the line to take a rest. Action cannot go on forever, because it defeats itself, and we have to be thankful for those generations that we shall now deal with for having rendered the invaluable service of being quiet and thus permitting once more the growth of the power of reserve force. There is value in just sitting still and letting the soil rest, even if the garden is not cultivated as it might have been. And such a service Joseph[8] Crosby seems to have rendered. His father had felt the inward push to grow into newer and wider fields, Joseph Crosby probably felt the need of contraction into narrower limits, and both in their way fulfilled their destiny. There is a great difference between absolute idleness, a useless waste of one's opportunities, and the calm repose that contemplates life without an over-participation in it, and it must not be supposed that Joseph Crosby was an entirely shiftless and indolent man, just from the fact that in his old age he had to petition the court for support from his children. Such an incident may merely have meant that his failure to adapt himself to life was on the side of practical affairs. But, whatever he was or was not, we can only set him forth as the records show him to have been, and assign the rest to the realm of conjecture, merely reminding those who may have construed his life to have been over-quiet and non-productive, that there is a value in quiet daily accomplishment of little things.

Joseph[8] Crosby was the fourth child and third son of Simon[7] and Rachel Crosby. His father was a man of activity, whose activity took the form of usefulness, and who seemed to be quite human in that twice he was held up for slight misdemeanors, as we have seen; for he was caught fishing in a place that belonged to the Indians. But it has always been known that *errare humanum est*, and certainly always the biggest and best fish lurk in the waters we can't fish in. Perhaps Joseph Crosby tried to be too good. It is possible.

Simon[7] Crosby, at the time he drew up his will in June 1717, designates that he has already given to his son Joseph "in land and help about building twenty pounds"; there remained, therefore, due him by his father's will the sum of sixty pounds. Simon Crosby treated all his children alike, and the fact that Simon and Joseph were not named as executors of his estate was undoubtedly due to the fact that each was busy in his own home and in his own way, for Simon lived in the home of his father as the eldest child, and Joseph had built himself his own home, as we see by his father's will and by Hazen's History of Billerica. It may well have been also that neither Simon nor Joseph had displayed the necessary business ability that would seem to warrant their choice as executors. However that may have been, Joseph[8] Crosby had secured from his father a considerable amount of land, and this is shown from the fact that whereas he bought little land he sold a good deal, perhaps all of it, and of this a considerable portion to his son William. As a matter of record and for the information of those who may be interested, a list of his real estate transactions, so far as it has been possible to secure them, is given:—

Middlesex Deeds.

1707 The earliest record in Mdsx deeds in the name of Joseph Crosby is 14 Nov. 1707 when he and the other heirs of Wm. French quit-claim their rights in certain lands.
1708 The same heirs sell 2 a. 10 poles land in Billerica.
1709 Sells 43 a. land for 23—13—8.
1710 Sells land in Billerica to Ralph Hill.
1713 Sells 2 parcels of upland and swamp, in Billerica
1714 Mortgages some land in Billerica to Mass. Commissioners.
1715 Sells land to Daniel Barney in Billerica.
1716 Sells land in Billerica to Samuel Ruggles for 113 LB.
1718 " " " " for 60 LB., 103 in one, 62½ a. in the other.
1718 Deeds to son Joseph of Worcester for love etc one third of a 40 a. lot.
1718 Sells land in Worcester 2/3 of 40 a. lot to Jonathan Waldo of Boston.
1719 Mortgages land in Billerica 38 a. 58 poles, to Massachusetts Bay Col.
1719 Sells 4 tracts of land 220 a., 200 a., 106 a., 150 a. for 123 LB. to Jonathan Waldo.
1720 Sells 35 a. in Billerica to son Wm. for 160 LB.
1722 Sells land in Billerica to Samuel Ruggles
1723 Sells 19 a. in Billerica to son Wm. for 54 Lb.
1723 Buys 25 a. in Lancaster
1727 Sells 21 a. in Billerica to Samuel Ruggles for 130 Lb.
1727 Sells 20 a., 3 a., 4 a. and a house in Billerica to son Wm. for 200 Lb.
1732 Sells ½ house and land in Concord to son Wm. for 100 Lb.
1728 Sells to brother Nathan all his land near Nutting's Pond, 68 a. and 75 a. for 157 Lb. 10 s.

Joseph[3] Crosby was born in 1669 in the log house of Simon Crosby on Bare Hill. He grew up in the town of Billerica among his brothers and sisters, securing such an education as the times furnished. The principal occupation of those days was tilling the soil, and to such Joseph Crosby lent himself, and apparently as well became proficient in the art of tailoring, for he is mentioned in some deeds as "husbandman" and "taylor." It is unlikely that his services as a tailor were much in demand, for most suits were home-spun and home-made. Nor was that occupation particularly remunerative to him. He married, on 6 May 1691, in his twenty-second year, a daughter of Lieut. William and Mary French. It was in Lieut. William French's house that the meeting of the Board of Selectmen of Billerica was held, to see if the purchase by Joseph Crosby's father of the lands of William Brown was to be allowed, and so, by the strange destiny that seems to be at work, the children of Lieutenant French and Simon Crosby decided to ratify still further the arrival in Billerica of the Crosby family.

Like his father, Simon, Joseph Crosby married into a family of distinction. The family of French, like that of Brackett, was given to action and apparently to military activity and the affairs of education. Lieut. William French or "Frenche" was born in Halstead, County Essex, England, 15 Mar. 1603. He married first in England, Elizabeth Symmes (said to have been the sister of Rev. Zachariah Symmes). Lieutenant French came to America in the ship *Defence* in the same company with Rev. Thomas Shepard in 1635. He settled first in Cambridge; in 1652 he was one of the original proprietors and settlers in Billerica; was a Lieutenant and afterwards Captain of the militia, but did not serve in any of the Indian wars. He was chosen the first man to sit in the "Deacon's seat," in 1659, and was a commissioner to establish country rates the same year. In 1660 William French was a Selectman, and served as such for nine years, "the first Board of Selectmen in Billerica." In 1661 he was on the committee in Billerica to examine children and servants in reading, religion, and catechism. Lieut. William French was the first Deputy from Billerica to the General Court in Boston, elected in 1660, taking his seat in 1661. Evidence of his activity in the cause of Indian instruction is found in a letter written by him to "a godley friend in England," published in London in the famous tract "Strength out of Weakness," and afterwards republished in the Massachusetts Historical Society Collection, 3d Series, volume 4, pages 149–196, in which he gives a detailed account of the testimony of an Indian convert. The main facts of above statements are taken from New Eng. His. & Gen. Reg., October, 1890.

His first wife died 31 Mar. 1668, and he married second, 6 May 1669, Mary (Lothrop) Stearns, widow of Capt. John Stearns of Billerica. Capt. William French died in Billerica, 20 Nov. 1681. His widow married third, 1684, Isaac Mixor, Jr., of Watertown, Mass. The property of Capt. William French was left by will to his widow, Mary, and daughters Mary, *Sarah*, and Hannah. By this will of Lieutenant French his daughter Sarah inherited £40–10–00, which was divided as follows:—

To Sarah French ye 2d daughter, 40 acres in ye old common field, at	06 00 00
To 4 acres in mill swamp according to ye records of it, at	12 00 00
To 3 acres division in mill swamp, granted to ye estate in 1685	04 00 00
To one acre in prospect meadow, according to ye record of it, at	01 00 00
To 14 acres of ye homestead, at ye east end, with liberty to pass upon Mary's land to it, at	14 00 00
To so much due from Daniel Champney of Cambridge,	03 10 00
	40 10 00

However much Lieut. William French may have been concerned with the education of the Indian, he seems not to have devoted much time to the instruction of his three daughters, for a perusal of the records shows that not one of them was able to sign her name for acknowledgment of her portion of the father's property, but made instead a mark. Perhaps Lieut. William French, being a military man, did not think mere women were obliged to write.

But, whether she could write or not, Sarah French Crosby assumed the duty of raising a family with such good results that she brought to Joseph Crosby twelve children, all of whom, except the youngest, who probably died young, contracted exceedingly good marriages.

Little appears in the Billerica records of the public activity of Joseph[3] Crosby. He seems, in July, 1696, to have been taxed £3-11-10 and also £1-0-11 on the meeting-house rate. The only public office he seems to have held was that of Constable, to which he was appointed in March, 1695/6, and it may have been that he secured that appointment upon his own request, either to protect his property, which was somewhat removed from the centre of the town, or else to preserve the peace in that part of Billerica and relieve his father of that duty.

In addition to the land he secured from his father, he was granted by the town of Billerica, in May, 1709, forty-two acres and ninety-six poles west of Concord River in the third range. But he was not destined to be a land owner, for before he died he had disposed of nearly all his property, although in 1735 shortly before his death a small tax of 8*s.* 10*d.* was levied on him.

While he was not so prominently active in the life of the Billerica church as his father had been, Joseph Crosby, like all the people of those times, attended worship in the meeting-house. Not to do so would probably never have occurred to them. And in 1712 he was "granted a place behind the womens seats to build a pue."

From his father he secured the bulk of the land he occupied, and on this land he built a home for the housing of his wife. The ancient map of Billerica in Hazen's history of that town gives the location of Joseph Crosby's house as being southeast of his father's house and near Nutting's Pond on Bedford Road; and here on his farm, helped out by some work at tailoring, he lived and spent nearly all his life. He left no will, for he had no property to bequeath. From time to time during his life he had deeded for love much of his property to his children, or, when exigencies required it, had disposed of it for money. One by one his children had married and had gone forth to seek their own fortunes. At last, somewhere before 1727, his wife Sarah died and left him a widower. The only remaining unmarried child was Hannah, and she married in 1728; for of Robert, the next to the youngest child, little is known.

On 31 Aug. 1736, at the age of sixty-seven, Joseph Crosby, finding that he had disposed of all his property, and not having the usual means to subsist, petitioned the court at Cambridge to have his children care for him. It is quite likely that he may have suffered some disability and have become physically incapacitated, and that the petition was entered so that an equitable and duly proportionate amount might fall upon all his children to pay. However that may be, the case was never brought to trial and was perhaps settled in the family. A copy of this petition is here given as follows:—

The petitioner is aged 68 years or upwards, and has for some time past been unable to support himself by business of any sort. That he has five sons now living, viz: David Crosby of Shrewsbury, Joseph of Worcester, both of the County of Worcester, William and Thomas, both of the town of Billerica, and Robert of Northtown, all living in the County of Middx: as also six daughters now living, viz: Sarah, the wife of Ephraim Abbot of Andover, in the County of Essex; Rachel, the wife of Thomas Wyman of Billerica afores[d]; Mary, the wife of Eleazer Ellis of Dedham; Prudence, the wife of Jeremiah Fisher of Needham, both in the County of Suffolk; Deborah, the wife of Peter Russell of Andover aforesaid, and Hannah, the wife of —— Watts of Boston, to and amongst whom to set them well forth in the world the Petit[r] has distributed his lands and estate to the value of several thousand of pounds as he accounts, not reserving to himself anything competent for his subsistence, nor being able to do it by his own work and labour; and therefore praying this Court would take the premises into their consideration and to direct that the Petit[r] may be maintained and relieved by his respective children or their husbands (being of sufficient ability), as the Province Law therein directs and that they may be respectively assessed thereto as the Court in their great wisdom shall see meet, and in order thereto that they be properly cited to appear before this Court to answer the premises, etc.

What thereafter happened to Joseph[8] Crosby is not clearly established. He probably went to live in the family of his eldest son, Joseph[9] Crosby, in Worcester, Mass., for there is a record which soon after appeared in that town of the death of a Joseph Crosby, which would closely correspond to the age that he would have been at that time. And, in addition to that, it is extremely unlikely he survived as late as 23 Dec. 1737, for, had he been alive then, his name would undoubtedly have appeared among those of his brothers, who on that date petitioned for a distribution of their father's estate.

And so lived and died Joseph[8] Crosby of Billerica, the first of a series of Crosbys that now follow that seem to have been contented to live quiet, peaceful lives, free from much action, and contented with lesser achievements.

WILLIAM[9] CROSBY (Joseph[8], Simon[7], Simon[6], Thomas[5], Anthony[4], Thomas[3], Miles[2], John[1]) was born in Billerica, 13 Feb. 1697/8, and died there 1 Jan. 1754. He married, before Jan. 1721 (date of birth of first child), Hannah, daughter of Thomas and Sarah Ross of Billerica. Hannah Ross was born there 13 May 1702, and died 4 Nov. 1756. Children, born in Billerica:—

> Hannah[10], b. 6 Jan. 1721/2; m. in Boston, 1 May 1744/5, Rev. Robert Cutler, son of James and Alice Cutler, b. 3 Apr. 1721, and d. in Greenwich, Mass., 7 Feb. 1786. He graduated at Harvard College in 1741, was first minister of Epping, N.H., preaching also at Canterbury, N.H., and Greenwich, Mass. She d. 26 May 1750, leaving Hannah[11], Millicent[11], Robert[11], and Prudence[11]. (Cutler Memorial, p. 50.)
>
> William[10], b. 27 Aug. 1723, and d. in infancy.
>
> Martha[10], b. 12 Jan. 1724/5; m. in Billerica, 26 Dec. 1745, Jacob, son of Jacob and Rebecca (Patten) Danforth, who was b. in Billerica 13 Aug. 1723, and d. there 9 Nov. 1748, leaving the widow with two children, Jacob[11] and Jesse[11].
>
> She m. second, in Billerica, 23 Jan. 1754, Matthew Mead, son of David and Hannah (Smith) Mead of Lexington, and d. there 8 Aug. 1792. Matthew Mead was b. in Lexington 9 Aug. 1717, and d. 1 Apr. 1796. They had Ward[11], Martha[11], Rhoda[11], Levi[11], Josiah[11], and Elias[11].

Prudence[10], b. 28 Nov. 1726, and d. young.

Jesseniah[10], b. 7 Oct. 1728; m. in Billerica, 19 Dec. 1751, Mary Hosley, daughter of Thomas and Martha (Richardson) Hosley, who was b. in Billerica, 6 Aug. 1730, and was living as late as 1763. He d. before 1774. They had Jessaniah[11], Mary[11], Isaac[11], Susanna[11], William[11], —— (son)[11], and Sarah[11].

Sarah[10], b. 27 June 1730; m. Timothy Swan (published in Cambridge, 24 Sept. 1748), son of John and Elizabeth Swan of Cambridge, who was b. 3 Aug. 1720, and d. 19 Oct. 1780. Sarah d. 2 Apr. 1756, age 26, and he m. second Sarah Spring.

Peletiah[10], b. 10 Mar. 1731/2, and d. 25 Mar. 1732.

Hezekiah[10], b. 31 Jan. 1732/3; m., 7 Feb. 1754, Anna, daughter of Samuel and Deborah (Hill) Whiting.

Seth[10], b. 8 Aug. 1734; m. 29 Apr. 1757, in Billerica, Rachel Hill, daughter of Peter and Rachel (Crosby) Hill, who was b. in Billerica, 4 Feb. 1736/7, and d. 19 Feb. 1814. He d. 18 Apr. 1814, in Billerica. They had (b. in Billerica) Rachel[11], Prudence[11], Sarah[11], Rachel[11], Rhoda[11], Seth[11], Alice[11], Hannah[11], Joshua[11], and Rhoda[11].

William[10], b. 9 May 1737, d. young.

Rebecca[10], b. 21 July 1738; m. in Billerica, 6 Nov. 1770, Samuel Lampson, son of Samuel and Abigail (Bryant) Lampson. He was b. in Reading, and probably d. between 5 Mar. 1777 (the date of his father's will) and 25 July 1778, the date of birth of his child Rebecca[11], as he is not mentioned then. In 1810 a Rebecca Lampson was living in Billerica on the Woburn road, southeast of Bare Hill.

William[10], b. 4 Jan. 1739/40, and was living at the time his father made a will in 1753.

Rhoda[10], b. 30 Nov. 1740, living in 1753.

Mary[10], b. 26 Apr. 1742, living in 1753.

William[9] Crosby was the fourth child and second son of Joseph and Sarah (French) Crosby. He was born in the house his father had built, not far from Nutting's Pond, in 1697, on Bedford Road. Unlike his father, Joseph Crosby, William seems to have had no other occupation in life than that of a simple farmer. Practically the only references to him in the town records of Billerica are to his having paid his taxes, certainly a commendable thing to have done, and a duty that grew on him as the years advanced, for he was a born accumulator of land, whereas his father had been a disposer.

A reference to the earlier part of this chapter will show that William Crosby bought from his father, generally for a consideration, although it is supposed his father deeded him property "for love," a considerable portion of land. And, as the community grew in size, land in "The Wilderness" was becoming constantly more valuable, and, as more and more of it came under cultivation, more and more time was required by the simple farmers to look after it. But Billerica was not even in the time of William Crosby what could be called a settled community, for it was only as late as 1695, two years before the birth of William Crosby, that another Indian massacre had taken place, in which the grandmother of the woman he married and five of her grandchildren had lost their lives. It is well to keep in mind the hardships of the times we are now dealing with, for it was in just such times that the Crosbys we are writing about lived; so naturally, in the midst of such surroundings, they did not remove far from the old Crosby home of Simon Crosby, which, as a garrison-house, had been prepared to withstand the attacks of the Indians.

In addition to the land he secured from his father, William Crosby from 1721 to 1730 bought at different intervals more land from Benjamin Thompson, John Blanchard, Benjamin Parker, Jr., Nathan Crosby, Jonathan Bowers, and Benjamin Wyman. For William Crosby had already married, sometime prior to 1721, Hannah Ross. The date of his marriage is not known, but 1721 records the birth of their first child, Hannah, and, with an eye to the future, William Crosby was adding to his holdings, for, like most of the families of the time, his own was growing apace.

William Crosby does not seem to have appeared to any great extent in the public life of his time. In March 1729/30 he was chosen Surveyor of Highways and again in 1730/1, an office that seemed to run in his family, and to which Simon Crosby, his grandfather, had given much time. As a further mark of his capacity along this line we find him in 1737 appointed to run the line between Bedford and Billerica. The only other reference to him is as tithing-man, to which he was chosen in 1752. He is recorded in the list of deaths in Billerica, Mass., as "*Mr.*," although why this prefix is before the name has not been discovered, but it would seem to indicate that somewhere in his life he did something that gave him a little distinction. There are not more than four other men whose names appear thus in Vital Records of Billerica. That he was a man of substance is proved by Middlesex Deeds.

But, as we have suggested in the case of his father, there was value in living a quiet life, for it tended to make for stability. These were still the days of the Colonies, and quite a little before the Revolutionary War, which did not come until the time of the next generation of Crosbys. The life and conditions surrounding William Crosby were therefore more like those of the time of his grandfather Simon than were the conditions which surrounded any of the later Crosbys.

William[9] Crosby, like all the rest of the children of Joseph Crosby, contracted a good marriage, for he married, sometime in 1719 or 1720, Hannah Ross, of Scotch descent. She was the grand-daughter of one Thomas Ross, whose history being a little unusual, a brief account is inserted here, furnished by a member of the New England Historic Genealogical Society:—

After the execution of Chas. I in 1649, his son Charles in 1651 made an attempt to recover the throne of England by invading the country with an army of Scotch Highlanders. They were met at Worcester by the forces of the Commonwealth under Cromwell, and totally defeated, over 7000 of the Scots being taken prisoners. By order of the government, these prisoners were sold into servitude for eight years and deported to the American colonies and the West Indies.

Some speculators bought a party of 272 of these prisoners for servitude in New England, and arrangements were made with Capt. John Greene, master of the ship *John and Sarah* of London, to transport them to Boston; and on 8 Nov. 1651, at Gravesend a list was made of the names of these 272 Scotch prisoners, a copy of which is preserved in Suffolk Co. Deeds, Boston, vol. 1, pp. 5 and 6.

These Scots could speak little or no English, and the recording clerk being unfamiliar with Scotch names and pronunciation, made many gross errors in writing their names, like calling "Gilchrist," "Killecross," etc. Also the copy in Suffolk deeds is illegible in some places and in others cannot be made out with certainty. In the list of 272 names appear 7 of Ross, viz: Alester Ross, Dan Ross, David Ross, James Ross, John Ross, James Ross, and *Jonas* Ross; at least this is the list as *printed* from the original. All of these men are later found in New England records, except *Jonas;* this name was so illegible in the original that the reading *Jonas* is uncertain, and I have no doubt it was really *Thomas* Ross who in 1655 is mentioned as a servant in Cambridge where he married as soon as his term of service expired, and later settled in Billerica.

This Thomas Ross, the "servant of Mr. Edward Winship in 1656," married, on 16 Jan. 1661, Seeth Holman, daughter of William and Winifred Holman. Just before the birth of Seeth Holman, her mother, Winifred, had undergone a long and arduous trial for witchcraft in Cambridge in 1659, from which she was finally acquitted.* But Seeth Holman herself, whose birth was thus clouded by what might have been a tragedy, was destined to end her life at the hands of the Indians on 5 Aug. 1695, in Billerica.†

And it was into this family that William Crosby married. He and Hannah, his wife, had fourteen children, four of whom died soon after birth, all the rest attaining maturity.

It was along in 1734–5 that William Crosby's father, Joseph, began to feel the pinch of necessity crowding him, and it is pleasant to find that William Crosby sold his father, undoubtedly "for love," land in Concord.‡ In this deed he mentions his father as his "honoured father."

On the thirty-first day of December, 1753, he drew up his will, a copy of which has been preserved. Any original document or piece of writing by an individual furnishes to those who can properly appraise it a better idea of the character and personality of that individual than any amount of description by some one else of the character of another person, and for that reason it is included here. From it may be seen a gentle nobility, a philosophical resignation, and a thoughtful provision of those who were to come after

---

*See files of the county court, 1659.   † Billerica Vital Records, p. 390.
‡ Middlesex Deeds, Book 36, p. 409.

him. A careful study of this document is well worth while, especially noteworthy being his solicitude over his younger son William.

WILL OF WILLIAM[9] CROSBY.

In the Name of God Amen the Thirty first Day of December in the year of our Lord one thousand Seven hundred and Fifty three I William Crosby of Billerica in the County of Middlesex within his Majesties Province of the Massachusetts Bay in New England, being sick and weak of Body but of sound mind and memory Praised be God for the same and Calling to mind the Mortallity of my Body and knowing that it is appointed for all men once to Die, Do make and ordain this my last Will and Testament in Manner and form following that is to say Principally and first of all I Give and Recommend my Soul into the hands of God that Gave it Hoping to Receive the pardon of all my Sins and Salvation through the Merrits of Jesus Christ my Redeemer, and my Body to the Earth to be Buried in such Decent Manner as my Executors whom I shall hereafter name may think proper; and as for Such Worldly Estate wherewith it hath pleased God to Bless me with in this life, I Give Demise and Dispose of the Same in the following Manner and form.

Imprimis I Give unto my well Beloved wife Hannah Crosby the one half of my Dwelling house (viz) the East End thereof Reserving Liberty to my other Heirs and Executors Room in the Chichin for Baking and Brewing and going to the well for water and Reserving the Sellar under the East Room for the use of my other Heirs that Remains in the other end of the house, Also I Give unto her my said wife three good Cows to be Brought up to her yard and my Best Mare and Conveniancy in the Barn and to be kept Summer and Winter out of my Estate and Liberty to keep two Hoggs, and thirty Bushels of Indian Corn and ten Bushels of Rie yearly and three Bushels of Malt and six Barrels of Sydar and the Barrels to put the Sydar in yearly and all the household stuff within Doors that she stands in need of and Also my Negro woman Jenney I give unto my said wife and her young Child During her natural life and to be at her Disposal, the Child if it should live to be Given by my said wife to any of my Daughters which my sd. wife shall think proper, and also I allow my Executors to let my sd. wife have a priveledge in the Gardens and what Sauce is needfull yearly and one Bushel of Salt to be Brought to her yearly, I also allow my Executors to provide for my sd. wife sufficient fire wood and pine brought to her Door Ready Cut; and also ninty weight of good Beef and two hundred weight of good pork to be Laid up for her yearly and Liberty in the Barn and to the well to pass and Repass at all times when it is needfull for her; and Six Sheep to be Kept for her and she to have the Benefit and priveledge of the wool yearly and also twenty pounds of flax from the Swinge all the above articles to my well Beloved wife During her natural life.

Item I give unto my three well Beloved sons Jesseniah, Hezekiah and Seth Crosby to them and their Heirs for ever all my Real Estate in Lands Scituate and Lying in Billerica and Bedford in the said County of Middlesex, and also all my Buildings Excepting what I have willed to my wife and when my said wife has Done with her part of the Buildings the same to Return to my said three sons, and also my will is that my said three sons shall have all my utensils out Doors and all my stock of Creaturs together with all my moveable Estate to be Equally Devided between them

Item My will is also that my Beloved Son Jesseniah shall not Come in for any more of my Estate above mentioned than his Equal part with his said Breethren, for I have already Given him by a Deed of Sale as much as I think is his part or proportion for his Double portion out of my Estate; and what of my Estate I have Given to my said son Jesseniah by a Deed of Gift my will is that it shall come into the apprisement with any other estate and that to be took out of his part or proportion of the Remainder of the same, and also my negro man Robin I Give to my said three sons to be at their Disposal.

Item I Give unto my well beloved Son William all my Lands in Townsend in the County aforesaid Lying in Two Lotts Containing about one hundred & Twenty five acres in Both Lots to him the said William Crosby his Heirs and assigns for Ever and my will is that my above named three Sons Jesseniah, Hezekiah and Seth Crosby shall go up and Clear and help him Build and give him stock and make him Equal to one of them as near as it Can be Esteemed by Reasonable men.

Item I Give unto my Grand Children, Hannah Cuttler, Millesent, Robert and Prudence Cuttler; Children of my Daughter Hannah Cuttler— Deceased, the sum of Twenty Six pounds Thirteen Shillings and four pence Lawfull Money of this Province to be paid Equally to them as they arive to Lawfull age by my Executors hereafter named, which sum with what I have already Done for their mother in her life time shall be their full part and portion out of my Estate

Item I give unto my Beloved Daughter Martha Danforth to her and her Heirs for Ever the sum of Thirty two pounds three Shillings Lawfull Money to be paid to her and her Heirs at or before the End of five years after the Date hereof which together with what I have already Done for her shall be her full portion out of my Estate

Item I give unto my well Beloved Daughter Sarah Swan to her and her Heirs for ever the Sum of Thirty four pounds one Shilling and four pence Lawfull Money to be paid to her and her Heirs by my Executors hereafter named at or before the End of Five years after the Date hereof, which with what I have already Done for her shall be her full part or portion out of my Estate

Item I Give unto my Beloved Daughters, Rebecca Crosby, Roada Crosby and Mary Crosby my three youngest Daughters the Sum of Sixty Six pounds thirteen Shillings and four pence Lawfull Money to Each of them to be paid to them by my Executors out of my Estate as they arive to age or marrige if sooner, which sum shall be their full portion out of my Estate, also my will is that my said three Daughters shall have Room and Liberty to Live in my Dwelling house so Long as they Live unmarried, they to pay or provide for their Board when they work for themselves

Item my will is that my Beloved son William shall have Liberty of Living and Room in my house so Long as he lives unmarried he to provide for himself after he Comes to age or when he goes to work on his place—my

Item will is that my Executors shall have all my money, Bonds, notes and Debts that I shall Leave after my Decease, and I Do order and allow them to pay all my Just Debts out of my Estate; And I Do Nominate, Appoint and Fully Impower my well Beloved Sons Jesseniah and Hezekiah Crosby before named to be Executors of this my last Will and Testament, Hereby Revoking and Dissanulling all and Former Wills and Testaments and Bequests whatsoever. In Wittness Whereof I the said William Crosby have hereunto set my hand and seal the Day and year above written

Signed Sealed Published
Pronounced and Declared   WILLIAM CROSBY   (SEAL)
by the Said William Crosby
to be his Last will & Testament
in the Presence of us the Subscribers

NATHANIEL DAVIDSON   SAMUEL BLANCHARD   SETH WILLSON

Commonwealth of Massachusetts }
Middlesex ss. Registry of Probate }
    A true copy.
              Attest,   W. E. ROGERS (Signed)   Register
(Entrd. Lib. 26, p. 237.)

And so on New Year's Day, 1754, William[9] Crosby departed this life and was laid to rest alongside other Crosbys that had preceded him into the great Unknown.

Chapter VI.

TWO OF THE CROSBY FAMILY IN BILLERICA DURING THE REVOLUTIONARY PERIOD.

An Account of Hezekiah and Jeremiah of the Tenth and Eleventh Generations.

Hezekiah[10] Crosby (William[9], Joseph[8], Simon[7], Simon[6], Thomas[5], Anthony[4], Thomas[3], Miles[2], and John[1]) was born 31 Jan. 1732/3; married, in Billerica, 7 Feb. 1754, Anna Whiting, daughter of Samuel and Deborah (Hill) Whiting, who was born in Billerica, 29 Mar. 1736, and died there 26 Feb. 1764. He married second, 6 Apr. 1765, in Medford (also recorded in Tewksbury), Lucy Kittredge of Tewksbury, probably daughter of William and Mary (Wright) Kittredge, and born 12 Aug. 1743, in Tewksbury, which town was set off from Billerica in 1734. Hezekiah Crosby died in Billerica, 26 July 1817, and she survived him.

He had the following children, born in Billerica (by the first wife, Anna):—

> Anna[11], b. 11 May 1755; m., in Wilmington, 28 July 1778, Nathan Jaquith, son of Benjamin and Hannah Jaquith, who was b. in 1755, and d. in Wilmington, 11 Nov. 1788, aged thirty-three years. They had recorded in Wilmington, Anna[12], Abigail[12], Nathan[12], Jeremiah[12], Nathaniel[12], Alice[12], and James[12].
> Timothy[11], b. 5 May 1756. (No further record.)
> Deborah[11], b. 25 Feb. 1758, and d. 18 Jan. 1811.
> *Jeremiah*[11], b. 20 Mar. 1760; m., 13 Oct. 1783, Abigail Jaquith, daughter of Deacon Benjamin and Hannah (Walker) Jaquith.
> Rhoda[11], b. 3 Jan. 1764, and d. 11 Jan. 1764.

Children, born in Billerica (by second wife):—

> Lucy[11], b. 10 Nov. 1765; m., 19 Dec. 1782, in Billerica, James Lewis, son of James and Rebecca (Brown) Lewis, b. in Billerica, 26 Jan. 1761, and d. in Groton, 24 Dec. 1828. She d. in Groton,

30 Dec. 1828. They had James[12], Aaron[12], Levi[12], Andrew[12], Lucy[12], and Merric[12].

Hezekiah[11], b. 8 Nov. 1767, removed to Missouri, where he became a large land-owner.

William[11], b. 3 June 1770; m., 12 Oct. 1804, in Billerica, Sally Davis, daughter of Benjamin and Mary (Mann) Davis, b. in Billerica, 27 June 1783, who d. in Belfast, Me., 2 Nov. 1877, a widow.

William Crosby graduated from Harvard College in 1794, and was a pioneer in settlement of Belfast, Me. He was Senator of the Maine district in the Massachusetts Legislature and Chief Justice in the Court of Common Pleas, 1811–23. This family was most distinguished in the State of Maine. His son, William George Crosby, was Governor of Maine, 1853–54.

Levi[11], b. 2 Oct. 1772. (No further record.)

Mary[11], b. 2 Mar. 1783. (No further record.)

Achsah[11], b. 2 Oct. 1786; m., in Billerica, 26 Oct. 1809, David Parker, son of John and Mary (Shattuck) Parker, b. in Billerica, 16 May 1786, and d. 5 Feb. 1824. She d. there 22 Oct. 1857. They had John Henry[12], Caroline[12], Augusta[12], William Crosby[12], Charles Edwin[12], Achsah Crosby[12], Norman[12], Mary Ann[12], Edward David[12], James Lewis[12].

The tenth and eleventh generations, represented by Hezekiah and his son Jeremiah, were the generations of the Crosby family that passed through that period in the history of this country that was marked by the struggle of the Colonies for independence from England; and so they were the connecting links between those early days when Billerica was known as "The Wilderness," and bring the family down to fairly modern times, when the dangers of attack by Indians and the struggle for existence in a new and wild land were succeeded by the struggle for existence that is found in all times and places, but in a well-settled and peaceful community.

Hezekiah Crosby, born in 1732, was too old to take active part in the Revolutionary War, but, as we shall see, did his part in his way, leaving to his son Jeremiah the active participation in the war. Hezekiah Crosby, as a younger man, saw active service for a few weeks in the expedition to Crown Point, for he enlisted 6 Apr. 1759, in Col. Eleazer Tyng's regiment and served until 19 April,* not a very long

* Massachusetts Archives, 97: 163.

service, to be sure, but possibly all that was required of him, and showing plainly enough he could meet his duty when it was necessary, and also showing perhaps where Jeremiah Crosby got his fighting blood, although fighting blood is not peculiar to any race or nationality, as may plainly be seen by the great war now raging in Europe in which nearly all the so-called civilized nations are in deadly combat.

Billerica in the time of Hezekiah Crosby had become more settled and a more comfortable place in which to live. The old Crosby home was no longer needed as a garrison-house for defence against "ye Indian enemy." The farms were well established, and most of the arable land was under cultivation. The families then living there held their estates, and instead of being scattered and worked piecemeal were concentrated into well-established estates. The roads were good and the means of communication much better. Isolated dwellings with rather small clearings around them had given over to many well-regulated farms. There was some joy of living, at least as much as the still considerable religious feelings handed down from Puritan times permitted. Of course, there was not that well-balanced living that contemplates the hard necessities of life and the compensating earned pleasures, an almost ideal state of affairs that is seldom or never found; but at least there was not the over-joy in living that has succeeded it, nor the struggle for over-existence that too often has been mistaken for a real struggle for existence. The life of the farmers was simple, and simple requirements were simply furnished, and some of the austerity of previous times had been softened, without losing any of the feeling of the necessity for freedom along the lines of progress in liberal thought —liberal as compared with what had preceded it.

William[9] Crosby had been a careful farmer who had husbanded his resources and by dint of careful and frugal ways had added materially to his patrimony. It is not known at exactly what time the possession of the original home, built by Simon Crosby, again came into the possession of this line of Crosbys, although it is known that Hezekiah Crosby lived and died there, and it may well have been that it came under the control of his father, William, in his lifetime, as a part of the added possessions he secured, for, as we have seen, Hezekiah's grandfather, Joseph, had established his own home near Nutting's Pond.

To gain any idea of the personality of Hezekiah Crosby we have to rely upon those references to him that are contained in the records of the town of Billerica, and by a perusal of his will, which will later appear.

After two generations of comparative quiet, so far as life outside the domestic circle and the studious attention to the details of the cultivation of the farm are concerned, we have in the tenth generation a return to a life of activity in the public service, but not such a complete reversion to those interests as was found in the case of Simon[6] Crosby, who gave so much time to public affairs of the newly settled district, nor yet so much as is later found in the son and grandson of Hezekiah Crosby, namely, Sumner[12] Crosby. Indeed, if we can judge at all of Hezekiah Crosby, especially from the kind of man his will would seem to indicate he might have been, it was more owing to force of circumstances, or perhaps from that natural capacity which always makes itself felt and exacts corresponding obligations, or from the position as head of a family that had theretofore rendered invaluable service to the town, rather than from natural inclination, that brought Hezekiah Crosby into a life of considerable active service outside the narrower family sphere. Of course, at this late day we can only conjecture as to his personality, but conjecture is a pleasant and harmless phase that somewhat relieves the tendency to monotony in the perusal of dry records. But in a careful study of his will, we don't seem to find that spontaneous elasticity of temperament that usually is found in a man of natural activity in life. There seems there to be found a more rigid planning for the future that wishes in the moment to establish things for all time, and that attitude is not usually the one that lends itself readily to the adaptation of events as they kaleidoscopically change in the actual circumstances of life.

Hezekiah[10] Crosby was the eighth child and third son of William and Hannah (Ross) Crosby. Three of the eight, however, had died in early infancy. Born in 1732, he lived through the Indian War of 1745-62, and went to Crown Point in 1759. He had already married, in 1754, Anna Whiting of Billerica when he joined the expedition to Crown Point. His boyhood and early manhood had been spent on the Crosby farm. He attended the school, which by that time was able to offer better facilities for an education, and here in the school and in the church of his ancestors he became acquainted with Anna Whiting, and now we will make a little digression to give a brief account of the Whiting family, for Anna Whiting was the mother of five of Hezekiah Crosby's children, among whom was Jeremiah[11] Crosby, of the next generation.

Rev. Samuel[1] Whiting, born in old Boston, county of Lincoln, England, 20 Nov. 1597, was a member of an ancient and distinguished family. His father, Hon. John Whiting, was mayor of Boston, England, 1600-08. He was graduated from Emmanuel College, A.B. 1616, A.M. 1620. He soon received orders, and became a chaplain in a family which was connected with the Bacons and Townsends of Norfolk, and continued in that parish three years. He was afterwards settled as a colleague with Mr. Price at Kings Lynn, in the same county. He remained three years at Lynn, but, complaint being made by the Bishop of Norwich of his nonconformity in administering the services of the Church, he was removed to the Rectory of Skirbeck, near Boston, where his nonconformity was also complained of, and led subsequently to his emigration to the American Colonies. He arrived in Boston, Mass., 25 May 1636, and settled in Lynn, Mass., the following November, where he was the first minister of the place, dying there 11 Dec. 1679, eighty-two years of age.

Rev. Samuel[1] Whiting was twice married. His second wife, mother of Rev. Samuel[2] Whiting of Billerica, was

Elizabeth (St. John) Whiting, daughter of Hon. Oliver St. John, member of Parliament. Her brother, Oliver[2] St. John, was one of the most distinguished lawyers of England, and was later Lord Chief Justice of England under Oliver Cromwell. The mother of Elizabeth (St. John) Whiting was Sarah Bulkeley, daughter of Edward Bulkeley of Odel, Bedfordshire, England, and sister of Rev. Peter Bulkeley, the first minister of Concord, Mass. She died in Lynn, Mass., 1677, age seventy-two years.

Rev. Samuel[2] Whiting was born in Skirbeck, England, 25 Mar. 1633, eldest son of Rev. Samuel[1] and Elizabeth (St. John) Whiting of Lynn, Mass. He was graduated from Harvard College in 1653 in the same class with Thomas[7] Crosby, brother of Simon[7] Crosby of Billerica. Admitted freeman 11 May 1656, and in 1658 he became the first minister of Billerica.

Rev. Samuel[2] Whiting married, 12 Nov. 1656, Dorcas Chester, who was born in Wethersfield, Conn., 1 Nov. 1637; she was daughter of Leonard and Mary (Wade) Chester. Her father was a nephew of Rev. Thomas Hooker, D.D. After living for a year or so in Watertown, Mass., he removed with Dr. Hooker's company to the Connecticut Valley, and was helpful in establishing settlements there, and died in Wethersfield, 11 Dec. 1648. His widow, Mary, married Hon. Richard Russell, one of the foremost citizens of Charlestown.

The happy marriage of Rev. Samuel[2] and Dorcas (Chester) Whiting continued forty-six years.

Oliver[3] Whiting, fourth child of Rev. Samuel[2] and Dorcas (Chester) Whiting, was born in Billerica, 8 Nov. 1665; married there, 22 Jan. 1689/90, Anna Danforth, born 8 Mar. 1667/8, in Billerica, daughter of Jonathan[1] and Elizabeth (Poulter) Danforth; and died 22 Dec. 1736. His widow died 13 Aug. 1737, also in Billerica.

Oliver[3] Whiting was Representative in the General Court three years, 1719–20, 1728; Town Clerk seventeen years, 1705–11, 1714–23; Selectman twenty years, 1692, 1699, 1702, 1704–11, 1714–20, 1722–23.

Samuel[4] Whiting, sixth son of Oliver and Anna (Danforth) Whiting, was born in Billerica, 6 Sept. 1702; married, 8 May 1729, Deborah Hill, daughter of Samuel[3] and Deborah Hill. She was born in Billerica, 21 Nov. 1705, and died there 5 Sept. 1745. He married second, 2 Nov. 1749, Mrs. Elizabeth Winchester. Samuel[4] Whiting was deacon for many years in the first church in Billerica, of which his grandfather, Rev. Samuel Whiting, was the first minister. He died there 4 Nov. 1772.

It was this Samuel[4] Whiting who was the father of Anna, the wife of Hezekiah Crosby.

> I give unto my three well Beloved sons Jesseniah, Hezekiah and Seth Crosby to them and their Heirs for ever all my Real Estate in Lands Scituate and Lying in Billerica and Bedford in the said County of Middlesex, and also all my Buildings excepting what I have willed to my wife and when my said wife has Done with her part of the Buildings the same to Return to my said three sons, and also my will is that my said three sons shall have all my utensils out Doors and all my stock of Creatures together with all my moveable Estate to be Equally Devided between them.

Thus wrote William[9] Crosby in his will, dated 1753, one year before he died. And what he willed was undoubtedly carried out, for nothing more was heard of it. And so at the age of twenty-two Hezekiah Crosby got his start in life.

In 1754 appears the first reference to Hezekiah Crosby in the town records of Billerica, when he was taxed £9–3–0 for the Province tax, £4–10–2 for the minister's rate, and £8–1–0 for the town rate. So by this time he must have been well established in his patrimony and have taken his place in the community as head of his family. Up to 1765 he held only a few minor and unimportant town offices, but in that year was chosen one of the highway surveyors, an office that the Crosbys had filled before his time.

In the previous year he had lost his first wife, Anna, who died less than two months after the birth of their fifth child. This left him with four small children on his hands, for the fifth and youngest, Rhoda, had died almost at birth. After he had come back from the expedition to Crown Point, Hezekiah Crosby had lived quietly on his farm, helping

AUTOGRAPH SIGNATURE OF HEZEKIAH[10] CROSBY

out in public affairs to some extent, but mostly devoting his energies to his farm and family. His ten years of married life from twenty-two to thirty-two years of age with Anna Whiting had been years of great beauty to Hezekiah Crosby, and the loss that suddenly faced him when his wife died must have seemed an unusually hard blow to bear. But a year later he found Lucy Kittredge of Tewksbury willing to assume the care of his four small children (for the oldest was only ten), and not only did she care for these motherless children, but in turn became the mother of six children of her own, of whom four at least reached maturity and the records of the others are lost. They may have died in infancy.

The Indian wars were now over, and the great Revolutionary War had not yet come to harass the Colonies. During these ten years 1765–75 Hezekiah continued quietly in his occupation of farmer, applying himself to the needs of his family, and giving a little time to the public service.

In 1770 he was chosen as one of the petit jury to serve at the Inferior Court of Common Pleas at Concord, and in 1771 he was Constable, and again in 1773, an office that, like that of Surveyor of Highways, was much held in the family.

When the war broke out between England and her American colonies, Hezekiah Crosby was fifty-three years old, and, perhaps feeling the effect of so many years spent in arduous labor, did not feel able to undergo the rigors of active military campaigning, but gave much time and thought to the affairs of the Continental Army, although he was not in the field.

Hazen in his History of Billerica* gives a very good account of the great enthusiasm shown in that town at the outbreak of the war. Billerica, from the small settlement of a dozen or two families in the time of Simon[7] Crosby, had grown into a town with a population of fifteen hundred people, and of this fifteen hundred there are records to show that three hundred and seventeen enlisted for service, to

* Page 246.

which possibly might be added the names of fifty or a hundred more, if the records could be found. In this connection Hazen says:—

> The lists of Revolutionary Soldiers are necessarily incomplete. Many of the Rolls are lost; and it would take months of labor to go over the mass which is preserved, but imperfectly indexed, with such care that no name from any town would be likely to escape. The town had representatives in various directions where no rolls of such service are found.
>
> If we had these lost records, they would probably add fifty, and perhaps one hundred to the three hundred and seventeen enumerated above. When we remember that the census of 1776 gave the town a population of 1500, we can see in part to what extent these patriotic fathers gave service and life to found a nation. Their children should never forget at what a price they gained freedom for themselves and coming generations.

But it was not in any of these lists, either of those existing or missing, that Hezekiah Crosby's name would be found enrolled. Instead, his oldest son, Jeremiah, then a mere boy, did all the active fighting.

In 1776 the town of Billerica levied a special tax for the purposes of the war, and in the list of those assessed we find "Hezekiah Crosby taxed £4–8–2, Crosby place east of Nutting's Pond." *

There was great patriotism among the members of the different families, fanned and kept alive by the soldiers as they returned from active service. They were also greatly influenced by the example of their minister, Rev. Henry Cummings, so it is with no surprise that we find the son of Hezekiah[10] Crosby (Jeremiah[11] Crosby) in the list of soldiers from Billerica in 1778.

This Rev. Henry Cummings, D.D. (born 16 Sept. 1739), graduated from Harvard College, 1760, was ordained in Billerica, Mass., 1763, and preached there sixty years, where he died 5 Sept. 1823, age eighty-four. He became the Father of the town, and was the representative head of every advance movement for the benefit of the State and town. He was greatly beloved and revered by all the people, who adopted

* Hazen, p. 248.

his opinions and followed in a great measure his advice during the stormy days of the American Revolution. It was also this Rev. Henry Cummings who had charge of the church in Billerica, together with his colleague, Rev. Nathaniel Whitman, during the change in the church from orthodoxy to Unitarianism.

As the earlier Crosbys had followed the call for a more liberal belief in religious matters in the seventeenth century, so the Crosbys of the eighteenth century kept abreast of the changes that many parishes underwent in that period, and seem all of them, without exception, to have accepted the new faith.

In 1778 Hezekiah Crosby became a Selectman of the town of Billerica and one of the Assessors, both of which offices he filled again in 1779; and on 3 Aug. 1779 he was chosen, with Capt. Edward Farmer, to meet with men of other neighboring towns to regulate the price of produce and manufactures. He served as Selectman, not only in 1778 and 1779, but also in 1780, 1781, and 1785, and in these late years he filled once more the offices he had formerly held, viz., Constable in 1782 and Surveyor in 1787.

And so, while war between England and the Colonies waged with varying success until in the end the Colonies were successful, Hezekiah Crosby did what he could at home, not only by contributing what funds he could spare for the cause that lay near his heart, but as well by serving on committees which were appointed in 1781 and 1782 to procure beef and clothes for the army in the field, and meanwhile in these trying years lent his voice and judgment to the affairs of the town in which he lived.

Thus it may perhaps fairly be said that Hezekiah[10] Crosby was in a considerable degree an exponent of a life of activity in the public service. He always thought of himself as a farmer, and such he essentially was. In his will he designates his station in life as that of yeoman.

During the life of Hezekiah Crosby he had to face the effects of two wars, which were very disastrous upon property and the value of property; and it took a careful and steady hand in the management of his affairs not to become lost in the vortex which every war creates.

Hezekiah Crosby lived until 1817, and, despite the hard times in which he lived, he died only four years before his son Jeremiah, having reached the advanced age of eighty-five. It can be said without the danger of contradiction that he made the most of his opportunities, and in the creating of his destiny he appears not to have shirked any of his duties.

In 1800, being then sixty-eight years of age, he made his will. We give his will, as we have done with some of his ancestors, not that the face value of the document itself is of great importance, but because it has generally been the case that the will was the only piece of original writing now in existence, and more is *felt* concerning the personality of an individual by the perusal of a bit of original writing than is often to be discovered in volumes of appraisement by others. And it has been the intention in this book to try, so far as possible, to present to the reader merely what seems to be as fair a picture of the persons under consideration as could be reasonably supposed to be an accurate and just presentation, dissociating him or her from the personalities that surrounded them, and letting them stand on their own feet. Such a task is not easy in the absence of original documents, but, where they have been available, it has been endeavored to make the most of them, and, with that object in mind, the will of Hezekiah Crosby is inserted here:—

In the Name of God Amen.

I Hezekiah Crosby of Billerica in the county of Middlesex and commonwealth of Massachusetts, yeoman—Calling to mind the uncertainty of life, and willing to provide against all unforeseen casualties by an Equitable distribution of such worldly estate as providence has seen fit to bless me with, do make this my last will and testament.

1 After Commending my soul to God who gave it, I will that my mortal part, whenever I shall be called in providence to put it off be decently and honorably interr'd, by my executor hereafter named at his own proper charges.

2 I give unto Lucy my beloved wife all such household furniture and cloathing as I shall be possess'd of at my discease also the use and improvement of one undivided moiety of the garden North of my dwelling house, during her natural life.

3 I give unto my said wife and my Daughter Deborah the use and improvement of the west end of my said Dwelling house includeing the westardly garrett chamber, Room, Kitchen Chamber, kitchen on, and cellar under the same, together with the privilege of drawing water at the well at the eastwardly end of said house and all other privileges which may be necessary to the enjoyment of the same; Provided, Nevertheless it is my will that my daughter Achsa do have, and that my said wife and daughter Deborah do permit her to occupy and enjoy said westwardly end of said house, equally with themselves, untill her marriage and they permitting her to enjoy the same as aforesaid may have and enjoy the same during their natural lives and the longer liver of them.

4 I direct my said Executor to furnish my said wife and Daughters, Deborah, and Achsa with seats in the pew now occupied by the family, my said wife and Daughter Deborah during their lives, and my said Daughter Achsa untill her marriage.

5 I give unto my son Timothy one hundred dollars to be paid within one year from my decease.

6 I give unto my son Hezekiah one hundred dollars, provided my said son shall personally demand the same of my said executor within five years after my decease.

7 I forgive unto my son, William all notes and obligations which I now hold against him.

8 I forgive unto my said son Timothy & my son Jeremiah all notes and obligations which I now, or may hold against them at my decease.

9 I give unto my daughter Anna fifteen dollars to be paid within one year from my decease.

10 I give unto my daughter Lucy fifteen dollars to be paid within one year from my decease.

11 I give unto my daughter Achsa two hundred dollars to be paid within one year from my decease.

Provided, nevertheless that if my said Executor shall pay and discharge any or all of said legacies in my life time, then said legacies to be void so far as they shall appear to have been discharged by receipts to my said executor.

12 And in case any of said pecuniary Legacies undischarged in my life time, by reason of death or otherwise, shall not go as above directed, my will and pleasure is that they should be equally divided among my children surviving at the time any of said legacies shall lapse or fail of going as above directed.

13 My will is that my said Executor pay and discharge all Just debts and demands that shall be due and owing from me at my decease to all persons whatever out of the surplus of my estate after deducting each and every of the aforesaid legacies.

14 And as to all the rest and residue of my personal Estate, whether in possession or in action I give and bequeath the same to my son Jeremiah.

Also I give and devise unto my said son Jeremiah all my real estate wherever the same may be situated, except what is above devised to my said wife and Daughters Deborah and Achsa, which I likewise devise unto him after the termination of their several estates.

To have and to hold the same to him the said Jeremiah his heirs and assigns for ever.

Provided Nevertheless that each and every benifit, legacy, and Devise to my said son Jeremiah is on the following conditions, i. d.

1 That my said son Jeremiah duly take on himself the execution of this my last will and testament.

2 That within three months after my decease he will enter into a penal bond of three thousand dollars to my said Wife and Daughter Deborah, with sufficient sureties, to their acceptance under the following conditions, i. d.

1 That during their lives and the longest liver of them he will keep said westwardly end of said dwelling house in good and comfortable repair.

2 That during the same time he will supply them with sufficient fuel for the maintenance of one fire, at the door ready cut, and fit for burning.

3 That during that time he will furnish them with an able bodied, gentle horse to ride when and where they or either of them shall wish for one.

Also a good milch Cow to their separate use, both to be pastured, housed & fodered by him at his own expence.

4 That during that time he will furnish them with a boy or girl or both of them to be always ready at the call of either of them if they or either of them shall wish for said boy & girl or either of them.

5 That during that time he will supply them with household furniture, utensils, cloathing and bedding suitable to their degree and former habits, as the same shall become necessary by reason of the wear and loss of such household furniture, utensils, cloathing and bedding on hand at the time of my decease.

6 That during that time he will at all times promptly and without delay bring in to and supply them with all necessary Bread, Meat, sauces, cyder spirits, and all such necessaries, comforts, and conveniences of life as are suitable to their degree and former habits. Hereby meaning that they shall be so supplyed as aforesaid as that they shall be able to keep a separate table make such little presents, and entertain their friends as they have hereto fore been accustomed to do.

7 That during that time he will relieve comfort and support them in sickness and in health, with all necessary Physic watchings, and attention at all times demean himself towards them as a loving brother and dutiful son—

8 That he will give both and each of them a decent christian burial.

15 I make and appoint my said son Jeremiah sole executor of this my last will and testament.

In testimony whereof I have hereunto set my hand and seal this 10th. day of March A. D. 1800.

ABEL BOWMAN
SETH CROSBY Junr.   HEZEKIAH CROSBY   (Seal)
JOHN LEWIS Junr.

Signed sealed and published in presence of us, we also subscribing as Witnesses in the presence of the testator and each other.

Commonwealth of Massachusetts }
Middlesex ss. Registry of Probate }

(Vol. 128, p. 374.)

It was a fortunate thing for Jeremiah[11] Crosby that, as he lived but a very few years after the death of his father, he was not called upon long to carry out all the details of conduct imposed upon him. There was a benevolent breadth of contemplation upon life and the future in the will of William[9] Crosby which somehow seems to be missing in this document we have just set forth, and this rather narrow outlook upon life which carries so many imposed conditions upon those who come after can perhaps only mean that Hezekiah felt the need of them, and, of course, the need was in himself. So that is the reason why we said that, although he did lead a life of much active usefulness, the impression is got that Hezekiah Crosby's outlook upon life was not essentially a broad one and his life of activity not probably of his own choosing, and we could have wished that he did not feel it necessary to call to the attention of his son Jeremiah that he was to support his mother and sister "in sickness and in health, with all necessary Physic watchings, and attention at all times demean himself towards them as a loving brother and dutiful son."

Hezekiah Crosby's father died when Hezekiah himself was just reaching manhood, and it may be that this narrow vision was partly the result of his own struggle for life.

In his second marriage, that to Lucy Kittredge, Hezekiah Crosby seems to have made a most fortunate choice, for they lived together happily over fifty years. It is not known just when she died, but it is known that she survived him.

Jeremiah[11] Crosby.

Jeremiah[11] Crosby (Hezekiah[10], William[9], Joseph[8], Simon[7], Simon[6], Thomas[5], Anthony[4], Thomas[3], Miles[2], and John[1]) was born in Billerica, 20 Mar. 1760, and married first in Wilmington, 23 Oct. 1783, Abigail Jaquith, daughter of Deacon Benjamin and Hannah (Walker) Jaquith. She was born in Wilmington, 13 Feb. 1761, and died 12 Jan. 1810, in Billerica.

Jeremiah Crosby married for his second wife, Lucy, widow of Edward Winship of Cambridge, and daughter of Amariah Learned of Watertown. Amariah Learned had by his second wife, Susanna Norcross, a daughter Lucy, who was baptized in Watertown, 5 Mar. 1769. She married in Cambridge, 22 Nov. 1788, Edward Winship, and had a son Edward, baptized 25 July 1790, who died 13 Nov. 1790. On 9 Oct. 1791 another son was baptized Edward, and on 9 Jan. 1795 Edward Winship the father died, age twenty-nine years.

Lucy Winship was admitted to full communion in the Cambridge church, 12 Apr. 1795, and on the record of the same church is found the marriage of Jeremiah Crosby of Billerica and Lucy Winship, 25 Dec. 1810. The old Bible gives her birth as 17 Feb. 1769, and her death 11 Apr. 1841, age seventy-two. Jeremiah[11] Crosby died in Billerica, 19 Oct. 1821. Children by first wife, born in Billerica:—

> Jeremiah[12], b. 15 Aug. 1784; m., 26 Nov. 1812, in Billerica, Ruth Bowman, daughter of Abel and Lucy (Needham) Bowman, b. in Bedford, 4 Apr. 1786, and d. in Billerica, 11 Oct. 1830. He m. second, Lucy Goodwin, who was b. in Hillsborough, N.H., and d. in Billerica, 18 May 1846, age fifty-four. He had, by his first wife, Albert[13], Leander[13], Ambrose[13], Abigail[13], Abel Bowman[13], and Emily[13], and one child, Renslow[13], by the second wife.
>
> Abigail[12], b. 4 June 1786; m., in Billerica, 4 Feb. 1808, Jeremiah Hobson of Deering, N.H., and mentioned in her father's will in 1815 as Abigail Hobson. Jeremiah Hobson of Buxton, Me., Amherst and Deering, N.H., had by wife Lucy a son, Jeremiah, b. 28 Oct. 1779, who was doubtless the one who m. Abigail Crosby.
>
> Silence[12], b. and d. 25 May 1788.
>
> Hannah[12], b. 1 May 1790, and d. 28 Feb. 1796.
>
> Zoa[12], b. 27 May 1792, and d. 18 Mar. 1796.
>
> Lucy[12], b. 23 Aug. 1794, and d. 12 Mar. 1796.
>
> Hannah[12], b. 7 Apr. 1797; m., in Billerica, 8 Apr. 1819, Joshua Learned, son of Joshua and Sarah (Coolidge) Learned, b. in Hallowell, Me., 5 Dec. 1796, and d. in Watertown, 24 Oct. 1867. She d. there 5 May 1880. They had in Watertown, Albert[13], Stephen[13], Sarah Ann[13], Harriet W.[13], Joshua S.[13], William Bonney[13], Abigail[13], Lucy E.[13], and Emma Augusta[13].

Sumner[12], b. 21 Mar. 1801, and m., in Nov. 1826, Harriot Blanchard, daughter of Joseph and Sarah (Brown) Blanchard.

Alonzo[12], b. 22 Mar. 1803, and d. 17 Jan. 1860, in East Boston. He m., 12 Nov. 1828, Rutha Bemis, who d. 2 May 1834, leaving Rutha Elizabeth[13], Adelaide[13], and Mary Frances[13]. He m. second, 1 Feb. 1835, Mrs. Hannah (Mordough) Walker, and had Clarissa[12], Lucy Submit[13], and Alonzo[13], Jr.

Lucy[12], b. 15 May 1805; m., in Billerica, 7 Oct. 1831, John Osborn of Belfast, Me. They had one son, John S., b. in Belfast, and d. in Billerica, 24 May 1845, age twelve years, nine months, and six days. John Osborn d. in New Orleans, La., in 1860; she m. second John Tomlinson, and she m. third John B. Leach. She d. in Oct. 1886.

Jeremiah[11] Crosby is the last one of the line of the Crosbys we have started to deal with that may be of interest to those of the Crosby family not directly descended from him, for his life covered the Revolutionary War, and he was himself a personality quite different from any of those who had preceded him, and holds some value as a person outside of his place merely in a line of male Crosbys.

Jeremiah[11] Crosby was born on the old Crosby farm in Billerica and in the original Simon[7] Crosby house, which was built in 1678. By the terms of his father's (Hezekiah's) will Jeremiah, being his eldest son (for all record of Timothy[11] Crosby is lost, the supposition being that he died young), inherited in his turn the Crosby farm and buildings that had been so long in the family. Although his father, Hezekiah, lived to be eighty-five years of age, it is quite likely that Jeremiah Crosby ran the farm in an independent capacity during the late years of his father's life, after the end of the Revolutionary War had released his time for more peaceful employment and pursuits.

Jeremiah Crosby was married in 1783, being then twenty-three years old, and it is almost beyond question that, as the eldest son and destined to possession of the farm, he lived with his wife and children in the same house with his father and stepmother, for his own mother had died when he was only six years old, and such recollection as he may have had of her was necessarily very slight. At the time of his marriage he had completed his duties as a soldier and was ready for a different kind of a life.

As stated above, the influence of Rev. Henry Cummings upon the town of Billerica during the troublous times caused by the Revolutionary War was very great, and it was under this influence that Jeremiah Crosby came, so that his martial spirit was fired as a mere boy of sixteen, leading him to enroll at that rather tender age to be a soldier. But the remarkable thing to notice is that he kept enlisting and re-enlisting for a return to the war, as if to show that it was not merely the influence of Mr. Cummings that was exerted upon him, but that also there was in him a certain considerable amount of energy that had to be worked off in that way.

His record as a soldier is an honorable one. Like those Crosbys who had preceded him, he worked in an humble capacity as a soldier, in fact as a private. Although it is interesting to note that, when the new church in Billerica was built in 1797, he was described in the church records as "Lieut. Jeremiah Crosby," and as at that time he subscribed for two pews in the edifice, pews 10 and 35, it is more than likely he was thereupon raised to the rank of lieutenant. But, none the less, he was just Private Jeremiah Crosby, as his father had been Yeoman Hezekiah Crosby. As a matter of record, we give the following references to Jeremiah[11] Crosby's services in the Revolutionary War:—

Jeremiah Crosby: Appears with the rank of *Private* in a return of Capt. Solomon Kidder's Co., Col. Brooks's regt. endorsed "1776" and probably made up at White Plains. Residence Billerica. Reported at White Plains fit for duty. (Massachusetts Soldiers and Sailors in the War of the Revolution, vol. 20, p. 179.)

Jeremiah Crosby: Appears with the rank of *Private* on Muster and Pay Roll of Capt. Edward Farmer's Co., Col. Jacob Gerrish's reg. Enlisted 20 Feb. 1778. Service to 20 May 1778. Time of service 3 mos., at Bunker Hill. Roll sworn to in Middlesex Co. (*Ibid.*, vol. 19, p. 76.)

Jeremiah Crosby: Appears with rank of *Private* on Muster and Pay Roll of Capt. Solomon Pollard's Co., Col. Samuel Denny's regt. Enlisted 23 Oct. 1779. Discharged 4 Dec. 1779. Time of service 1 mo.

12 days. Company detached to march to Claverack and join Continental Army for 3 mos. (*Ibid.*, vol. 21, p. 185.)

Jeremiah Crosby: Appears in a description List of men raised to reinforce the Continental Army for the term of six months, agreeable to resolve 5 June 1780; returned as received Justin Ely, Commissioner by Maj. Peter Harward of the 6th Mass. regt. at Springfield, 3 July 1780. Age 20 years: Stature 5 ft. 8 in.: Complexion Light: Town Billerica. Arrived at Springfield 3 July 1780, marched to camp 3 July 1780, under command of Lieut. Frye of the Artificers. (*Ibid.*, vol. 35, p. 184.)

Jeremiah Crosby: Appears among a list of men raised for the six months' service and returned by Brig. Gen. Paterson as having passed muster in a return dated Camp Toto'way, 25 Oct. 1780. Residence Billerica. (*Ibid.*, vol. 25, p. 225.)

Jeremiah Crosby: Appears in a Pay Roll for Six Months Men raised by the town of Billerica for service in the Continental Army during 1780. Marched 29 June 1780. Discharged 9 Dec. 1780. Time of service 5 mos. 22 days. (*Ibid.*, vol. 4, p. 5.)

Jeremiah Crosby: Appears with rank of *Private* on Muster and Pay Roll of Capt. Samuel Jay's Co., discharged 29 Nov. 1781. Time of service 3 mos. 22 days, including 11 days' (220 miles) travel home. Residence Billerica. Regt. raised in Suffolk and Middlesex Counties to reinforce the Continental Army for 3 mos. Roll dated Woburn. (*Ibid.*, vol. 23, p. 125.)

As well as this activity in times of war, Jeremiah Crosby took a little more than a mere passing interest in public affairs in times of peace, for he became a deacon in the Billerica church when that institution, under the lead of Rev. Henry Cummings and his colleague, Rev. Nathaniel Whitman, decided to follow what was then the radical move of the day, and to follow into the ranks of Unitarianism. On the civic side he held the office of Selectman of Billerica in 1806, 1807, and 1810.

Although Jeremiah Crosby was married twice, his first wife, Abigail Jaquith, was the mother of all his children. The Jaquith family, like the Crosby family, had been long in the Colonies, and there is inserted here a brief account of the line of Abigail Jaquith.

Abraham[2] *Jaquith* was the son of Abraham[1] Jaquith of Charlestown, Mass., "and Anna dau. of James Jordan of Dedham, Mass." Abraham[2] Jaquith was born 19 Dec.

1644; went from Charlestown to Woburn, and settled in that part which afterwards became Wilmington; was taxed there 1666; married Mary Adford, 13 Mar., 1671; had children, *Abraham³, Elizabeth³, Sarah³*. (Woburn records.)

Abraham³ Jaquith, born 17 Feb. 1672/3, married, 26 Dec. 1700, Sarah Jones, born 10 July 1681, in Wilmington, daughter of Hugh and Mary (Foster) Jones. (For pedigree of Mary Foster Jones, see New Eng. His. and Gen. Reg., vol. 61, p. 151.) Abraham and Sarah Jaquith had fifteen children, the ninth being Benjamin. (See Sewall's History of Woburn, Mass., p. 618.)

Benjamin⁴ Jaquith, born 27 June 1716, married July 1739, Hannah Walker, daughter of Capt. Samuel and Hannah (Fowle) Walker of Woburn. Hannah (Walker) Jaquith died in Wilmington, Mass., 20 Feb. 1801, at age of eighty-two years. Deacon Benjamin Jaquith died in Wilmington, 29 Aug. 1801, at age of eighty-five years. (Town records and gravestones.) They had ten children.

Abigail⁵ Jaquith, born 13 Feb. 1761, married 23 Oct. 1783, Jeremiah Crosby of Billerica, Mass., and died in Billerica, 12 Jan. 1810.

Abigail (Jaquith) Crosby was the tenth child of Deacon Benjamin and Hannah (Walker) Jaquith. In her Bible it is recorded in connection with the death of her parents that they "lived together in a marriage state 62 years and one mo."

Deacon Benjamin⁴ Jaquith lived and died on the homestead farm of his father in Wilmington. It does not appear that he was ever in civic life. For many years he was deacon in the Congregational church of Wilmington. All public records connecting him with the town name him as Deacon Benjamin Jaquith. He marched on the alarm of Lexington, 19 Apr. 1775, as a private in the Militia Company of Colonel Greene's regiment, at the age of fifty-nine; service, two days. He further furnished soldiers during the war, for what reason is not stated, paying for such service, for he was probably too old to serve. (See Massachusetts Soldiers and Sailors in the War of the American Revolution.)

In 1815 Jeremiah Crosby made his will, a copy of which is inserted below. It is a document notable in its brevity, directness, and equitable disposition of his property. In it is found a quiet security as to the future that is apt to indicate a command of the present, and from it we may fairly suppose Jeremiah Crosby to have been a pretty well-balanced man. He died in 1821, at the age of sixty-one years.

Will of Jeremiah[11] Crosby:—

In the name of God Amen. I, Jeremiah Crosby of Billerica in the County of Middlesex and Commonwealth of Massachusetts, gentleman;—

Calling to mind the uncertainty of Life and willing to provide against all unforseen Casualties by an Equitable distribution of such worldly Estate as Providence has seen fit to bless me with, do make this my last will and testament.

1st. After Commending my soul to God who gave it I will that my mortal part whenever I shall be called in Providence to put it off be decently and honorably inter'd by my Executor hereafter named at his own proper charges.

2d. I give unto my Beloved wife Lucy D. (already quoted)

3d. . . .

4th. I give to my Daughter Abigail Hobson twenty Dollars, together with what she has had to be paid in two years after my decease.

5th. I give to my Daughter Hannah two Hundred Dollars to be paid at the age of twenty-one unless needed before by marriage.

6th. I give to my Daughter Lucy two Hundred Dollars to be paid at the age of twenty-one unless needed before by marriage.

7th. I give to my Son Sumner three Hundred Dollars to be paid at the age of twenty-one.

8th. I give to my Son Alonzo three Hundred Dollars to be paid at the age of twenty-one, provided nevertheless that if my said Executor shall pay and discharge any or all of said Legacies in my Lifetime, then said Legacies to be void so far as they shall appear to have been discharged by Receipts to my said Executor.

9th. My will is that my said Executor pay and discharge all just Debts and demands that shall be due and owing from me at my Decease to all persons whatever out of the surplus of my Estate after deducting each and every of the aforesaid Legacies.

10th. And as to all the Rest & Residue of my personal Estate whether in possesion or in action, I give and bequeath to my son Jeremiah. Also I give and Devise unto my said son Jeremiah all my Real Estate wherever the same may be situated to have and to hold the same to him the said Jeremiah to his Heirs and assigns forever. Provided nevertheless that each and every Benefit, Legacy and devise to my said son Jeremiah is on the following Conditions, i. e. that my said son Jeremiah duly take on himself the Execution of this my last will and Testament.

11th. I make and appoint my said son Jeremiah Sole Executor of this my last will and Testament.

In testimony whereof I have hereunto set my hand and seal this sixteenth day of September in the year of our Lord one thousand eight hundred and fifteen.

JEREMIAH CROSBY (Seal)

SETH CROSBY
JOSIAH CROSBY, Jr.
ABEL BOWMAN, Jun.

Signed, sealed and published in presence of us, we also subscribing as Witnesses in presence of the Testator and each other.

Will No. 5345,
Lib° 140. Fol. 350
Dec. 4, 1821.

And with Jeremiah Crosby expired the line of four generations of this family we started to deal with in this book who were born and lived and died in Billerica, as well as the founder of the branch in Billerica, Simon[7] Crosby, who, although not born in Billerica, spent nearly all his life there and died there.

These five generations of Crosbys were all men of a simple life, mostly farmers and principally doing nothing else. Where opportunity offered or conditions seemed to require it, they gave time to public affairs. They did not live in a large centre of population, and so had no opportunity to accumulate even a moderately large property, but probably were none the less contented with life in the sphere they found themselves in, and satisfied to meet their duties as they presented themselves. They were not generals, admirals, or capitalists, and were accordingly spared the hardships that attend upon fame and fortune. They took an interest in the religious and civic affairs of the town of Billerica, and, when occasion demanded it, fought for the country they believed in. It is the people who live out their destiny in just such a manner that form the backbone of any country, and those who most nearly live at the general average of the race most nearly come to know what real living is.

Chapter VII.

THE FIRST MERCHANT IN THE FAMILY.

An Account of Sumner Crosby of the Twelfth Generation.

Sumner[12] Crosby (Jeremiah[11], Hezekiah[10], William[9], Joseph[8], Simon[7], Simon[6], Thomas[5], Anthony[4], Thomas[3], Miles[2], and John[1]) was born 21 Mar. 1801, in Billerica, and married there, 26 Nov. 1826, Harriot Blanchard, daughter of Joseph and Sarah (Brown) Blanchard, who was born in Billerica, 16 Sept. 1803, and died in South Boston, Mass., 16 Dec. 1880. Sumner Crosby died in South Boston, 10 Apr. 1875. Children, born in Boston:—

> Joseph Blanchard[13], b. 5 Feb. 1829, m. Mrs. Rachel Maria (Sears) Gleason, and d. 20 Jan. 1903, in Boston.
> Eliza Harriot[13], b. 11 July 1830, and d. 10 Mar. 1886, in Boston.
> *William Sumner*[13], b. 22 Apr. 1844, and m., in South Boston, 11 Oct. 1877, Eleanor Francis Davis, daughter of Almon Hemenway and Elizabeth (Everett) Davis.

All that remains now to tell of this particular line of the Crosbys will prove of interest probably only to those connected directly with the descendants of Sumner[12] Crosby now living or yet to be born, for all the descendants of Sumner[12] Crosby now surviving are comprised in the thirteenth, fourteenth, and fifteenth generations of this line of the family we started to trace from 1440.

The twelfth generation of Crosbys in America brings us to Sumner Crosby, the seventh child of Jeremiah[11] of Billerica, and the last of the line we are dealing with, who was born there on the old Crosby place, where his forebears for several generations had lived and reared their families.

Having a brother much older than himself, to whom the

farm was destined to go, and possibly feeling that lure of the city which apparently appealed more to him than it had to his ancestors, and perhaps foreseeing the life of public service which was in store for him, and which he came by naturally perhaps through inheritance from many families on both sides,—at all events he removed to Boston somewhere about 1820, that city being then in process of awakening from its slumbers which set in after the activities of the Revolutionary War, and beginning to show the symptoms of its future mercantile development. And here we find once more the signs of that restless activity and stretching out in newer fields which brought the first Crosbys to America.

Sumner Crosby was the first Crosby in the direct line we are writing of who turned his attention to the mercantile side of life; and, while only fairly successful as a merchant compared with others of those and later days, he nevertheless established a business which has lasted to the present day, and, what was of far greater importance, a reputation for integrity which has remained after him.

But it was not as a merchant that Sumner Crosby left his mark on the community in which he lived, but as a public-spirited citizen, who gave freely and unstintingly of his time and best thought for the public good.

After attending the "little red school-house" (which in this case actually was red and may still be seen near the Crosby farm, although now in a state of sad neglect), where he secured as much education as was possible in those days in rural districts, he worked a few years on the ancestral farm, and at about the age of twenty he went to Boston, where he secured a position as a clerk in a store at the West End. He must have filled this position with credit and saved some money, for in 1826 he went back to Billerica to claim for a wife Harriot Blanchard, whom he had known from earliest childhood, and took her back to Boston to live. In addition to what he may have saved, he received the sum of $300 from his father, Jeremiah Crosby, as we learn from the latter's will. With this saving and heritage

Sumner Crosby was enabled to start a store in the West End of Boston.*

The varying life of a merchant contains little of interest, except that on the whole he was successful and might have been much more so had not a too trusting confidence in humanity proved somewhat incompatible with a strictly business career. In 1841 he quitted business to accept the position of Superintendent of the State Institution for the Insane in South Boston, which position he held with much credit to himself and much advantage to the institution until 1853, when once more he embarked upon a business life.

Hardly was he again in business for himself when he was prevailed upon to represent his ward in the Boston Common Council, and in 1856 he was elected as the Representative of Ward 12 and re-elected in 1861, 1862, and 1865.

It was during these years that the first discussion started over the expediency of establishing a City Hospital,† and from the start Sumner Crosby evinced the greatest interest in the project, and he appeared before many hearings on the subject in behalf of the proponents, until finally the dreams of those interested were realized and the Boston City Hospital was opened to the public in 1864. And on the first Board of Trustees, elected in 1863 by concurrent vote of the Common Council, under ordinance of 23 Dec. 1862, was Sumner Crosby himself at that time, not a member of the Council, but chosen as one of three citizens-at-large‡ for a term of three years.§ He was immediately placed on the Building and other important committees. And so he gave all his time and ability to study the needs of the institution he was so much interested in.

After serving his last term as a member of the Common Council, in 1865, he was persuaded to serve the community in a larger sphere, and was elected a member of the legisla-

---

* "I give to my Son Sumner three Hundred Dollars to be paid at the age of twenty-one." (Will of Jeremiah Crosby, dated 16 Sept. 1815; admitted to probate 4 Dec. 1821. Lib. 140. Fol. 350. East Cambridge Probate Office.)

† "History of the Boston City Hospital 1864–1904," p. 103 et seq.

‡ Ibid., p. 113. § Ibid., p. 163.

ture in 1866, and in the following year he was elected a member of the Senate of Massachusetts. This completed his activities in public office, and it was truly said of him, "In whatever capacity he served, it was with that strict regard for the public good that characterized the service of men of his day."*

In religion he was a Unitarian, as his father before him had accepted that belief in Billerica, and, like his ancestors, Sumner Crosby was very active in all that pertained to the church. He was chairman of the Board of Trustees of the First Hawes Church of South Boston, and as such gave his vote to sustain Theodore Parker as against the decision of the Boston Association of Unitarian Ministers, when that body disqualified Parker from further fellowship with it because of his sermon at the occasion of the ordination of Mr. Shackford as pastor of the Hawes Church, thus showing his independence of thought and his ability to forecast public opinion, which in after years freely vindicated Theodore Parker from all charges of extreme radicalism.

In business, Sumner Crosby was a prominent member of the Corn Exchange of Boston, where he was much respected by his business competitors; but he gave his time to other matters than business and politics, serving the South Boston Savings Bank for many years as trustee. He was a useful member of St. John's Lodge of Masons, at one time being elected Master, but not being able to serve, through stress of other duties.

It appears to have been quite a natural thing for Sumner Crosby to have married Harriot Blanchard, for her family had been intimately acquainted with his for over one hundred years by reason of close proximity of residence in Billerica, and by reason of a previous intermarriage between the two families, John Blanchard having married, in 1701, Mary, the daughter of Simon[7] and Rachel (Brackett) Crosby.

The Blanchards, like the Crosbys, were principally

* "History of the Boston City Hospital, 1864–1904," p. 174 *et seq.*

farmers, with some military service and some service in public office. The principal facts concerning them follow:—

Thomas[1] Blanchard was born in England, and came to America in 1639 in the ship *Jonathan*, apparently from Penton, Hants, England. Otherwise, little is known of the family prior to their coming to this country. Thomas[1] was married three times: first, to some one in England who is not known, and who died before he left there, and by whom all his four sons were born, viz., George[2], Nathaniel[2], Thomas[2], and Samuel[2]. His second wife was Agnes Bent (Barnes), the widow of one Barnes, who died on shipboard, and never reached America. For his third wife he married Mary ——, whose family name has been lost. Thomas[1] Blanchard settled in Charlestown, and in 1648 went to Braintree for a short while, returning to Charlestown about 1651, having bought a farm in the latter place, consisting of two hundred acres of land and some houses, from Rev. John Wilson and his son, in that part of Charlestown known as "South West of Mystic River," now called Malden. Thomas[1] Blanchard died 21 May 1654. The appraisers of his estate reported:—

> The house and land valued at £300.
> The whole amount of inventory 642/0/0.
> Taken on the 25th of 4. mo. 1654 by us.
>
> JOSEPH HILLS,
> EDWARD COLLINS.

Samuel[2] Blanchard, as we have seen, was the last of the children of Thomas[1] and his unknown first wife, and was born in England, 6 Aug. 1629. He lived for several years in Charlestown with his father, but finally settled in Andover, where he was identified with the civic life of that town. He married first, 3 May 1654, Mary, daughter of Seth and Bethia Sweetser of Charlestown, by whom he had seven children. She died 20 Feb. 1669, and he married second, 24 June 1673, Hannah Doggett, daughter of Thomas Doggett and his second wife, Elizabeth, daughter of Jonas and Frances Humphrey, and widow of William

Fry. She was born in Weymouth in 1646, and died in Andover, 10 July 1725. Samuel Blanchard died in Andover, 22 Apr. 1707. The Doggett Genealogy (page 345) says the four children of Samuel and Hannah (Doggett) Blanchard were born in Charlestown, and refers to an old document, in which it says, "I Samuel Blanchard came to Andover with my family upon the 10th of June 1686," etc.

John[3] Blanchard was born in Charlestown, 3 July 1677, son of Samuel and Hannah Blanchard, and was married, 7 Aug. 1701, to Mary Crosby, daughter of Simon[7] and Rachel (Brackett) Crosby.

John[3] Blanchard lived in Billerica, where he died 10 Apr. 1750, and his wife died there 7 May 1748. He was Representative to the General Court at Boston in 1725.

Simon[4] Blanchard, twelfth and youngest child of John and Mary Blanchard, was born in Billerica, 16 Mar. 1725/6, and married, 17 Dec. 1746, Rebecca, daughter of Samuel and Sarah (Hutchinson) Sheldon, who was born in Billerica, 28 July 1727, and died there 3 Mar. 1814. Simon died there 19 Apr. 1796.

They had ten children, the ninth being Joseph[5].

Joseph[5] Blanchard was born in Billerica, 17 Oct. 1765, and was married first, 10 June 1788, to Mehitable Waters of Carlisle. She died 7 June 1794, age 28. He married second, 15 Nov. 1798, Sarah, daughter of Col. Jonathan and Mary (French) Brown of Tewksbury, Mass. She was born in Tewksbury, 24 Mar. 1774, and died in Marshfield, Mass., 27 Feb. 1856. Joseph[5] Blanchard was Selectman of Billerica four years,—1808 to 1810, inclusive, and 1812,—and died there 11 Sept. 1828.

Harriot[6] Crosby, fifth child of Joseph[5] and Sarah (Brown) Blanchard, was born 16 Sept. 1803 in Billerica, and was married, 26 Nov. 1826, to Sumner Crosby, the subject of this chapter.

It was in the little school-house in Billerica and the meeting-house in which Rev. Henry Cummings had preached in the Revolutionary times that Sumner Crosby used to see Harriot Blanchard, and this early attachment of the years of youth ripened into a love that lasted during forty-nine years of married life.

Sumner Crosby was a quiet, unassuming man, of great nobility of character and simplicity of deportment. He was generally loved by all who knew him, and much mourned when he died on 10 Apr. 1875.

He marked a return from the life of a farmer, which his ancestors had led before him, to the life in a larger centre of population. His personality was well rounded and well balanced. While his success as a merchant, a calling for which he was not especially adapted either by temperament or inheritance, was not particularly noticeable, he succeeded in doing good as he went, and adding something to public progress and help and comfort to individuals. With him we take leave of the line of Crosbys that have passed into the mysterious Beyond. For an unbroken line of twelve generations who seemed in a simple way to have tried to do their best, we have no apologies to offer.

Chapter VIII.

THE PRESENT-DAY CROSBYS OF THIS LINE OF THE FAMILY.

A Very Brief Account of the Thirteenth, Fourteenth, and Fifteenth Generations.

William Sumner[13] Crosby (Sumner[12], Jeremiah[11], Hezekiah[10], William[9], Joseph[8], Simon[7], Simon[6], Thomas[5], Anthony[4], Thomas[3], Miles[2], John[1]) was born in South Boston, Mass., 22 Apr. 1844, and married, 11 Oct. 1877, in South Boston, Eleanor Francis Davis, daughter of Almon Hemenway and Elizabeth (Everett) Davis. Eleanor Francis Davis was born in Dedham, Mass., 14 Mar. 1845. Child:—

> Sumner[14], b. in South Boston, 12 Nov. 1878; m., 6 Aug. 1901, in Alameda, Cal., Idolene Snow Hooper.

The old saying "*De mortuis nil nisi bonum*" presupposes, perhaps, the opposite to be the case of the living, and, as those who may come in future generations of this branch of the Crosby family can easily inform themselves of those Crosbys now living, to whatever extent their interest may be aroused, we will deal but briefly with the representatives of the last three generations.

William Sumner[13] Crosby was the third child of Sumner[12] and Harriot Blanchard Crosby. He attended the Hawes School of South Boston and later graduated from the Boston English High School at the age of sixteen. He then went into business with his father, to which business he has since devoted constant attention.

On 11 Oct. 1877 he was married to Eleanor Francis Davis,* by Rev. James Freeman Clarke, D.D. In June,

---

* For an account of the Davis family, see "Dolor Davis—Richard Everett," by the author of this book, and published by Geo. H. Ellis Co., Boston.

1889, they removed to Brookline, where they have since lived.

Sumner[14] Crosby (William Sumner[13], Sumner[12], Jeremiah[11], Hezekiah[10], William[9], Joseph[8], Simon[7], Simon[6], Thomas[5], Anthony[4], Thomas[3], Miles[2], John[1]) was born in South Boston, Mass., 12 Nov. 1878, and married in Alameda, Cal., 6 Aug. 1901, Idolene Snow Hooper,* daughter of Charles Appleton and Idolene Geneva (Snow) Hooper. Idolene Snow Hooper was born in San Francisco, 2 Feb. 1883. Children:—

> Charles Hooper[15], b. in San Francisco, Cal., 28 Nov. 1902.
> Barbara Appleton[15], b. in Alameda, Cal., 8 May 1904.
> Beatrice Blanchard[15], b. in Alameda, Cal., 17 Mar. 1907.
> Sumner[15], b. in Alameda, Cal., 10 June 1911.

Sumner[14] Crosby graduated from Harvard College in 1901 and received the degree of M.A. in 1902. He removed in July 1902 to California, where he was engaged in business in San Francisco for eleven years. He was Councilman of the City of Alameda, 1909-11; Assemblyman from Alameda in the California Legislature, 1911-13; delegate from California to the National Republican Convention in Chicago; and was at one time president of the Alameda Board of Education. In 1913 he retired from politics and business in California and returned to live in the East.

And of the fifteenth and last generation of this Crosby line we have been following through so many years, what shall we say? We have come a long way from John[1] Crosby of Holme-on-Spalding-Moor, in York County, England. To those who are given to believe that a person's destiny is greatly, if not wholly, influenced by their inheritance and environment, we would call attention to the fact that in the fifteenth generation of any family there is only one sixteen-thousandth part, presuming that from all ancestors an equal amount of good and bad is inherited.

* For an account of the ancestors of Idolene Snow Hooper, see "A Biographical Sketch of Eight Generations of Hooper in America," by Mrs. William Sumner Crosby. Boston, 1904. Published by Geo. H. Ellis Co.

Just what part inherited predispositions play in the personality of an individual will probably always be a matter of speculation. The author of this book does not believe they have much influence in determining the character of individuals, but believes that each individual creates his own destiny in the exact proportion to his own inward capacity to adapt himself to his surroundings and hence to the greater destiny that manages all things. The constant rotation of all that exists brings things always around once more to a point about where they were before, but in a different form, and this law applies as well to genealogy as to other studies of human nature or to the wide field of the nature of all things.

But there is a certain interest and pardonable curiosity as to what those who have borne a certain name in an unbroken line may have been like provided one does not become lost in the achievements of the past or in hopes of the future to find an excuse for the failure to meet present requirements. Destiny, like time, is always at work, and never ceases her labors, and the more individuals are able to do the same, the nearer they come to living in the present and adapting themselves to the greater destiny.

And so we will take leave of the Crosbys past and present, hoping that the lives of quiet usefulness lived by past Crosbys may augur its continuance in future generations.

Owing to the rapid multiplication of ancestors, if every collateral branch should be considered, as one goes constantly back into the past, it has been necessary to adhere to one general scheme of presenting the subject, and so only those in the direct male line of descent have been dealt with and the families into which they directly married.

APPENDICES

Appendix A.

EARLY CROSBYS IN YORKSHIRE.*

The earliest mention found of the place "Crosby" in Yorkshire is in Domesday in 1086, when one Bernulf as undertenant to Alan, Earl of Brittany, held lands in Crocsbi.

The earliest mention found in Yorkshire of the surname "Crosby" is in 6 John (1204). "Nottinghamshire. Watele, the land of Radulphus Taxon. The jurors say that Odo de Crosseby, constable of Tikehill, and his servants, took from said manor, after said manor was taken into the hands of our Lord the King, of land, men, and goods £23-8-4, to which he declines to answer except to our Lord the King, as he says." ("A Crosby Family," by Judge Nathan Crosby, p. 4.) Tikehill is now known as Tickhill, a parish in Southern Yorkshire on the borders of Nottinghamshire.

In 24 Henry III. (1240), Ralph, son of William de Crosseby, and Robert his brother, granted lands in Eskelby, County York, to Hugh the rector and the brethren of St. Leonard's Hospital in the city of York. (Yorkshire Archæological Journal, vol. 10, fol. 272.)

In 44 Henry III. (1259–60), William, son of Bartholomew de Eskelby, had a tenement in Crosseby, County York; and Henry de Crosseby and William de Crosseby were sued by Iseult de Massam as to a tenement in Eskelby. (Assize Rolls, Yorkshire, No. 1049, Public Record Office, London.)

In 30 Edward I. (1301–02) John de Crosseby of Scrueton (Scruton, County York) was assessed xviij$d$. (Lay Subsidy, North Riding of Yorkshire, 211–2.)

Among the early freemen of the city of York (of which the rolls commence in 1340) the following Crosbys appear in the fourteenth and fifteenth centuries: John de Crosseby,

*Compiled by J. Gardner Bartlett.

tailor, 1350; Robert de Crossbi, blacksmith, 1357; John de Crosseby, draper, 1382; Thomas de Crosseby, fletcher, 1386; Robert de Crosseby, armourer, 1396; John Crossby, vintner, 1413; William Crosseby, carpetmaker, 1415; Robert Crosseby, fletcher, son of Thomas Crosseby, fletcher, 1421; William Crosseby, dyer, 1439; William Crosseby, cartwright, 1449; John Croseby, yeoman, 1458; Thomas Crosseby, baker, 1464.

In 1 Richard II. (1378), Thomas de Crosseby, laborer of Cottenesse,* was assessed iiij$d$. (Poll Tax 1378, East Riding, Yorkshire, Lay Subsidy, 202-69.)

The will of John de Crosseby, citizen of York,† dated 28 Aug. 1397. To be buried in Church of St. Dionis, York. To John de Crosseby,‡ draper of York, 3s. 4d. To wife Alice my term in my messuage in Bootham Bar, city of York. All residue to said wife. Executors, my said wife, Thomas de Scamston, and John de Crosseby, draper. Witnesses: Thomas Catour, Will. Muston. Proved by executors 17 Nov. 1397. (Prerogative and Exchequer of York Wills, vol. 2, fol. 7. Translated from the Latin.)

The will of Robert de Crossby of Bolton Percy, County York, proved by his widow Joane and son Thomas de Crossby, 3 May 1400. (This will is not preserved.) (P. and E. York Wills, vol. 3, fol. 37. Translated from the Latin.)

The will of Margaret Crosseby of the city of York, "semsteer," dated 14 Mar. 1431/2. To be buried in church of St. Helen in Stayngate, city of York. To the high altar of said church, to the Cathedral, etc. All residue to Sir Robert Galtresse, chaplain, and Thomas Crossby of Coxwold, they to be executors. (No witnesses.) Proved by executors 17 Mar. 1431/2. (P. and E. of York Wills, vol. 3, fol. 603. Translated from the Latin.)

The will of William Crosseby, citizen and dyer of the city of York, dated 30 Sept. 1466. To be buried in church of St. John the Evangelist, Ouse Bridge, York. To an honest priest to celebrate masses for my soul for a year in the

---

* Cotness in the parish of Howden.   † The freeman of 1350.   ‡ *Ibid.*, 1382.

parish church of Crosseby Raveswathe £3-6-8. To my poor workwomen 20s. To my brother John Crosseby living in the parish of Crosseby Raveswath, a gown, a hood, 100s. etc.; and to his child 3s. 4d. To my sister Alice 3s. 4d. To each of my apprentices 3s. 4d. To my kinsman John Smyth 13s. 4d. To my kinsman Thomas Smyth, dyer, 26s. 8d. To my kinswoman Margaret Fownays 8 marks. To my wife Sibel £10. All residue to wife, Sibel, John Marshall, draper, John Tyesdale of York, upholsterer, and Thomas Smyth, dyer, they to be the executors. Supervisors, John Mychell, grocer of London, and Thomas Wyles, chaplain. Codicil dated 1 Oct. 1466: To Thomas Croseby, son of John Croseby 5 marks. To Sir John Darley, monk 6s. 8d. To Robert Edson 5 marks. To Alice Warde 3s. 4d. To wife Sibel for life a messuage in North Street, York, bought of William Stokton, to revert at her death to St. John's Church, York. Witness, Thomas Wyles, chaplain. Proved 21 Nov. 1466 by widow Sibel Crosseby, John Tesedale, and Thomas Smyth, executors named, power reserved for the other executor John Marshall, when he shall appear. (P. and E. of York Wills, vol. 4, fol. 70. Translated from the Latin.) This testator was doubtless a native of Crosby Ravensworth, County Westmoreland; was freeman of city of York 1440, chamberlain 1461, and sheriff 1463–64. In 1459 he and his wife Sibel joined the Guild of Corpus Christi, York.

The will of Hugh Crosby of Whitgift, County York, dated 25 Jan. 1473/4. To son John and daughter Julian a heifer each. To Elizabeth Husband a ewer. All residue to wife Alice, sole executrix. Sons William Crosby and Richard Crosby supervisors. Witnesses, Thomas Herpham, chaplain, William Kay, chaplain. Proved 12 May 1474 by executrix. (P. and E. of York Wills, vol. 4, fol. 11. Translated from the Latin.)

Appendix B.

DEED OF THOMAS AND SIMON CROSBY TO SIR MARMADUKE LANGDALE AND RICHARD MEADLEY.

THIS INDENTURE mad the fower and twentith day of March in the Ninth yeare of the raigne of our Soueraigne lord Charles by the grace of God King of England, Scotland, ffrance and Ireland Defender of the faith &c Betwene Sr William Constable of fflamburgh als fflamborough in the County of yorke Barronet Thomas Crosby of / Holme in Spaldingmoore in the said County yeoman and Symond Crosby of the same sonne of the said Thomas Crosby of the one part. And Sr Marmaduke Langdaile of North Dalton in the said County K^t and Richard Meadley of Sancton in the said County gent of the other part Whereas ye sade Sr William Constable by his Indenture / under his hand and seale bearing date the seuenteenth day of September in the Eight yeare of his said Maties Raign that now is ouer England &c Did for the / Consideracons therein menconed demise grant bargaine sell assigne and sett ouer vnto the said Thomas Crosby and Symond Crosby their heyres Executors Administrators & / Assignes, All that one Messuage or Tenemte in Holme in Spaldingmoore aforesaid and all other the p^{r}misses with the appurtenncs thereunto belonging then in the tenure / and occupacon of William Hewley or his assignes. One other Messuage or tenemte and other the p^{r}misses with the appurtenncs then in the tenure and occupacon of John / Varnill or his assignes One other Messuage or Tenemte in Holme aforesaid and other the p^{r}misses with the appurtenncs then in the tenure and occupacon of George / Atkinson or his Assignes One other Mesuage or tenemte there and other the p^{r}misses with the appurtenncs then in the tenure and occupac̕on of William Johnson/ or his assignes One other Messuage or Tenemte in Holme aforesaid and other the pʳmisses with the appurtennces then in the tenure and occupacon of Thomas Acklam/ or his assignes Together with all Comons and Comodities profitts and advantages wayes easemts patches, passages, waters and water-courses and all yearely rents and reuercons thereof/ and all other the pʳmisses with the Appurtenncs whatsoeuer to the said Mesuages or tennemts and other or any of the aforesaid pʳmisses with their or any of their appurtenncs whatsoeuer/ belonging or in any wise appertaining all which said Mesuages or tennemts and other the pʳmisses with the appurtenncs are scytuate lyeing and being within the town feilds and Territoryes of Holme in Spaldingmoore aforesaid TO HAUE AND TO HOLDE occupye possesse and enioy all the aforesaid mesuages or tenemts and all and euery other the before recyted Demised/ pʳmisses with their and euery of their appurtenncs vnto the said Thomas Crosby and Symon Crosby their heyres executors administrators and assignes from the feast of the Annunciacon/ of our blessed Lady the virgin Mary then last past before the date of the said Indenture for Dureing and vntill the full end and tearme of Three hundreth yeares from thence next/ after following and fully to be compleate and ended yeilding and paying theirfore yearely and euery yeare dureing the said tearme vnto the sade Sʳ William Constable his heyres or/ assignes the anuall or yearely rent of two pence of lawfull English money att the feast of Easter onely if it were asked or demaunded with A Prouiso or Condicon that if the sade/ Sʳ William Constable his heyres executors administrators or assignes or any of them did well and truely Content and pay or cause to be contented satisfied and payed vnto the/ said Thomas Crosby and Symon Crosby or either of them there or either of there executors administrators or assignes the true and Just summe of fower hundreth pounds of/ lawfull English money att and vpon the feast day of the Anunciacon of our blessed Lady St. Mary the virgin or within forty dayes next after the saide feast att any time or times/ within the space of seauen yeares next ensueing the date of the sade Indenture without any drift or further delay as also did pay or cause to be payed vnto the said Thomas Crosby/ and Symon Crosby or to the one of them their or either of their executors administrators or assignes the true and just summe of Thyrtie and two pounds of good and lawfull/ English money yearely and euery yeare att the seuerall feasts of St Michaell the Archangell and the Anunciacon of St. Mary the virgin by equall portions or within forty dayes next/ after either of the said feasts vntill the said summe of fower hundreth pounds were vnto the said Thomas Crosby and Symon or the one of them there or the one of their/ heyres, executors administrators or assignes fully satisfied or payed as aforesade the first paymte thereof being syxteene pounds to begin at the feast of St. Michaell the Archangell/ then next and so consequently from feast to feast as aforesaid Dureing the non paymte of the aforesade summe of fower hundreth pounds according to the true intente of the/ sade Indenture, And that then and from thencefoorth vpon paymte of the said seuerall summes as well the aforesaide summe of fower hundreth pounds as the saide sume of thirty/ and two pounds in manner and forme aforesaide the said Estate of bargaine and sale demise and grant to be vtterly voyde and of none effect to all intents Constructions & purposes/ as though the same had neuer bene had or made, the sade Indenture or any thinge therein conteined to the contrary in any wise not withstanding as in and by the sade Indenture/ with diverse other Couennts therein conteined more att large appeareth whereunto reference be hat NOW THIS INDENTURE WITTNESSETH that they the said Thomas Crosby/ and Symon Crosby for and in consideracon of A certaine competent sume of good and lawfull English money to them or the one of them in hand well and truely payed by the/ sade Sr Marmaduke Langdaile before the ensealing and Deliuery of these p^{r}sents whereof they doe acknowledge the receipt and thereof and of euery part thereof doe clerely and freely/ acquite release and discharge the sade Sr Marmaduke Langdale his executors, administrators and assignes and euery of them for euer by these p^{r}sents, And for diuerse other good/ causes and Consideracons thein thereunto especially moueing haue by the Dereccon and appointemte of the sade Sr William Constable and together with him granted bargained/ solde assigned ouer releassed and confirmed, and by these p^{r}sents doe for thelselues, their executors administrators and assignes clerely and freely grant bargaine sell assigne/ set ouer release and Confirme vnto the sade Sr Marmaduke Langdale and Richard Meadley their executors administrators and assignes All that the saide Mesuage or/ tenemte with the appurtenacs in Holme in Spaldingmoore aforesaid now or late in the tenure or occupacon of the said William Hewley or his assignes and the said other Mesuage or tenemte and p^{r}misses/ with the appurtenncs now or late in the tenure or occupacon of the sade John Varnell or his assignes, and the said other Messuage or Tenemte and p^{r}misses with the appurtennces in Holme afore saide/ Now or late in the tenure or occupacon of George Alkinson or his assignes, and the said other Messuage or tenemte and p^{r}misses with the appurtenncs in Holme aforesaid now or late in the tenure/ or occupacon of the said William Johnson or his assignes and also the sade other Messuage or Tenemte and p^{r}misses with the appurtenncs in Holme aforesaide now or late in the tenure or occupacon of the/ said Thomas Acklam or his assignes. And also all and singuler houses Edifices buildings barnes stables Orchards garths gardens Lands Tenemts Meadowes feedings pastures wayes Easemts pathes passages/ waters watercoursses profitts Comons Comodities aduantages Emolumts & Hereditamts with the appurtenncs whatsoeuer to the said seuerall messuages or tenemts farmes and p^{r}misses or any of them belonging/ or apperteining or therewith used or enioyed and all rents reuercons and yearely profitts of the same or any part there of and also all the Estate and Estates right tytle interrest tearme of yeares/ claime and demaund whatsoeuer of them the saide

APPENDIX B

Sr William Constable Thomas Crosby and Symon Crosby or any of them in or to the said messuages lands and p^{r}misses or any part of/ them, or any of them, with there and euery of their appurtennes together also with the said grant or Indenture of lease and all other grants leasses assignemts and writeings wch they/ them, or any of them haue or hath touching or concerning the said Mesuages or Tenemts lands and p^{r}misses or any part thereof TO HAUE AND TO HOLD the said messuages or tenemts and all and singuler/ other the p^{r}misses hereby graunted and assigned or menconed or intended to be granted and assigned and euery part and parcell thereof with their and euery of there appurtennes, and also the said recyted/ Indenture of lease and other writeings and Euery of them, vnto the said Sir Marmaduke Langdale and Richard Meadley their executors administrators and assignes for and dureinge all/ the rest residue and remainder of the said tyme and tearme of three hundred yeares in the said recited Indenture of lease menconed and yet to come and vnexpired and for and/ dureing all such other estate and estates right tytle interrest tearme of yeares clame and demaund whatsoever as they the said Sir William Constable Thomas Crosby and Symon/ Crosby or any of them haue or hath or may, can, might, or ought to haue, or clame in or to the said messuages or tenemts lands and p^{r}misses or any part or parcell of them or any of them/ & by force or vertue of the said recited Indenture of lease or by any other wayes or meanes whatsoeuer And the said Sir William Constable Thomas Crosby and Symon Crosby doe seuerally and/ respectiuely for themselues there seuerall and respectiue heyres Executors administrators and assignes and not one of them for the acte of another couennte promisse and grant to and with the said/ Sir Marmaduke Langdale and Richard Meadley their Executors administrators and assignes and to and with euery of them by these presents That it shall and may be lawfull to and for them/ the said Sir Marmaduke Langdale and Richard Meadley their Executors administrators and assignes and euery of them att all and every time and times hereafter for and dureing all the rest/ residue and remainder of the said tyme and tearme of three hundreth yeares in the said recyted Indenture of lease menconed and yet to come and vnexpired, peaceably and quietly to haue/ hold use occupy possesse and enioy the said messuages or Tenemts herdytamts and all and singuler other the p'misses hereby granted and assigned or menconed or intended to be/ granted and assigned and euery part and parcell thereof, with their and euery of there appurtenncs without the lawfull lett sute troble Euiccon ["eviction"] expulcon incumbrance or interrupcon of/ them the said Sir William Constable Thomas Crosby and Symon Crosby or any of them there or any of their heyres executors administrators or assignes or any of them or of any/ other person or persons whatsoeuer lawfully clameing the saide messuages or tenemts and p'misses or any part or parcell thereof by from or vnder them or any of them And that the said messuages or Tenemts lands/ tenemts heridytamts and all and singuler other the p'misses and Euery of there appurtenncs now are is and be and soe for and dureinge all the rest residue and/ remainder of the said time & tearme of three hundreth yeares in the said recyted Indenture of lease menconed and yet to come and vnexpired shall remaine Continue and be vnto the saide Sir Marmaduke Langdale and Richard Meadley theire/ executors administrators and assignes cleare and free and clerely and freely acquited Exonerated and discharged or otherwise vpon reasonable request well and sufficiently saued and kept harmlesse by them/ the said Sir William Constable Thomas Crosby and Symon Crosby, there heyres Executors administrators or assignes or some of them of and from all ["every" left out] manner of former and other guifts grants/ bargaines sailes leases assignments Estates rents, arrearages of rents, Statutes, Recognizances, Judgemts, Execucons, forfeitures, seisures, fynes, Issues amercimts and of and from all other tytles troubles/ charges demaunds and incumbrances whatsoeuer heretofore had made comitted Suffered or done or hereafter to be had made Committed

152   APPENDIX B

suffered or done, by them the said Sir William Constable/ Thomas Crosby and Symon Crosby their executors administrators or assignes or any of them or of or by any other person or persons whatsoeur lawfully clayming or p'tendinge to haue or which at/ any time here after shall lawfully Clame or p'tend to haue any Estate right tytle tearme or Intterrest in or to the said Mess land or p'misses or any part or parcell there of by from/ or under them or any of them or by their or any of their meanes Consents or procuremts the rents and seruices hereafter to growe due and payable to the Chiefe lord or lords of the ffee/ of fees of the said p'misses for the same onely excepted and fore prised: IN WITNESSE whereof the parties aboue said to these p'sent Indentures Interchangablye have set their hands/ and seales the day and yeare first aboue written

    WILLIAM CONSTABLE

    Thomas Crosbye   Simon Crosby

[Endorsed on the back]

Sealed Signed & delivered in
the p'sence of vs

    Tho: ffugill
    christopher Jackson.

GENEALOGICAL INDEX.

EXPLANATORY NOTE.—Wherever the same name has been found to have been given to more than one person in the same generation, the name itself has not been repeated in this index, but all such references have been combined under one heading.

Abbott, Daniel[10], 92.
—— Ebenezer[10], 92.
—— Elizabeth[10], 92.
—— Ephraim, 92.
—— Ephraim[10], 92.
—— John, 92.
—— Joshua[10], 92.
—— Josiah[10], 92.
—— Martha[10], 92.
—— Mary[10], 92.
—— Peter[10], 92.
—— Sarah (Barker), 92.
—— Sarah[10], 92.
Adford, Mary, 128.
Appleton, Mary[5], 41.
—— Robert[6], 41.
—— Simon, 41.

Bell, Widow Jannett, 9–12.
—— John, 9, 10.
—— Thomas, 10.
Belt, Jasper, 32.
—— Sir Robert, 32.
—— Robert[2], 32.
—— Sarah[3], 32.
Bemis, Rutha, 125.
Bennett, Elizabeth, 35.
Bent, Agnes, 135.
Blanchard, Abigail[9], 67.
Blanchard, Benjamin[9], 67.
—— David[9], 67.
—— George[2], 135.
—— Hannah[9], 67.
—— Harriot, 125, 131, 132, 134, 136, 138.
—— John[3], 67, 134, 136.
—— John[9], 67, 104.
—— Joseph[5], 125, 131, 136.
—— Mary[9], 67.
—— Mary (Sweetser), 67.
—— Nathaniel[3], 135.
—— Rachel[9], 67.
—— Samuel, 67.
—— Samuel[3], 135, 136.

Blanchard, Samuel[9], 67.
—— Sarah[9], 67.
—— Sarah (Brown), 125, 131, 136.
—— Simon[4], 136.
—— Simon[9], 67.
—— Thomas[1], 135.
—— Thomas[2], 135.
Bower, William[1], 32.
—— William[2], 32.
Bowman, Abel, 124.
—— Lucy (Needham), 124.
—— Ruth, 124.
Brackett, Alice, 66, 90.
—— John, 73.
—— Peter, 73.
—— Rachel, 66, 71, 74, 80, 89, 91, 96, 134, 136.
—— Capt. Richard, 50, 66, 71, 73, 74, 75, 89, 90, 91.
Brigham, Anne, x, xi, 19, 25, 46, 50, 56, 57, 59, 62, 63, 70.
—— Elisabeth[5], 61.
—— Francis[4], 61.
—— Henry[3], 60.
—— Isabell (Watson), 56, 62, 63, 64.
—— Jennett[4], 61.
—— John[5], 61, 62.
—— Peter[4], 61.
—— Richard[4], 61.
—— Richard[5], 62.
—— Robert[5], 29, 62.
—— Thomas[1], 60.
—— Thomas[2], 60.
—— Thomas[3], 60, 61.
—— Thomas[4], 61.
—— Thomas[5], 56, 62, 63.
—— William[4], 61.
—— William[5], 62.
Brown, Col. Jonathan, 136.
—— Mary (French), 136.
—— Susanna, 93.
Bulkeley, Edward, 115.
—— Rev. Peter, 115.
—— Sarah, 115.
Burley, Alison, 61.

154 GENEALOGICAL INDEX

Chester, Dorcas, 115.
—— Leonard, 115.
—— Mary (Wade), 115.
Crosby, Abel Bowman[13], 124.
—— Abigail[9], 35, 66.
—— Abigail[12], 124.
—— Abigail[13], 124.
—— Achsah[11], 111.
—— Adelaide[13], 125.
—— Agnes[3], 5.
—— Albert[13], 124.
—— Alice[11], 103.
—— Alonzo[12], 125.
—— Alonzo[13], 125.
—— Ambrose[13], 124.
—— Anna[9], 67.
—— Anna[10], 93.
—— Anna[11], 110.
—— Anne[8], 58.
—— Anthony[4], 12, 13, 14, 16.
—— Anthony[6], xi, 20, 21, 29, 42.
—— Dr. Anthony[7], 14, 19, 27–29, 31–35, 65.
—— Barbara A.[15], 139.
—— Beatrice B.[15], 139.
—— Benjamin[9], 66.
—— Bulah[10], 93.
—— Catherine[8], 67.
—— Catherine[10], 92.
—— Charles H.[15], 139.
—— Clarissa[13], 125.
—— Widow Constance, xi, 56, 59, 62–65.
—— David[9], 93.
—— David[10], 93.
—— Deborah[9], 94.
—— Deborah[11], 110.
—— Dorothy[9], 67.
—— Ebenezer[8], 58.
—— Eleazer[8], 58.
—— Eliphalet[9], 67.
—— Eliza Harriot[12], 131.
—— Elizabeth[9], 35, 67.
—— Elizabeth[10], 93.
—— Ellen[6], 12.
—— Emily[13], 124.
—— Emma[2], 5.
—— Ephraim[9], 67.
—— Esther[9], 67.
—— Hannah[7], 63, 65.
—— Hannah[8], 67.
—— Hannah[9], 35, 66, 92, 93, 101.
—— Hannah[10], 93, 102, 104.
—— Hannah[11], 103.
—— Hannah[12], 124.
—— Hepsibah[10], 93.
—— Hezekiah[10], 103, 110–120, 123, 125, 126.
—— Hezekiah[11], 111.
—— Increase[8], 58.
—— Isaac[9], 67.

Crosby, Isaac[11], 103.
—— Jacob[10], 93.
—— James[9], 66.
—— Jane[7], 32, 63, 65.
—— Jane[9], 67.
—— Jeremiah[11], 110–112, 114, 118, 120, 123–132.
—— Jeremiah[12], 124.
—— Jesseniah[10], 103.
—— Jesseniah[11], 103.
—— Joanna[9], 67.
—— John[1], 2, 5–7, 139.
—— John[2], 5, 6.
—— John[3], 7.
—— John[7], 63, 65.
—— John[8], 58.
—— John[9], 66.
—— John[10], 93.
—— Jonathan[8], 35.
—— Jonathan[9], 35, 67.
—— Joseph[7], 31, 44, 56, 58, 63.
—— Joseph[8], 58, 66, 92, 95–98, 100–103, 105, 106, 113.
—— Joseph[9], 92, 102.
—— Joseph[10], 92.
—— Joseph B.[12], 131.
—— Joshua[11], 103.
—— Josiah[8], 67.
—— Josiah[9], 67.
—— Katherine[7], 32.
—— Leander[13], 124.
—— Levi[11], 111.
—— Lucy[11], 110.
—— Lucy[12], 124, 125.
—— Lucy Submit[13], 125.
—— Martha[10], 102.
—— Mary[7], 63, 65.
—— Mary[8], 67, 134, 136.
—— Mary[9], 66, 67, 93.
—— Mary[10], 103.
—— Mary[11], 103, 111.
—— Mary Frances[13], 125.
—— Mehetabel[9], 35.
—— Mercy[8], 58.
—— Miles[2], 5, 8, 9.
—— Miles[4], 9, 11, 12, 13.
—— Nathan[8], 67.
—— Nathan[9], 67, 104.
—— Nathaniel[8], 35.
—— Nathaniel[9], 66.
—— Nicholas[4], 9, 12.
—— Oliver[9], 67.
—— Peletiah[9], 94.
—— Peletiah[10], 103.
—— Persis[10], 93.
—— Phineas[9], 66.
—— Prudence[7], 32.
—— Prudence[9], 35, 93.
—— Prudence[10], 93, 103.
—— Prudence[11], 103.
—— Rachel[8], 66, 75.

GENEALOGICAL INDEX 155

Crosby, Rachel[9], 66, 67, 93.
—— Rachel[10], 93.
—— Rachel[11], 103.
—— Ralph[4], 9, 12.
—— Rauf[3], 7.
—— Rebecca[10], 103.
—— Relief[10], 93.
—— Renslow[12], 124.
—— Rhoda[10], 103.
—— Rhoda[11], 103, 110, 116.
—— Richard[2], 5, 6, 7.
—— Robert[2], 5, 6, 7.
—— Robert[5], 56, 63.
—— Robert[7], 63, 65.
—— Robert[9], 94, 101.
—— Rutha Elizabeth, 125.
—— Samuel[9], 35, 66.
—— Samuel[10], 93.
—— Sarah[8], 58, 67.
—— Sarah[9], 67, 92.
—— Sarah[10], 92, 93, 103.
—— Sarah[11], 103.
—— Seth[10], 103.
—— Seth[11], 103.
—— Silence[12], 124.
—— Simon[6] the Emigrant, ix, x, xi, 1, 14, 16-18, 20, 22-25, 27, 29, 31, 42-50, 54-57, 59, 63, 67-69, 113.
—— Simon[7], of Billerica, 31, 44, 56, 58, 63, 66-71, 73-85, 89, 91, 96, 98, 104, 105, 112, 115, 117, 125, 130, 134, 136.
—— Simon[8], 58, 66, 75, 96, 97.
—— Simon[9], 66.
—— Solomon[9], 66.
—— Solomon[10], 93.
—— Sumner[12], 113, 125, 131-134, 136-138.
—— Sumner[14], 138, 139.
—— Sumner[15], 139.
—— Susanna[10], 93.
—— Susanna[11], 103.
—— Thomas[3], 7, 8, 9, 10, 11, 12.
—— Thomas[5], ix, x, xi, xiv, xviii, 12, 14, 16, 19-29, 31, 33, 35, 41, 44, 63, 69.
—— Thomas[6], xi, xiv, 20, 22, 27, 29-32, 42, 44.
—— Thomas[7], 31, 33, 44, 56, 58, 63, 74, 115.
—— Thomas[8], 35, 58, 66.
—— Thomas[9], 93.
—— Thomas[10], 93.
—— Timothy[11], 110, 125.
—— William[2], 5, 7, 8.
—— William[3], 7, 8.
—— William[6], xi, 20, 27, 29, 31, 32, 42.
—— William[8], 58.
—— William[9], 93, 97, 102-106, 109, 112-114, 116, 123.
—— William[10], 93, 102, 103.

Crosby, William[11], 103, 111.
—— Gov. William George[12], 111.
—— William Sumner[13], 131, 138.
—— Zoa[12], 124.
Cutler, Alice, 102.
—— Hannah[11], 102.
—— James, 102.
—— Millicent[11], 102.
—— Prudence[11], 102.
—— Robert[11], 102.
—— Rev. Robert, 102.

Dales, Constance[6], 42.
—— John, 22, 42.
—— John[6], 42.
—— Peter[6], 42.
—— Phillippa[6], 42.
—— William[6], 42.
Danforth, Abigail[9], 67.
—— Anna, 115, 116.
—— Elizabeth[8], 67.
—— Elizabeth (Poulter), 67, 115.
—— Hannah[9], 67.
—— Jacob, Sr., 102.
—— Jacob, 102.
—— Jacob[11], 102.
—— Jesse[11], 102.
—— Jonathan, 67, 73, 115.
—— Jonathan[9], 67.
—— Lydia[9], 67.
—— Rachel[9], 67.
—— Rebecca (Patten), 102.
—— Samuel, 67.
—— Samuel[9], 67.
Davis, Almon H., 131, 138.
—— Benjamin, 111.
—— Eleanor Francis, 131, 138.
—— Elizabeth (Everett), 131, 138.
—— Mary (Mann), 111.
—— Sally, 111.
Doggett, Hannah, 135, 136.
—— Thomas, 135.

Ellis, Eleazer, 93.
—— Eleazer[10], 93.
—— Hannah[10], 93.
—— Mary[10], 93.
—— Mehitable[10], 93.
—— Rachel[10], 93.
—— Timothy[10], 93.
—— William[10], 93.

Fisher, Elizabeth[10], 93.
—— Hannah[10], 93.
—— Jeremiah, 93.
—— Jeremiah[10], 93.
—— Jesse[10], 93.
—— Capt. John, 93.
—— Joseph[10], 93.
—— Josiah[10], 93.
—— Prudence[10], 93.

GENEALOGICAL INDEX

Fisher, Rebecca (Ellis), 93.
—— Rebecca[10], 93.
—— Samuel[10], 93.
—— Sarah[10], 93.
—— Timothy[10], 93.
—— William[10], 93.
Foster, Hepsibah, 93.
—— Sarah, 93.
—— Thomas, 93.
French, Hannah, 99.
—— Mary, 66, 92, 98, 99.
—— Sarah, 66, 92, 98–101, 103.
—— Lieut. William, 66, 73, 75, 92, 98, 99, 100.
Fry, William, 136.

Gleason, Rachel Maria (Sears), 131.
Goodwin, Lucy, 124.

Hammond, Rev. Peter, 42.
Hesaye, Everill, 61.
Hewiey, George, 42.
Hill, Deborah, 116.
—— Peter, 103.
—— Rachel (Crosby), 103.
—— Rachel, 103.
—— Samuel[2], 116.
Hobson, Jeremiah, Sr., 124.
—— Jeremiah, 124.
—— Lucy, 124.
Holman, Seeth, 106.
—— William, 106.
—— Winifred, 106.
Hooker, Rev. Thomas, 47, 72, 115.
Hooper, Charles Appleton, 139.
—— Idolene G. (Snow), 139.
—— Idolene Snow, 138, 139.
Hosley, Martha (Richardson), 103.
—— Mary, 103.
—— Thomas, 103.
Humphrey, Elizabeth, 135.
—— Frances, 135.
—— Jonas, 135.
Hunt, Mary, 92.
—— Samuel, 92.
—— Sarah[10], 92.
—— Thomas, 92.

Jaquith, Abigail, 110, 123, 127, 128.
—— Abigail[12], 110.
—— Abraham[1], 127.
—— Abraham[2], 127, 128.
—— Abraham[3], 128.
—— Alice[12], 110.
—— Anna[12], 110.
—— Anna (Jordan), 127.
—— Deacon Benjamin, 110, 123, 128.
—— Elizabeth[3], 128.
—— Hannah (Walker), 110, 123, 128.
—— James[12], 110.
—— Jeremiah[12], 110.

Jaquith, Nathan, 110.
—— Nathan[12], 110.
—— Nathaniel[12], 110.
—— Sarah[2], 128.
Johnson, Elizabeth[8], 65.
—— Hannah[8], 65.
—— Capt. John, 63, 65.
—— John[8], 65.
—— Robert, 65.
—— Samuel[8], 65.
Jones, Hugh, 128.
—— Mary (Foster), 128.
—— Sarah, 128.
Jordan, James, 127.

Kidder, Alice[9], 66.
—— Anna (Moore), 66.
—— Benjamin[9], 66.
—— Dorothy[9], 66.
—— Enoch, 67.
—— Ephraim[8], 66.
—— Ephraim[9], 66.
—— Hannah[9], 66.
—— James, 66.
—— Joseph[9], 66.
—— Rachel[9], 66.
—— Richard[9], 66.
—— Thomas[9], 66.
Kittredge, Lucy, 110, 117, 123.
—— Mary (Wright), 110.
—— William, 110.

Lambert, Constance, 20, 28, 29, 32, 40, 41, 44.
—— Richard, 40.
—— William, 40.
Lampson, Abigail (Bryant), 103.
—— Rebecca[11], 103.
—— Samuel, Sr., 103.
—— Samuel, 103.
Lathrop, Thomas, 67.
Leach, John B., 125.
Learned, Abigail[13], 124.
—— Albert[13], 124.
—— Amariah, 124.
—— Emma Augusta[13], 124.
—— Harriet W.[13], 124.
—— Joshua, Sr., 124.
—— Joshua, 124.
—— Joshua S.[13], 124.
—— Lucy, 124.
—— Lucy E.[13], 124.
—— Sarah Ann[13], 124.
—— Sarah (Coolidge), 124.
—— Stephen[13], 124.
—— William B.[13], 124.
Lewis, Aaron[12], 111.
—— Andrew[12], 111.
—— James, Sr., 110.
—— James, 110.
—— James[12], 111.

GENEALOGICAL INDEX 157

Lewis, Levi[12], 111.
—— Lucy[12], 111.
—— Merric[12], 111.
—— Rebecca (Brown), 110.
Longhorne, Bethia[6], 65.
—— Constance[8], 65.
—— Elizabeth[3], 65.
—— Richard, 63, 65. 55n
—— Richard[8], 65.
—— Samuel[8], 65.
—— Sarah[8], 65.
—— Thomas, 26.
—— Thomas[8], 65.
Lume, Anne, 65.
Luse, William, 58.

Manning, Abiall (Wight), 67.
—— Mary, 67.
—— Ensign Samuel, 67.
Mead, David, 102.
—— Elias[11], 102.
—— Hannah (Smith), 102.
—— Josiah[11], 102.
—— Levi[11], 102.
—— Martha[11], 102.
—— Matthew, 102.
—— Rhoda[11], 102.
—— Ward[11], 102.
Miller, Rev. John[1], 58.
—— John[2], 58.
—— Lydia, 58.
Millington, Anne[6], 42.
—— Barbara, 61.
—— Jennett, 61.
—— Marmaduke, 21, 38, 42.
—— Peter, 21.
—— Peter[5], 42.
—— Phillippa[6], 42.
—— Robert, 42.
—— Thomas, 36, 38, 42, 61.
—— Wilfred, 38.
—— William, 20, 21, 38, 42, 61.
Mixor, Isaac, Jr., 99.

Norcross, Susanna, 124.

Osborn, John S., 125.
—— John, 125.

Palmer, Edward, 61.
Parker, Abigail, 66.
—— Achsah Crosby[12], 111.
—— Anna, 93.
—— Augusta[12], 111.
—— Caroline[12], 111.
—— Charles Edwin[12], 111.
—— David, 111.
—— Edward David[12], 111.
—— James Lewis[12], 111.
—— John, 66.
—— John, 111.

Parker, John Henry[12], 111.
—— Jonathan, 93.
—— Mary Ann[12], 111.
—— Mary (Danforth), 93.
—— Mary (Shattuck), 111.
—— Norman[12], 111.
—— William Crosby[12], 111.
"Peploe," John, 93.
"Pepple," John[10], 93.
Pickard, Anne[8], 65.
—— Hannah[8], 65.
—— Jane[8], 65.
—— John, 33, 63, 65.
—— John[8], 65.
—— Mary[8], 65.
—— Rebecca[8], 65.
—— Samuel[8], 65.
—— Sarah[8], 65.

Rawson, Anne (Glover), 67.
—— Anna[9], 67.
—— Edward, 67.
—— Perne[9], 67.
—— Rachel[9], 67.
—— Sarah[9], 67.
—— Thomas[9], 67.
—— Capt. William, 67.
—— William, 67.
—— William[9], 67.
Ross, Hannah, 93, 102, 104, 105, 106, 114.
—— Sarah, 102.
—— Thomas, 93, 102, 105, 106.
Russell, Deborah[10], 94.
—— Peletiah[10], 94.
—— Peter, 94.
—— Peter[10], 94.
—— Phebe, 94.
—— Phebe[10], 94.
—— Rachel[10], 94.
—— Rebecca[10], 94.
—— Hon. Richard, 115.
—— Thomas, 94.

Sears, Silas, 58.
Shed, John, 67.
—— Sarah (Chamberlain), 67.
—— Sarah, 67.
Sheldon, Rebecca, 136.
—— Samuel, 136.
—— Sarah (Hutchinson), 136.
Sotheron, Agnes[2], 36, 61.
—— Alison[4], 38.
—— Anne[4], 22, 42.
—— Anne[5], 42.
—— Beatrix[3], 37.
—— Christopher[3], 36.
—— Elisabeth[5], 42.
—— Isabel[5], 41.
—— Isabel[5], 42.
—— Jane[5], 20, 22, 28, 29, 35, 41, 63.

Sotheron, Jane[6], 42.
— Janet[4], 38.
— John[2], 36.
— John[3], 37, 38.
— John[5], 29, 38, 42.
— Margaret[3], 37.
— Margaret[4], 38.
— Matthew[4], 42.
— Philip[6], 42.
— Phillippa[3], 38.
— Phillippa[5], 42.
— Robert[2], 36, 37.
— Robert[3], 37.
— "Sir" Thomas[2], 36.
— Thomas[2], 37.
— Thomas[6], 42.
— Thomas[7], 42.
— William[1], 36.
— William[2], 36.
— William[3], 37.
— William[4], 20, 28, 29, 32, 38–41, 44, 49.
— William[5], 42.
Spring, Sarah, 103.
Stearns, Benjamin[10], 93.
— Elizabeth (Bigelow), 93.
— Elizabeth[10], 93.
— John, 67, 92, 93, 99.
— Mary[10], 93.
— Prudence[10], 93.
— Rachel[10], 93.
— Samuel, 93.
— Samuel[10], 93.
St. John, Hon. Oliver, 115.
— Oliver[2], 115.
Swan, Elizabeth, 103.
— John, 103.
— Timothy, 103.
Sweetser, Bethia, 135.
— Mary, 135.
— Seth, 135.
Symmes, Elizabeth, 98.
— Rev. Zachariah, 98.

Thackwray, Thomas, 42.
Thorley, Richard, 65.
Tomlinson, John, 125.
— Peter, 61.
Tompson, Anne[7], 57.
— Benjamin, 74, 104.
— Joseph, 73.
— William, 74.
— Rev. William, 25, 49, 57, 58, 63, 70, 71, 74.

Wade, Jonathan, 35.
— Prudence, 33, 34, 35.
— Susanna, 35.
Walker, Hannah (Fowle), 128.
— Hannah (Mordough), 125.
— Capt. Samuel, 128.
Waters, Mehitable, 136.
Watson, Constance, 61, 62.
— James, 62.
Watts, Samuel, 93.
Westobie, George, 12.
Whiting, Anna, 103, 110, 114, 116, 117.
— Deborah (Hill), 103, 110, 116.
— Elizabeth (St. John), 115.
— Hon. John, 114.
— Oliver[2], 115, 116.
— Rev. Samuel[1], 114, 115.
— Rev. Samuel[2], 80, 114, 115, 116.
— Samuel[4], 103, 110, 116.
Whittaker, John, 66.
Wilsh, Margaret, 61.
Winchester, Elizabeth, 116.
Winship, Lucy, 124.
Wright, Anne, 33.
— Elizabeth, 61.
Wyman, Lucy[10], 93.
— Prudence (Putnam), 93.
— Simon[10], 93.
— Sybil[10], 93.
Wyman, Thomas, 93.
— Thomas[10], 93.
— William, 93.

GENERAL INDEX.

Alne, town in Yorkshire, xiv, 5, 6, 7, 8.
Bartlett, J. Gardner, ix, x, xi, 2.
Belt family, xi, xiv.
Billerica, Mass., 58, 66–85, 89, 92–96, 98–100, 102–106, 110–119, 123–128, 130–132, 136.
Blanchard family of Bubwith, 15.
Blodgett, George B., 64.
Bower family, xiv.
Braintree, Mass., 25, 56–59, 66–75, 90.
Brigham family, xi, 20, 59, 60 et seq.
Brown, William, 73, 75–77, 98.
Bubwith, 3, 8, 10, 12, 13, 15, 16, 20.
Bursea, 3, 10, 13.
Buttercrambe, 18, 45.

Cambridge, Mass., x, 17, 19, 22, 24, 25, 26, 31, 42, 47, 56, 63, 66, 69, 70, 72, 85, 98, 101, 102, 103, 106.
Coats-of-arms, xiii, xiv.
Concord, Mass., 89, 106, 115.
Constable family, 4, 5, 7, 9, 22, 36, 38.
Crosby in Ayrshire, Scotland, xviii, xx.
Crosby Cannonby, town in Cumberland, xviii, xix.
Crosby, place in Cumberland, xviii, xix.
—— derivation of the name, xiv–xvii.
—— Garret in Westmoreland, xviii, xix.
—— Great, town in Lancashire, xvi, xviiii, xx, xxi.
—— Hall, xxi, xxii, xxiii.
—— town in the Isle of Man, xviii, xx.
—— Sir John, xxi, xxii, xxiii.
—— Lighthouse, xx.
—— town in Lincolnshire, xi, xviii.
—— Little, town in Lancashire, xviii, xx.
—— Ravensworth in Westmoreland, xviii, xix.
—— town in Yorkshire, xii, xviii, xx, xxi, 6.
Crosseby, Odo de, xv.
Crown Point, Expedition to, 111, 114, 116.
Cummings, Rev. Henry, 118, 119, 126, 127, 136.

Day, Steven, 25, 70.
Defence, ship, 17, 98.

Domesday Book, xi, xii.
Dudley, Gov. Thomas, 35, 72.

Ellithorpe family, xi, 9, 10.

Flynt, Henry, 57, 90.
Freeman's Oath, 48.

Gribthorpe, 3, 10, 12, 13.

Hill, Capt. Ralph, 80.
—— Ralph, Sr., 71, 73.
Holme Manor, 5, 9, 22, 23, 36, 37, 38, 60.
Holme-on-Spalding-Moor, x, xi, xiv, 2, 3, 4, 7–10, 12, 13, 14, 18, 20, 21, 28, 29, 30, 32, 33, 36–42, 44, 56, 58–64, 68, 139.

Lambert family, xi, 4, 13, 20.
Langdale family, 5, 22, 36, 44.
License, Inn-keeper's, 83.

Millington family, xi, 4, 20.

Newtowne, Mass., 69, 72, 73.

Payne, Capt. Edward, 45, 46.
Printing-press, 23, 24.

Rogers, Rev. Ezekiel, x, 16, 17, 18, 23, 24, 25, 44, 64, 65.
Rowley, Eng., 17, 18.
—— Mass., ix, x, xi, 17, 19, 20, 23, 25–28, 31, 33–35, 42, 44, 54, 56, 59, 63–65.

Shepard, Rev. Thomas, x, 16, 17, 18, 25, 44, 45, 47, 48, 49, 71, 72, 90, 98.
Sotheron family, xi, 4, 20, 36.
Stillingfleet, 5–8.
Susan and Ellen, ship, 45–47.

Testa de Nevill, Crosby mentioned in, xvii, xviii, xx.

Watson family, xi, 20.
Wheldrake, 8, 14, 16.
Whitman, Rev. Nathaniel, 119, 127.
Winthrop, Gov. John, 72, 89, 90.

CPSIA information can be obtained
at www.ICGtesting.com
Printed in the USA
LVHW080025110922
728083LV00025B/503